Seatramps

Seatramps
Five years of ocean life

SHEILA MARTIN

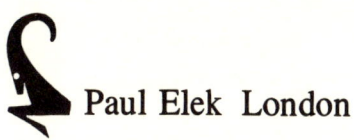
Paul Elek London

To my skipper

First published in Great Britain 1977 by
Elek Books Limited
54-58 Caledonian Road, London N1 9RN

Copyright © 1977 by Sheila Martin

All rights reserved. No part of this publication may be reproduced, stored in a retrieval system or transmitted, in any form or by any means, electronic, mechanical, photocopying, recording or otherwise, without the prior permission of the publishers.

ISBN 0 236 40090 8

Printed in Great Britain by
Unwin Brothers Limited
The Gresham Press, Old Woking, Surrey
A Member of the Staples Printing Group

Contents

List of Illustrations		6
Acknowledgements		8
1	'If he can't find Start Point how's he going to find the Canaries?'	11
2	Islands in the Sun	21
3	Bandidos and Cunas	34
4	Enchanted Seas—and Enchanted Isles	43
5	To the Marquesas	60
6	Atoll Paradise	68
7	The Land of the Frangipani	77
8	Hurricane Bebe	90
9	Australian Homecoming	105
10	'Missus, we don't eat people no more!'	115
11	The Ways of the Solomon Islanders	124
12	Papua New Guinea	138
13	Indonesia, Here We Come ... We Hope	148
14	Bali to Swaziland	160
15	Cape Town to Rio	175
16	Home—via Revolution	185
Postscript		192

List of Illustrations

PHOTOGRAPHS
Between pages 96 and 97

Shebessa sails North from Bequia, West Indies
Splendour in poverty—Cuna Islanders
The author with sea lions, Galapagos
The author with Tom in party mood, Tuamotu style
Hurricane Bebe reaches the Bay of Islands, Suva, Fiji
Norman with Alan Jacobson and Noel Wilkinson on the Yarra, Melbourne
Loyalty Island mother with her children
Lopevi volcano, near Epi, New Hebrides
Norman trading with islanders, Malaita, Solomons
Shells for sale in a Malaita street
Are Are Lagoon, Malaita
Shebessa, hung with fish, at anchor off the Cosmoledos
The author with priest and student at the Roman Catholic Mission on Garove Island, off New Britain
Landscape of the Atlantic island of Trindade
New Year fertility ceremony of the Incwala, Swaziland
North Atlantic passage

MAPS AND DIAGRAMS

	page
The voyage of *Shebessa*, 1970–75	endpapers
Shebessa's accommodation plan	16
Shebessa's sail plan	24
Shebessa's course Grenada-Panama	35
Takaroa atoll	70
Vatoa Island	93
Suva Harbour	98
Shebessa's course through New Caledonia, the New Hebrides and Solomons	117
Shebessa's course Rabaul-Samarai	141
Shebessa's course Samarai-Bali	150
Shebessa's jury rudder	152

Acknowledgements

First, we would like to thank my mother who has patiently waited for our return, never failing to encourage us on our travels with letters and home news at every mail stop; our children, Bri, Chris and Carrie, who have each helped us in countless ways, ironing out problems at home and arranging for spares to be sent to us; and our nephews and their wives in Melbourne, Neil and Irene, Bruce and Jeannie, who gave us such a rousing welcome to their city, and endless hospitality.

Johnny and Peggy Finlinson had faith in our dreams and our voyaging. They came to the launching of *Shebessa* in Medemblik, to Tenerife in 1971, the Seychelles in 1974 and both were there to welcome us back to England. Their love and kindness to my mother and our children while we were away meant a great deal to us, as did the many reassuring letters we received. Johnny and Pegs, thank you.

In England, Captain Watts and his staff, particularly Mr Ford, contributed a great deal to the success of our voyaging. Captain Watts, however busy, always made time to give Norman advice before we left, and Mr Ford never failed to fulfil our urgent requests for spares and charts. We had the finest service from Brian Blake of Volvo Penta in London, from Miss Covell of the British Seagull Company, and from Mr Barber of Pinta Auto Pilots. On our return 'Wattie', Mr E. P. C. Watson and his wife Jean, of the Royal Thames Yacht Club, welcomed us back, then did, and still do, everything possible to help us acclimatise to shore living. Thank you, Wattie and Jean.

From Holland, Jongert the builders, Sihi (electric bilge pumps), Fasto (water heaters) and Bolinders, the Volvo Penta agents in Rotterdam, sent us spares all over the world—often complimentary, as did Verheys, makers of our propeller shaft. From the United States, Zenith Radio and Groco Toilets gave excellent service.

To the countless people throughout the world who helped us on our way we should like to say 'Bless you and thank you'. We cannot possibly acknowledge you all by name but we'll never forget your warmth of heart and kindness. To name but a few, Captain Stephen Despretz of *Amiral Charnier,* French Navy who welcomed us to French Polynesia, assisting us with repairs; the Durouchoux family in Tahiti, with whom we often played bridge—in French; Monsieur and Madame Angelier, of Raiatea; the Williams family in Nuie; John Barraclough on *Camdella* in Suva, Fiji, who dived for our lost anchor the morning after the hurricane was over.

Friends and complete strangers welcomed us to Australian shores. Thank you, Peter and Natasha Coghlan, Doug and Joan Johns, Peter and Betty Dyce, Laurie LeGuay, Rod Cook and John Hawley, John and Norma Gleeson—you all made us at home. At Sandringham Yacht Club, Commodore Lou Abrahams, Ray Elsegood and many members made sure we were happy. Alan Dean sorted out our teeth, Dr Brian Woodward checked our medical supplies; Ken Crossley, Noel Wilkinson, Len Morgan and Jack McKeddie, Norman's rowing pals, and good friends Elsie Mitchell, Victor and Cy Cater, Keith Dunkley, Alan Church, Ron and Gay Baillieu, Hugh and Pauline McLean gave us wonderful hospitality and made sure we were never lonely or hungry. Olaf Christiansen and Nancy and Bob Haynes assisted me greatly with my shell collection. Many firms provided us with food and supplies with their compliments: Heinz, Plumrose, Kraft Foods Ltd, Nestlés and Johnson & Johnson—so many goodies that made all the difference to our life in 1973.

In Nouméa, Claire Mersadier mended our torn mizzen on her domestic machine. Monsieur and Madame Wahnapo, Lifou, Loyalty Islands treated us like royal guests. Nan and Mike Townsend, acting High Commissioner, Vila, New Hebrides brought us back to civilisation, inviting us to an English tea. Frank Haskins, NZ, headmaster of Epi senior primary school, welcomed us to his shores. Jimmy Jones and his wife Violet allowed us to taste the joys of his island. Edward Faka I, son of Number 2 Chief, Tikopia, helped to make our stay there so enjoyable. Colin Thackra and Bob Gordon gave us a glimpse of Auki Malaita, Solomon Islands, arranged for our anchor stock to be straightened and put our anchor winch into action again. In Honiara, Eric Legg, Commodore of the Yacht Club, and many members befriended us;

Ron Naylor fixed our instruments and Bill and Betty Culver on *Kia Kia* became dear and ever helpful friends.

New Guinea: Rabaul—the friendliest yacht club in the world, thank you all for being so marvellous, and especially Bryan and Lyn Cooper on *Shi Bui* who adopted us as Mum and Dad, and Alan Smith, Manager of the National Bank, a great guy. We'd like to thank Lionel and Shirley Fox, Wilmur and David Chambers of Madang for their wonderful hospitality. In Cairns Vince O'Brien helped us with engine problems. In Gan, Indian Ocean, the RAF gave us a little bit of home when we were badly needing it. Our thanks go to all the officers and men we met there, and in particular to Squadron-Leader Peter Haigh, W/O Abbott, and Sergeant Ron Peters.

South Africa. In Durban, Arthur Jones, the Secretary of the Royal Natal yacht club, was kindness itself, and Norma and Bob Lambert befriended us– great people. In Cape Town, Margot gave us great hospitality at her beautiful home and willingly carted a great many stores to *Shebessa*. We will never forget the generosity of the South African people and the firms there who provided us with food and drink and other provisions and services. Bull Brand (canned meat), Joko (tea), Castle (beer), Stollenburg (wine), Rothman, Kodak and Captain Coltham Grimrod (shipping) serviced our dinghy and life raft for free. Viking Bakeries gave us double baked bread. Shell Oil supplied our needs with their compliments.

Our thanks to the Brazilian Navy for their constant hospitality and assistance, to Commander Cyro, Trindade and Captain Matoso Maia, Salvador. Phyl and Sue Wade, good yachting friends, helped us fit our new Hydrovane self-steering gear in Rio. Aldoh Cunha introduced us to his beloved town Salvador, and Newton Salles allowed me to look at his beautiful shell collection, presenting me with a box of exquisite Brazilian specimens. Finally, our thanks to Peter at Café Sport and Othom, a highly talented scrimshaw artist, both of Horta, Azores.

S. and N.M.

1
'If he can't find Start Point how's he going to find the Canaries?'

I count myself one of the luckiest women on earth. I've stopped signing myself 'housewife' on documents: my occupation is now 'seawife'. We no longer own a house; our home is our yacht. We've been at sea for almost five years, roaming the oceans in *Shebessa,* sometimes alone, sometimes with crew, seeking out remote places and meeting small communities that rarely have contact with the outside world. We've said goodbye to a great many luxuries and comforts, things we accepted before as necessities of living. We're neither young, nor wealthy, nor very strong, but we're happier and healthier than we've ever been before.

This is how it all began.

One afternoon someone suggested we might be tired of waterskiing around Lake Windermere so why didn't we try sailing? By the end of that afternoon we were the proud owners of a duck egg blue 11 foot Heron dinghy with red sails which we christened *Waltzing Matilda*. We knew absolutely nothing about sailing but decided that the best way to learn was baptism by fire. Our first attempt to sail across the lake took five hours—after capsizing and the loss of our rudder. Ignominiously we were towed by a passing motor boat to the shore. We bought a beginner's guide to sailing and persevered.

After many weekends of practice Norman, who loved competition, decided we would join the Royal Windermere Yacht Club to race. The lawn of the Club was packed with members watching our every move. I was sucking wine gums, my mouth dry with nerves. We cast off, the main and jib drawing well as we sailed away—but why was the boat filling with water at such an alarming rate? 'We've got a leak!' I cried. 'We're sinking!' We paddled a sadly water-logged *Waltzing Matilda* back to the jetty amid ripples of laughter from the spectators. Would I ever learn? I'd forgotten to push in those all-important bungs in the stern!

So ended our first sailing period.

When the Government reduced purchase tax on cars, with falling prices in the second-hand market Norman's hitherto successful car hire business was suddenly in serious difficulties, the value of his large fleet being drastically written down. He had to get outside capital into the business at the price of losing control, and we followed the new head office from Harrogate to London for a difficult few years. Norman led a stifled existence after running his own show for so many years, now having to work under supervision, while I battled with an old house and the dramas and love affairs of three late teenage children. Norman was full of muscular aches and pains, groaning each morning as he rolled out of bed; we had most of the creature comforts but were no longer happy or fit. Then one day Norman's remaining shareholding and service agreement were bought out by the controlling interest, and at the age of fifty-six he retired—with something to retire on. He took up sailing again, this time on the South coast, and in a larger class than before, 36 to 52 foot. I began to join in too, and we spent many weekends in various hired craft, mixing with yachting folk.

Once at sea I relaxed, loving the freedom, the peace and the open air life; I felt at home. But on shore I was ill at ease in nautical company, feeling very much a novice, not understanding a quarter of the stories in sailing jargon. Coming into port was always tense, Norman steering, me on the bow with a warp in my hand ready to leap for the jetty. Would I make that leap? And if I did, would I remember the right knot to tie, or at least make it look like one out of the book and do it in a casual manner so that no one could doubt my skill? It took time to learn not to mind making a fool of yourself at this sport where there would always be *someone* watching.

After a while Norman and I began to think of sailing our own yacht—perhaps away from England to warmer climes. We had no commitments; the children were all on the point of leaving home. We both had an urge for a more simple, natural way of living, away from the tensions and artificialities of cities. Some years previously Norman had visited the West Indies, Tahiti and Hawaii, loving their carefree way of life. We were both born beachcombers, and it didn't take long for Norman's rhapsodic reminiscences to fire me with the enthusiasm to live, one day, in the tropics. Could sailing our own yacht there be the answer? To me this sounded a glorious impossible dream—but with Norman you never knew.

This was a hectic time for him, trying to find out what ocean sailing was all about. He took four navigation courses concurrently at polytechnics and the Admiralty as well as Captain Watts' correspondence course, having long sessions with that wonderful gentleman, who, no matter how busy he was, always found time to help a new yachtsman, giving endless advice and assurance.

We searched the magazines and the marinas up and down the country looking for our dream boat. On a cold November day we found her—*Dionis*, a 31 foot fibreglass sloop, laid up ashore at Woolverstone marina; she was only six months old and had hardly been sailed. She looked spanking new and we both fell in love with her, a slender navy-blue swan of extraordinary grace. She had all we thought we needed, comfortable accommodation below with two berths forward, a bathroom and toilet, two settees and one pilot berth, navigation table, galley and a decent cockpit, and a 15 hp petrol/oil engine.

The decision to throw up our life on land and take to the sea, perhaps for years on end, was a tremendous cross-roads for us both. The children wished us well, but others thought we were mad. The conversation invariably followed the same pattern. 'Your husband's ex Navy of course—or ex Merchant Navy?' 'No.' 'Have you sailed on a boat this size before?' 'No.' 'Don't you think you should have an experienced naval man with you?' 'No.' We were both confident and determined we would make it in our own way. Norman had always been an active and hardy sportsman—a first-class oarsman in his younger days in Australia, and in latter years he had kept up his skiing; I reckoned we'd little to worry about.

Our plan was to head for the Mediterranean, and to get acclimatised there to living afloat. The winter of 1968/69 was spent rearranging our lives, selling or storing our possessions, getting the family organised, buying the necessary charts, pilot books and equipment. Norman tried to find out as much as possible about conditions, routes to take, and a myriad other things. He wrote for advice to Sir Alec Rose who had recently returned from his sail around the world in *Lively Lady*, and to Lord Riverdale who had sailed *Bluebird of Thorne* to New Zealand, and both these fine sailors were very helpful.

Together with the children we took *Dionis* on her maiden voyage from Warsash on the Hamble to Guernsey, where we would prepare for the next stage. It was a bumpy, wet overnight cross-Channel passage, with all of us wearing inflatable lifejackets. I felt like a blown-up Diana Dors, having an ample bosom anyway, so movement and cooking were most awkward. Bri, Chris and Carrie were marvellous, each taking a watch and loving the adventure.

There followed eighteen glorious months in the Mediterranean with the children joining us at various stages as we cruised to all the islands right through to Greece and Turkey. As the weeks flew by, we adjusted to our new mode of living. We felt fitter than we'd ever felt before. Our bodies became tuned to perpetual motion, our knees were more supple, gone were the aching muscles of the early days. We changed our priorities, accepting the fact that our boat was number one and we came second. The realisation that we were on our own—away from friends, the family doctor, dentist, shops and services we could call on when in need—drew us closer together than we'd ever been before. We simplified our life. I cut my hair short so the wind couldn't whip it into my eyes. We kept our clothes down to a few practical basics. We learned to conserve our 30 gallons of water, never certain when we'd get our next supply, by using sea water for cooking and washing and on hot days throwing buckets of it over each other on the foredeck to keep ourselves alert.

These eighteen months gave us experience and confidence. They were a good try-out, as the Mediterranean is not as most people think, always sunny and balmy—the weather can be very changeable, and between Siros and Tinos we found force eleven more than enough. On New Year's Day 1970 Norman said: 'This life suits us. There's no reason why we shouldn't sail further. What about the West Indies?' 'Well, why not?' I replied. It still didn't percolate through to me that he was already envisaging a world cruise.

Anyway, if sailing was to be our permanent way of living, we needed a bigger boat. Norman went to London to the Boat Show to see what was available, then at Port Hamble marina saw a Trewes class steel ketch which seemed ideal—40 feet, strongly built, well finished, with an aft cabin and an interior which could be altered to suit our needs. We ordered a slightly larger version to be built in Holland—42 foot over the deck, 33 foot waterline, 12 foot 3 inch beam, 5 foot 5 inch draft, displacement 21 tons—for delivery in November 1970.

In September *Dionis* reached Cannes to be laid up for sale, and sadly we said farewell. We were now homeless, with our worldly possessions heaped on the quay in Cannes old harbour—and how pathetic they looked. Then, piling everything into a hired van, we drove to the builder's yard on the old Zuyder Zee or IJsselmeer as it is now called, rented a couple of rooms nearby and took up shore residence while the vessel grew into a fine ship, our ship, our permanent home, under our supervision. What a crazy few weeks these were! There was so much to do, to organise and have made the way we wanted, and always there was the language barrier.

But at last came the day of launching. The sheen on the new boat's topsides was dazzling, the varnish gleamed; she was a delight to the eye. The yard workmen massed around us as Norman, determined to have the last word after the many misunderstandings from our not knowing Dutch, actually delivered a speech in Dutch (having been helped to prepare it by the local bank manager). There were gasps of amusement, an obviously touched silence, then a great ovation from the yard men. I cracked a bottle of champagne on the bow and named the ship *Shebessa* (combining my name and Norman's mother's—Bess). It was a heady moment.

After *Dionis* we felt as if we were driving a Rolls Royce after a Mini. There was so much to learn about *Shebessa*. And with a six cylinder Volvo Penta 75 hp engine after *Dionis*'s two cylinder two stroke engine—what a change! Somehow we had to get our ship across the North Sea to England to have most of the electrical navigation equipment, including the Necco compass and Pinta autopilot, fitted at a yard near Southampton to save transport costs and duties—and already we had snow and ice on the windscreen. Our water supply, 160 gallons, was in a cement-lined tank under the saloon. We were instructed to change the water at least five times to make sure it was sweet and pure.

Our insurers had insisted we must take at least two crew apart from ourselves on ocean crossings, so we had advertised. After some correspondence two young men came over from England to

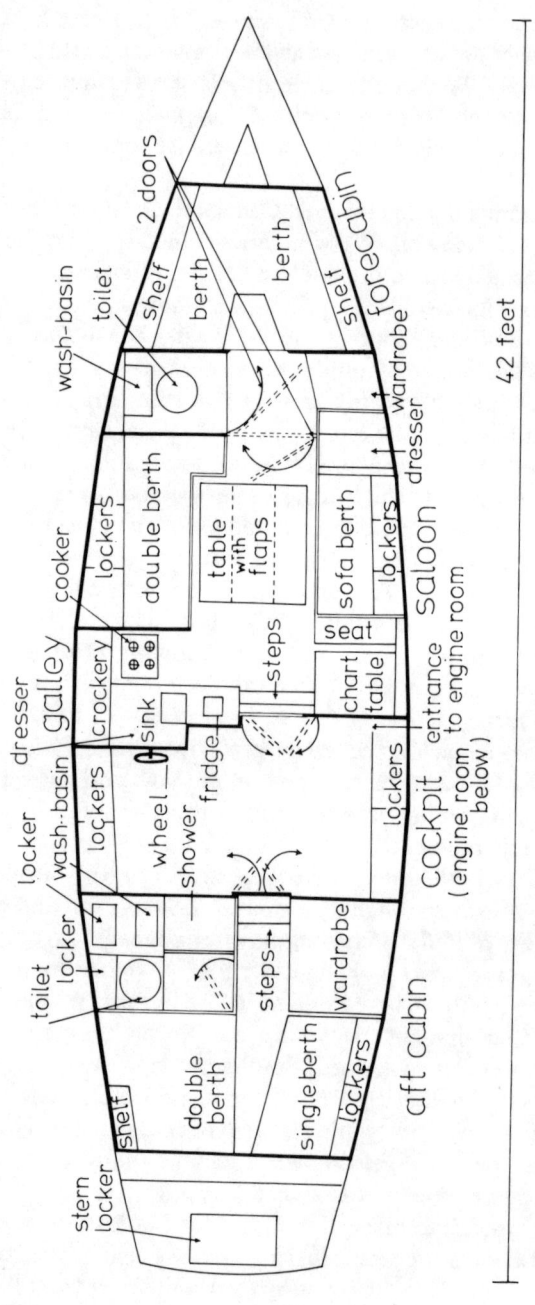

Shebessa: accommodation plan

sail with us to the West Indies: a twenty-five-year-old called Griffiths who had not done much sailing, and Ricky, a burly Cornish-American, younger but confident, forthright and a cook, who had sailed to Canada in a squarerigger. These two were the first in what was to prove a long succession of crew of widely varying characters and abilities whom we were to have stopping on and off *Shebessa* from one part of the world to another, each paying his keep in return for—the idea was, enjoyable cruising and experience.

All feeling highly apprehensive and strange learning the ropes of a new ship, we somehow shook down together and got our new beauty to Amsterdam, then through the locks to IJmuiden, the outlet to the North Sea. From there, taking our courage in both hands and with a favourable weather report, we set sail for the Solent. Within hours of leaving, a force eight gale blew up. It was freezing cold. We were pitching and tossing like mad. The cooker overgimballed, as it hadn't as yet had the protecting fiddles fitted. Our casserole supper landed on the floor, a greasy mass. I scooped it up and wiped the floor—but it was still very slippery. The pitching was crazier than ever and we were all grimly hanging onto the nearest handhold. I covered the floor of our exquisite new saloon with a packet of bread crumbs, which gave us some grip.

The water came out of the tap dark brown and looked undrinkable. Was it to be a dry voyage? We'd little else on board to drink. The next morning, for his first breakfast at sea, Norman asked for a large pot of tea and scoffed five beakerfuls, with all eyes watching him—and a wary eye was kept on him all day. When would he keel over? He didn't; he looked disgustingly healthy. So we all started quenching our thirst.

We battled on through gale force winds, down to a storm jib with those short steep waves of the North Sea smashing into us, crashing onto the coach roof and deck as the bow dived in. The mizzen pulled out of the boom track, the navigation lights were carried away. With soggy clothes and a biting wind, we started dodging ships as we crossed the main shipping lane. I had the oven on all day, not for cooking but crammed with wet clothes; at least they were warm to put on if not dry.

The crew man I shall never forget, on this diabolical maiden voyage for which even the worst excesses of the Mediterranean had not prepared us, was Griff who, despite all, kept smiling. He was a small man and dressed up in his yellow oilskins and hood looked just like a gnome. Fighting his way back from the foredeck in the gale after helping to reduce sail to a storm jib, he hung on to a stanchion for dear life as we heeled, the starboard deck well under water. As we rolled yet further, he disappeared under the foaming freezing sea and only the point of his hood was visible, while Norman screamed out at intervals from the foredeck, 'Hang on Griff!' as I held the wheel, shaking with fear and numb with cold. Time and again our yellow gnome went down and came up before he could make a break for it and reach the safety of the cockpit.

On the second night, still with storm jib only, we were wallowing around trying to hold our position when a freighter loomed out of the mist. We hadn't enough steerage way to take safe avoiding action so collision looked imminent. 'Send up a white flare!' screamed Norman at the wheel, but when Ricky threw it, instead of going up it landed in the cockpit. Norman grabbed it and threw it again, only to hit Griff in the chest as he came round the storm canopy to shelter (he'd been flashing a torch at the freighter). The flare bounced back again onto the cockpit seat, and had to be thrown a third time. The freighter was now only fifty yards away, looming it seemed a hundred feet above us. By some miracle we managed to get on a parallel course so that she slipped by alongside. We all sighed with relief.

Later that night, while I was crossing the cockpit, a violent lurch sent me flying, my head crashing heavily against the cockpit seat, and I came to dazed and shaken. 'What on earth am I doing here?' I asked myself. 'I must be out of my tiny mind.'

A very exhausted, wet crew sailed up the Hamble to Moody's boatyard at Swanwick.

Our game little Griff said to us: 'I'll let you know about the next voyage', but we somehow felt it was really goodbye. He'd been scared to death, we knew, yet he had never shirked anything, so we would have been happy to take him again. Norman was thankful that Ricky, an excellent crew with a deep love of the sea, was willing to stay with us—though ideally I could have wished for a quieter man than this noisy extrovert.

We had decided to head for the West Indies via the Canaries, and then if we were happy with our new way of living to keep heading West to Australia and visit Melbourne, Norman's home town, where he had a couple of nephews and a niece, whose parents, Norman's brother and his wife, had been killed in a car accident some years previously; they would be as pleased to see us as we would them.

Having set December 16th for *Shebessa*'s departure, we had three weeks of intense activity: taking out both masts, re-rigging, fitting the autopilot, a DF loop on top of the mainmast and a radar reflector on top of the mizzenmast, repositioning winches, provisioning and a host of other jobs.

But for the 1,900 miles passage to the Canaries Norman was going to be without his first mate. It was decided I should rest a while and settle a few loose ends, while Norman and his crew sailed *Shebessa* to Tenerife, where I would join them.

Together we interviewed new crew. Norman was in favour of two hands in addition to Ricky for the voyage across the Atlantic. He was giving a lot of thought, too, to the notorious Bay of Biscay. We advertised again in the yachting magazines and saw four applicants. We found it a difficult problem to choose crew; how were we really to know how it would work out for us or for them? The answer was—one couldn't really; one just had to chat, asking questions to try to find out the character of each man. Sailing experience is really immaterial in crew—it is character that counts, and that's always hard to judge in advance.

Compatibility is the other essential, an ability to converse intelligently, to have some interests for conversation, cheerfulness and a willingness to be told what to do without getting upset. Not being psychiatrists, we had to take pot luck on our instinct.

We picked Robin, a young man of twenty-five who had never sailed at sea but had experience on Thames barges, now had an urge to roam the world—and could play the mouth-organ. It turned out to be a happy choice. Robin was a bright yet easy-going, unassuming type with a good sense of humour, very willing to learn, and utterly reliable in carrying out orders—sometimes too reliable. In the early stages of the passage to Tenerife, Norman told me later, when Robin was steering a course given him—usually 240°—suddenly a banking and flapping of sails would be heard and the ship would slow down. Norman would come up and say 'The wind's changed, Robin—what course are you steering?' '240°, that's what you said skipper.' We also picked Simon, twenty-four years old, studious, careful, rather uncertain as to his own abilities and early on a little uncertain of his skipper's—especially in navigation. Then at the last moment

Norman was delighted when Bri got three weeks off from university and arrived at Swanwick to join him for the sail to Tenerife, so that with Ricky he now had a crew of four. Bri was more than welcome as he had proved a tower of strength on *Dionis*.

On December 16th, miraculously on schedule, *Shebessa* slid off down the Hamble to the Solent, following the course and timetable Norman had long and carefully planned so as to be at the Needles at ebb tide. With a strange feeling I got on with my jobs, constantly in my mind the awareness that I too would soon be on the ocean for an indefinite period to come. How often would we meet conditions like the savagery of the North Sea, or, no doubt, even worse?

On New Year's Eve, in a very mixed up frame of mind, I boarded the plane for Tenerife. It was one of the hardest decisions of my life. Still badly shaken by the buffeting of the North Sea, I had had to say goodbye to our family for probably a matter of years. I was fearful of what I'd let myself in for, and whether I could cope. At this stage I would have willingly chickened out, but deep inside me I knew I couldn't let Norman down now. Mustering my last ounce of courage I caught the flight.

For two days I haunted the waterfront of Tenerife, scanning the horizon for sight of a sail. On the third afternoon, while idly throwing stones into a pool on the rocky shore, I looked up to see *Shebessa* under full sail gliding towards the harbour. I'd never seen her at sea before and was spellbound by her line and beauty. Racing as fast as my legs would take me to the wharf, too breathless to shout, I waved my arms to catch her crew's attention. Within minutes *Shebessa* was alongside, and I jumped on board into the arms of Norman and Bri. Excitement and relief welled up in me. My fears were forgotten. I was home.

As there was a heavy swell in Santa Cruz harbour, when the customs men had gone we moved off to anchor in the more sheltered fishing harbour of San Andros nearby. As we sailed there I eagerly lapped up the details of the voyage from England. It had been a smooth passage this time—apart from the question of navigation. Norman had relied the first night out on seeing the light on Start Point to the south of Torbay, intending to continue to Falmouth to await a good wind for the Bay. But no light did anyone see! The sense control on the DF set wasn't working, and he couldn't tell if they were east or west of Start Point. Simon never got over this episode. 'If he can't find Start Point how's he going to find the Canaries?' he was heard to mutter. However, with a continuing spanking south-easterly they hadn't needed to stop at Falmouth but continued down the Channel, crossing the Bay of Biscay to put in at the Portuguese sardine fishing port of Leixões, then on to find the North-East trades—the wind up to force six, with *Shebessa* running directly before it, which made for exhilarating sailing at up to ten knots. On Madeira the boys enjoyed a colossal New Year's Eve binge ashore and Norman, worn out by all the excitement and responsibilities of his first ocean voyage proper, a sleep around the clock on *Shebessa*. The 1,875 miles from England had been covered in 18 days.

2
Islands in the Sun

San Andros fishing harbour was the meeting-place for many yachts making the trans-Atlantic crossing, and someone would always be dropping in to recount an experience or swap tools. Alongside us was Ted, a stocky Englishman in his sixties, in his 30 foot *Santa Lena*. Ted had owned a garage in Leicester, working hard all his life, never finding time for a holiday abroad. Year after year he had listened to his customers' tales of their travels. He bided his time till a petrol company bought him out, and then set out to realise his ambition to see the world in his own boat. It wasn't too late; he still felt fit. 'Had all my teeth out—my appendix too,' said Ted. 'No point in taking chances at my age.' There was no happier man in all Tenerife. An old friend, a master mariner in his late seventies, had agreed to sail with him to the West Indies.

Sadly we said goodbye to Bri who now had to go back to university. Simon too departed back to England with his parents who had been holidaying in Tenerife, so our extra crew was down to the regulation two again for the passage to the West Indies.

On January 19th, 1971 with *Shebessa* filled to the limit for the long curving route through the North-East trades to the South-West, we weighed anchor to leave sight of land for 2,720 miles to Barbados. I hadn't yet come to terms with *Shebessa* or myself as to ocean sailing. Each morning the struggle to get my legs into my pants almost finished me. Once I was flung onto the loo with such violence I split the seat. 'Are we both mad?' I wondered daily. If only the world below me would stop moving. Norman, Ricky and Robin after the voyage to Tenerife were acclimatised and had confidence in our ship. I felt a novice again, getting used to a wheel instead of a tiller, and everything seemed enormous. The Mediterranean was a pond in comparison to these seas. Norman was doing a fine job but I was ill at ease; this was a voyage of much soul-searching for me. I could always be a coward and fly home from Barbados—if we ever found it—and be a grass widow for a few years. Or I could become a better seawife and conquer my fears.

I knew really that, come what might, I could never leave Norman's side, even if I had to chase with him round the globe, so it was up to me somehow to earn my stripes. What was I worried about anyway? My main responsibilities to my children were over now they were grown-up. I'd already lived a great life if I were to die tomorrow. I was only the size of a grain of sand among the teeming millions on the earth. I was an idiot at mathematics, so wondered how I could ever learn to navigate—yet if I didn't what would happen if disaster hit Norman? In fact I never did learn to navigate, reckoning it would cause problems on board; my reading would never work out the same as Norman's so which course would we take? I preferred to stay totally dependent on the skipper, who had never let me down yet.

Gradually I got to grips with fear, often having long talks with myself: 'Never mind, we can't all be Chichesters', and so forth. Then when my sense of humour was sadly waning I drew comfort from talking in broad Yorkshire, 'Ee lass, ye're a bit oop tight, don't be daft, pull thee self together.' The tongue of my home county made me smile and broke the tension.

Day followed day in a regular routine of steering, watch-keeping, maintenance, resting and sleeping. Each of us filled in the rough log at the navigation table after our watch, marking down the exact time, mileage and course steered; this was an important duty, in case weather conditions became such that Norman couldn't take sights and had to rely on dead reckoning. The little daily crosses on the chart gradually inched their way towards our landfall. We experienced all sorts of weather—rain, squalls, calms, and strong winds as the North-East trades were blowing harder than we'd anticipated.

I didn't do any cooking on this voyage. Ricky insisted on doing it and I didn't argue—he was an experienced cook, he did it well, and he obviously enjoyed it. He himself had a vast appetite, the stores disappearing at an alarming rate. He was meticulous at looking after the ship as well as his own equipment, even bringing out his own sewing roll to mend his jacket and refusing my offer of help. He was fearless on deck and very useful to have on board I had to admit—but his larger-than-life style made him at times a difficult person for me to put up with on 42 foot of boat. Robin, quiet and good-natured, was still learning the ropes but revelling in his new occupation. He gleefully accompanied our sea shanties on his mouth organ.

As we passed the half-way mark it at last became warmer, with sunny days and balmy nights, the moon and seemingly every star ablaze, and I began to relax and gain confidence. The high spot of the day for me was the early morning, when the seas were always kinder. While at the helm I would gaze at the flying fish, half fish, half bird with their extended wing-like fins. Like silver darts in the dawn light, they skimmed the waves, missing crest after crest by a hair's breadth, finally diving into the dark blue trough below. Usually we would find five or six lying on the deck, the boys collecting them for breakfast, and how I savoured the smell that wafted up from the galley as they sizzled in the frying pan.

We steered *Shebessa* using the twin yankees on the booms and the mizzen. As she rollercoasted up and down the heaving Atlantic rollers, Ricky and Robin took it in turn to sit on the bowsprit platform with legs astride as we zoomed downwards, the sea surging in a froth round their legs. 'Better than cinerama!' Ricky called out in his loud grating voice.

On the sixteenth night out, there occurred another of the many dramas *Shebessa* and her crew were to experience. It was the kind of thing one dreamed about in fearful fantasy. I woke up at 0230 hours to hear Ricky scream: 'I think we're sinking!' Norman rose like a puppet on a string and was in the cockpit in five seconds flat.

Norman: Thoughts of the liferaft were in my mind. The engine room was flooded—it looked as if it was full with steam coming out! Splash! Down into it to find water two feet deep and steam pouring out all the time. What in heaven's name was the problem?

We must be holed, and yet the hull was steel, so what could hole us out here? A whale couldn't do that to us. Or could it? We had felt no bump. The priority was to get the water level down to see what was happening. I switched on the electric bilge pump, but it didn't seem to make much impression. I reckoned it was probably just keeping up with the water coming in. 'Get some buckets!' I yelled. Frantically I submerged these into the water, sloshing about and passing them up to be emptied. The old saying is certainly true that the best bilge pump is a frightened man with a bucket. After a couple of hours of frenzied work the level was under control and no more was coming in. So we couldn't be holed. So what was it?

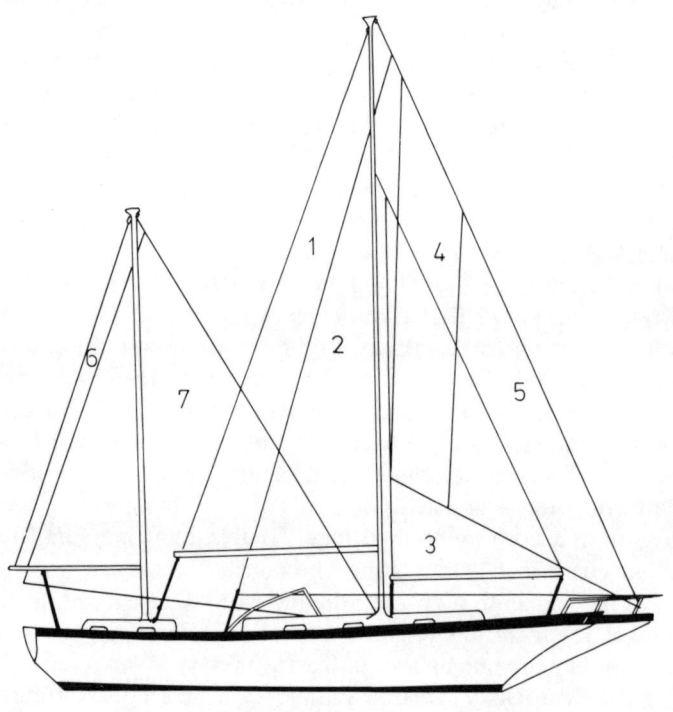

Shebessa: sail plan
1—Mainsail (298 sq. ft). 2—Genoa (558 sq. ft). 3—Boom staysail (148 sq. ft). 4—No. 1 yankee (252 sq. ft). 5—No. 2 yankee (140 sq. ft). 6—Mizzen (136 sq. ft). 7—Mizzen staysail (358 sq. ft)

Then I saw the trouble. The rubber hose in the wet exhaust line leading out of the engine along which the cooling water passed into the main exhaust was hanging off. Earlier in the night the wind had suddenly dropped so one of the crew, who shall be nameless, had started the engine, but without opening the exhaust cock. This cock is closed when the engine is stopped to ensure that sea water cannot run back up the exhaust pipe into the engine when the ship is heeled over. The exhaust fumes being unable to escape, pressure had built up; the hose was the weakest link so it blew off before the pressure caused the engine to stop. Later when the cock was opened, the engine had started and run normally but the cooling sea water from the heat exchanger had been pumped not into the exhaust for despatch overside, but directly out of the engine into the bilge, then when that had filled, into the engine room itself. How lucky we were that the engine had been stopped when it had been—in another few minutes the level would have reached the electrics and the alternator, then God alone knows what would have happened, a fire probably. We replaced the hose from the spares, washed everything down in petrol which dries quickly to get rid of the sea water, wiped it off, turned the key . . . and she started. No actual harm seemed to have been done.
Norman ends.

But we still didn't use the engine again until we reached the West Indies and had the opportunity of checking it thoroughly; fortunately the wind kept up and we had no real further need of it on this passage.

Excitement and anticipation gradually built up as our landfall—Barbados, hopefully—approached. From early morning on the twenty-first day from Tenerife we were all straining our eyes ahead when 'Land ahoy!' Robin shouted. A low faint outline had appeared on the horizon on the port bow. Barbados it was. Norman in particular breathed a sigh of relief, thankful that we had finally made it after his first real test of celestial navigation. It was a thrilling moment. We felt rather like Captain Cook discovering his first island.

We sailed down the western side of the beautiful tropical island of Barbados, past majestic beaches and large hotels blending quietly into the scenery, before dropping anchor opposite the Barbados Yacht Club, a lovely old colonial building in Carlisle Bay a few miles from Bridgetown. Amazing, I thought to myself as I counted the bruises on various parts of my anatomy, what the human body will stand.

Now followed, after twenty-one days at sea, twenty-one days of sheer pleasure and luxury: lying on hot sand with coconut palms waving gently above us, a drink in hand; swimming in warm water; visiting the local market and shops; listening to the noise and laughter of Barbadians. Wending our way South from St Vincent through the Grenadines, the little group of English-speaking islands stretching to Grenada, we anchored in a deserted bay off the west coast of Union Island. A local fisherman told us the village wasn't far away, just over the hill. As we needed stores, Norman and I decided to go there on our own. We took off, wearing canvas shoes for the first time for months. The track was overgrown so we had to fight our way through uphill jungle, arriving at the village scratched and dirty with sweat running off us.

Walking up the mud track we met a stocky little American woman; she looked about sixty and had a mop of white hair. She didn't mince words. 'Come and have some of my stew,' she said, 'You look tired', and thankfully we accepted her invitation, following her up the hill past little wooden shacks and three small stores to her home. She introduced herself as Millicent and quickly set about tending to our needs: water for our parched throats, some to splash on our faces, and then some for our feet—the relief was so great when we removed our shoes that it overcame the embarrassment we might have felt at their colour and smell. Two buckets of water appeared, doctored with boric acid, and the pair of us sat with our tired blistered feet in the buckets eating our lunch. With the balmy water, the delicious stew and home-made lemonade we began to recover.

Millicent's home was an old stone house with walls about 18 inches thick, a house she had rented without furniture—in fact there were a lot of withouts, no electricity, gas or water laid on. She had decided to live among a 99 per cent black population to see how she made out alone before buying property on the island. Her living room was welcoming and homely, with masses of windows thrown open wide to catch all the breezes. There were only three pieces of conventional furniture—an old rocking chair and two hard chairs picked up in the village. The table, the central piece, was a sheet of formica fixed on top of beer crates. The sofa consisted of crates covered with foam, a rug and cushions. The back door, which was always open, was a frame for her garden, cultivated from a wilderness in the three months she had been there. It was a mass of highly coloured tropical flowers, which she tended with loving care morning and evening. She had started a vegetable garden too with pigeon peas, lettuce and tomatoes growing in abundance, and this was an island where practically nothing else grew. Her water supply was in four strategically placed wine barrels. A latch door in the living room led to the loo where, balanced on top of the cistern, was an enormous trap to catch the rat that lurked there. Water was in short supply so the loo was flushed only once a day. Using it was a nerve-racking experience, furtively looking over your shoulder for the rat, remembering not to pull the chain, retreating fast and latching the door quickly.

As my feet were badly blistered Millicent asked me to spend the night with her, and I gladly accepted, feeling rather strange. All I had was what I was wearing, a bikini and a shirt, both looking the worse for wear. Norman returned to *Shebessa*, to sail with Ricky and Robin to the main harbour close to the village next day. I slept that night like a log until dawn . . .

Millicent had a maid. She came at eight a.m. until noon and for two hours at dusk. Her main job was to carry water from the well half way down the hill, a daily task six days a week. Balancing an old tin on her head, she walked to and fro, filling up the barrels; she was just a slip of a girl but she carried the tin with such poise. She also did the washing, sitting on her upturned tin with two buckets beside her. The clothes were subjected to a great deal of battering on the hard concrete but came up spotlessly clean. Millicent objected bitterly to her smalls having such rough treatment, instructing her maid time and again not to slap them against the stone. She wasted her breath; as soon as Millicent's back was turned, the girl returned to her own method with a dreamy faraway smile on her face.

Dress standards were kept up even on this small island. Shorts were all right at home, but to go down the main street, the only street, the mud track, a dress was called for. Millicent insisted that I should take a pumpkin with me when I joined *Shebessa* that afternoon and she knew just where we could find one. She decked me up in one of her dresses and a pair of slip-ons four sizes too big, and we set off to see a lady who lived over the hill. A tall woman, heavy with child, her thirteenth, ushered us into her home, a small room downstairs with a kitchenette off and one room upstairs. Fourteen people lived in this house and there would soon be fifteen. I tried to work out how seven people per room could find space to lay down their bodies to sleep. The woman gave us an enormous pumpkin from her store. To offer money would have been an insult, and yet I couldn't help thinking of all those hungry mouths she had to feed.

I talked Millicent into joining us for a sail to a neighbouring island so after lunch she decided a bath was necessary. She produced a galvanised metal wash tub and filled it with buckets of water. There in her living room she stripped, lowered herself into this small tub and sat with her legs hanging out, vigorously scrubbing hereself, till she was a mass of suds. Twenty-four hours ago we had been strangers, and now as I watched her do her ablutions I felt we had been friends for years. I shall always hold the greatest admiration for this brave little woman, who at a mature age and alone turned her back on the comforts and sophisticated social life of New York to live on a sun-drenched island.

We pressed on South through the Grenadines to Grenada, where we said farewell to Ricky and Robin, whose voyage ended here. We were glad to be alone for a while to enjoy our new ship as you only can *à deux*. In these warm waters I finally shed my fears and forgot all about the discomforts of the North Sea and the first few days in the Atlantic. Sailing once again seemed not only a natural way of life, but *the* most desirable one. We lingered in the sunshine. Here was what we had been dreaming about for so many years. St George's, Grenada was a sleepy town, the little café on the front, The Nutmeg, a meeting place for shoppers. Grand Anse beach was only half an hour's sail away, a long crescent of talcum powder sand fringed with palms. We met Ted again, now sailing alone; his friend had flown back to England. Ted believed in simple living when alone—seven or eight bananas for lunch, bread, cheese and pickled onions for supper—and was thriving on this diet. How he had changed since we had last seen him in Tenerife. He now sported gaily coloured shirts and an enormous straw hat with strings attached that were firmly wound round his waist in case the wind blew it away. He was as happy as a king.

And who wouldn't be here, where there seemed to be all the good things of life? 'Go slow and live' was written on all the petrol attendants' badges and they believed in it.

We had never sailed *Shebessa* alone before, and now decided to have a real holiday, island hopping up through the Grenadines to Antigua. This was easy to do, with short hops and good anchorages, if we were careful to negotiate the reefs. We headed for the Tobago Cays, only half a day's sail away—two uninhabited islands surrounded by reefs with, we had been told, the clearest water imaginable and abounding in fish and crayfish, a spear-fisherman's paradise.

We anchored between the two islands, careful to lay out two anchors as the current was strong. We swam and relaxed, Norman delighting in spearing fish for supper. I felt there was a distinct caveman attitude in this desire to hunt the evening meal. The fish—blue-green docile-looking parrots, reddish-tinged garoupe with their hideous bulging eyes, and highly coloured angel fish almost too beautiful to eat—all proved delicious.

We threaded our way through further islands, carefully watching the colour of the water. Pale blue and sand colour spelt danger, in deep blue, we felt safe. One afternoon we sailed into Bequia, a small island near St Vincent, with a large secluded and very beautiful bay and a tiny village on the far shore. Here on a yacht lived an American doctor with his pretty blonde wife and four children, two to seven years old. He was responsible for the health of this and the neighbouring islands, receiving calls by radio telephone, then sailing to see his patients, combining work and pleasure. This was one of the happiest ships we'd met, peals of laughter coming from the decks each day. The children's home was a gymnasium, the sea their swimming pool. For hours they'd swing on ropes from the boom to the guard rail, hanging on by their feet upside down just like monkeys, the two-year-old keeping up with the rest. He couldn't swim but he'd run to the stern, pull in the dinghy with one hand and with the other grab the anchor chain, then wrap his little legs around the chain and slither down it into the boat unaided. It was quite extraordinary how self-reliant these small children were.

Sailing across the bay trailing our fishing line with a red rag as a lure, we had caught a 20 lb barracuda. We cut it up and took some ashore to give to the locals. In the corner of the bay was an old wooden house—Barclays Bank. Beside it was a shack the size of a garden hut, the bakery. Here an old woman made bread every day, using an oil drum as her oven. She was surrounded by her animals which wandered in and out as she worked, ducks, a lamb, a goat, cats, dogs, turkeys and hens. We bought some bread and offered her barracuda. Her eyes lit up: 'Missus—I want de 'ead. Rest no good.'

Blissful days were spent in Bequia, getting to know the people and their pattern of living. When the fishing boats came in, a large conch shell like a trumpet was blown to let the village know the catch was ready for sale. We'd drop everything, jump into the dinghy and row over fast to join the throng round the fishing boats, delighting just in the sight of the variety of fresh fish jumping around in the boat.

Bequia was one of the few places left where the locals—mostly one family—still hunted for whales using the same methods as Captain Ahab. When a whale was sighted from the lookouts on the coast, off went two whalers, open boats manned by six hardy men who sailed or rowed in the direction indicated by flashing mirror signals from the lookouts. They came up dead behind the whale's tail, alongside the body, then zing! In went the harpoons by hand, to mortally wound the animal, later to be towed across to Petit Nevis, a small islet close by where the whale was cut up for local food and boiled for oil. As we sailed into the tiny harbour the stench of the whale meat being cooked in vast cauldrons nearly overpowered us; the shallow water and the beach were a mass of huge bones, some half as long as *Shebessa*. In Kingstown, St Vincent, a few miles away, the stalls along the street sold whale meat, small lumps cooked with what looked like a piece of yellow fat on top. With the smells of Petit Nevis still in our nostrils we didn't try it. Flying fish in abundance were sold here, and cheap. Our diet was gradually changing to fish rather than meat, which was of poor quality in these parts.

We sailed on North to English Harbour, Antigua—a very picturesque place steeped in history, many of the old buildings still standing from Nelson's day when he used the harbour as his main base. It was a crowded spot, with hundreds of yachts moored.

Soon after we arrived, I heard a caricature English voice booming alongside us: 'Malcolm Parker here. Are you thah?' I went up into the cockpit to behold, in a dinghy, a middle-aged man with a trim moustache, wearing spotless duck trousers and a reefer jacket. 'Everyone calls me Parky,' he announced. 'Come aboard my schoonah for a drink at six bells.' We'd arranged to meet friends that night, the 'six bells' flawed me—and yet I was intrigued to get to know this character and see his schooner. I went below to ask Norman what time Six Bells was, not wishing to air my ignorance. 'Well yes or no?' the voice rang out. I accepted the invitation. 'Six bells then. You know our yacht *Yackshima*? Everyone does. She's lying thah.'

On the dot of Six Bells we arrived and were introduced to another English couple, a tall droopy female who reminded me of a bloodhound, and her flabby-looking husband. We were ushered below. Climbing down the companionway, Norman drew my attention to an old desk and muttered something about having antiques aboard. 'Neturallah,' said Parky. 'The old girl was built in 1870.' Silently we entered the roomy saloon to be confronted with the brassy stare of a great bell. In the centre was a refectory table with bunk beds on one side, a replica of a park bench on the other, and a large comfortable carver's chair at the head—Parky's seat. We arranged ourselves round the table with Parky heading it, the only one in comfort. I felt a board meeting was about to commence. A small severe-looking woman, his wife, with back as stiff as a ramrod, served the drinks.

Parky opened the board meeting. His first target was Norman. 'Suppose you're British?' 'Australian.' 'Oh my god—dreadful stupid people. Friend of mine was going to settle thah—very famous man ectuallah—built his own yacht, sailed it there and they had the cheek to charge him purchase tax. Didn't pay. Sailed away and they lost a first class citizen.' Silence reigned. Then Parky fired his second shot at Norman. 'Employed any of the natives heah?' We'd had a boy cleaning the decks; he had worked hard and we were pleased with him. 'We employed a lad for a day,' said Norman. 'What'd you pay him?' 'Ten BW dollars.' 'Ten!' exploded Parky, spluttering gin, and the long droopy woman came to life and looked quite vicious: 'I pay five. And you've got to be jolly careful who you have aboard.' Silence once more.

We had given up any hope of having anything like a normal conversation. Parky continued to our amazement: 'Picking up a charter tomorrow. Frightful bore, but you have to slum it occasionally to make the odd pittance. Going to Bermuda ectuallah—taking on water heah first thing—if it runs out on the way they'll have to do without. Ha ha ha.' Eventually we made our getaway. It was quite the oddest drinks party we'd ever attended.

We sailed to the more northerly islands, a number of which were under French administration. In the duty free port of St Barts we met Tom Shortall, an American in his twenties on his yacht *Deneb*. He was having a spot of bother the day we arrived. He'd jumped into his old dinghy and gone clean through the bottom, losing his specs. Diving for these, his traveller's cheques had fallen out of his pocket. Hours of searching went on but to no avail. Tom took it all philosophically. He and his shipmate were fun people to be with; Tom had a mop of black curly hair and big round laughing eyes that captivated the girls. Wanting to travel, Tom had been given leave for a year from his studies at Yale. He asked us if he could join *Shebessa* in December for our voyage to and across the Pacific, and happily we agreed to take him on at Grenada.

At Martinique we turned South once more, and set off to see the famed beach at Gros Islet Bay, St Lucia. It was one of those dream West Indian days with a good steady wind, yet clear skies, hot sun and gentle seas; we registered a steady seven knots. Norman got a line on Pigeon Island, the entrance to Gros Islet Bay, before dusk. It became very dark so we anticipated difficulty in finding the entrance. We decided we could motor in at slow speed rather than fast under sail.

Norman went forward to drop the sails, while I started the engine. I put the motor into gear and we shot forward at a strange speed, so I throttled back a little—but *Shebessa* flew! It was like being in the fastest speedboat I'd ever been in as we raced all over the ocean. A million thoughts flashed through me. I can't control her speed. I must keep in control. I can't leave the wheel. How can I stop her? What's gone wrong? I screamed for Norman, but my voice was carried away. I could see he was screaming at me, but I couldn't hear. Steer away from trouble, even if you're flying. Keep your head. My mouth was dry. I was shaking. Norman, please hurry back. I wanted to switch off, but then I'd ruin the engine. 'Never switch off when the engine's running fast; let her idle first.' I'd had those words dinned into me, but how could I make a racing engine idle? We were now in neutral and the engine was roaring. Suddenly there was a loud clunk—then silence.

Norman was back in the cockpit. He made a bee-line for the engine room, where there was water around and steam rising. Then he looked up at the ceiling and saw a snow-like substance, crystals, and smelt GAS.

In the port locker of the cockpit we had a spare gas bottle, standing upright, wedged in with spare sheets, warps and sail bags, that we had carried from England. We opened the locker. It was as if a hard frost had fallen on the contents. Everything was white over, crisp and sparkling, and there was an overpowering smell of gas. The bottle now lay on its side; somehow it had tipped over, the safety stopper had loosened and liquid gas was running out. The gas vapour had entered the air intake to the engine, which liked this fuel, causing it to 'run away'.

We were both terribly shaken, not speaking but our minds working overtime, running over events. Guilt too. What had I done wrong? Could I have avoided damaging the engine? Should I have switched off? Was it repairable? Was it going to cost a fortune? How could we get a major repair done on a little island like St Lucia? We were in dangerous waters, with no engine, and we had a lockerful of liquid gas. Still numb with fright, I stood there. Norman went into action. He took the fateful bottle to the stern, cleaned it down and lashed it on. The smelly, encrusted warps and sheets he tied on and streamed overboard. The locker and the engine room lid were left open.

During this drama the wind had almost died. We set the sails once more, straining our eyes in the pitch black for a sight of Pigeon Island, and late in the evening ghosted into the bay, dropping anchor a hundred yards from the shore. Tired and hungry, with spirits down to zero, we had a cold meal and fell sound asleep.

At dawn the following day we sailed South-West down the St Lucia coast for Castries. In the marina our engine had been dismantled by the afternoon, and to our great relief the only damage was a blown head gasket, which Norman immediately ordered to be flown out from Holland. So we had an enforced stay of two weeks waiting for the vital part to arrive. 'That's it,' said Norman. 'I'm finished with gas. We'll chuck out all the bottles and buy an alcohol or paraffin stove.' I held my tongue, dreading the change. But mercifully we never did chuck out our gas cooker, instead making wooden platforms to hold our spare bottles and lashing them to the stern.

3
Bandidos and Cunas

We spent ten unforgettable months in the West Indies—but the Pacific and Australia were calling. Tom joined us in his sawn off jeans that had four layers of extra patches sewn on the seat. 'So you reckon you're going to be sitting on your behind a lot?' we teased him. But he knew what he was doing. He was gradually to wear through each layer till he was on his last patch in Tahiti. For the second year of our voyaging our insurance company, under pressure, had reduced their crew requirement on ocean-going voyages from two to one, but a thirty-five-year-old Canadian called Steve Doyle, who had answered an advertisement we had put out before we met Tom, was to join us in Panama. On December 7th, 1971 *Shebessa*, loaded with stores for six months, sailed from Grenada for Panama via the Dutch Antilles.

We started off well, with a perfect night's sailing, warm, starry skies, a little wind from astern, and a calm sea—typical Caribbean weather with not a ship in sight the whole night through. Then before breakfast next day a large tanker and a freighter passed uncomfortably close to us, presumably on a course for Trinidad. We soon approached the first of the Dutch Antilles, Bonaire. This island, Aruba and Curaçao are quite modern and industrialised, especially Aruba with its huge oil refineries. Bonaire is famous for the clarity of the sea, visibility being up to 180 feet—a paradise for skin and scuba divers, while Curaçao is the capital and administrative centre, with fine Dutch buildings and bridges over the canals lined with houses as in Amsterdam. The harbour master in Curaçao worried us when he insisted on taking down a full description of *Shebessa* and our exact itinerary, address of next of kin, etc. It was all very scary—was the voyage going to be that dramatic?

Aruba was noteworthy as the centre of the smuggling industry to Venezuela and Colombia. The luggers loaded up with duty free booze, cigarettes, cameras, watches, etc, waited for a message to come through that the coast was clear, then made a dash for it. We saw six of them there. In Aruba we heard of the Colombian harbours Santa Marta and Cartagena as being lovely places to visit, if you could put up with the bandits. We heard the story of a catamaran which arrived at Santa Marta after a hard passage; the crew anchored, then slept. In the morning there was nothing on board except themselves! Sails, sheets, warps, blocks, fenders, dinghy, radios, instruments, even the sheet winches—all had gone.

Conditions were boisterous, giving us a wild ride to the Colombian coast with strong following winds on the quarter. With no main, just the twin boomed out yankees and mizzen, we were averaging seven knots with *Shebessa* surfing down the faces of the high following rollers so that the helmsman had to be very careful not to broach.

We passed the mountains of the Sierra de Santa Marta towering straight out of the sea to a series of permanently snow-capped peaks rising up to 18,000 feet, a magnificent sight visible 70 miles away. A lugger looking exactly like the smugglers' ships in Aruba passed to port, pounding to windward in the great seas. Apparently the conditions were always the same in this area, so we reckoned the smugglers earned their cash the hard way.

Cabo de San Juan de Guia, the last northerly point before turning South for Cartagena, was hard to get past. A strong current against us and heavy winds astern caused very steep following seas coming at us from two directions—from astern and others apparently bouncing back off the coast around the corner onto our port beam. Our motion was wild. I could no longer control the

Shebessa's course Grenada-Panama

wheel and screamed for help so Norman took over and had his work cut out to keep control. The harbour at Santa Marta looked terrifying, with huge waves crashing on the beach. Neither Tom nor Norman fancied trying to get the booms down in these conditions, so we decided just to keep going, trying to keep dead before the wind, and worry about our destination later.

Tom and Norman divided up the night between them, but there was no sleep for any of us. Only later did Tom tell us of his fears that rugged night. Lying in his bunk listening to the pounding, with enormous following seas and the wind dead behind us, he had come out in a cold sweat, and when at the helm he knew he had only to make one mistake and we should have been over. We were very glad when dawn came and we could turn into the coast to establish our position and find Cartagena. In the lee of the coast life was calmer, so we set to to strip the deck of everything movable, ready for the bandidos, and motored into Cartagena.

First we anchored off the small Club de Pesca, a poor-looking place with a couple of jetties for the many small launches of the fishing members and just one small finger for yachts. Someone shouted a welcome 'Don't stay there, the bandidos will get you!' We anchored stern to to the jetty, about ten yards out. The Club did all the paperwork with customs, as well as supplying a twenty-four hour guard armed with a ·45 revolver! But even in spite of this we were told people still lost anything loose on deck, and we must not leave the ship unattended at night. We had thought of spreading tacks on the foredeck as did Joshua Slocum in *Spray* to keep off the pirates in the Magellan Straits, but settled for two hour watches just as if we were at sea.

Cartagena turned out to be a charming old walled town with many reminders of Spain's great imperial past. There were colonnaded streets, fine squares and shops selling local crafts—old saddles and brass stirrups, Indian mats, Cuna Indian *molas*. I was fascinated to see a most unusual statue on a grassy mound on the outskirts of the town—two enormous boots in stone, 'Los Zapatos Viejos', a monument in memory of a famous Colombian poet who had said on his death bed 'I love Cartagena as I love my boots', and so his boots had been immortalised. We visited the market, a vast roof stretching over hundreds of trading stalls, a mass of narrow passages in semi-darkness, shoes, clothes, fruit and vegetables all jumbled up together. The further we penetrated, the stronger grew the heat and the stench. As a wave of claustrophobia swept over me I had a moment of terror that we'd never be able to find our way out of this maze.

It was Christmas week. The city bustled with the very rich, while pathetically poor people squatted in doorways selling peanuts, tinsel and fireworks, and high above these dirty streets large black buzzards circled in formation overhead. Turkeys were being sold in the streets—live! As I didn't fancy tackling a live turkey on *Shebessa* we settled for Christmas dinner out at one of the many small, intimate restaurants. Everyone seemed happy and willing to help us—except the bandidos.

Norman: Each night the three of us kept watch in turn. It was an eerie sensation standing on the deck in the darkness seeing the faint shadows of canoes paddling silently past, knowing the occupants' eyes were searching *Shebessa* for signs of life before perhaps boarding us. Sure enough, one night Tom shook me awake. 'Skipper, I think they're coming aboard ...' Armed with our staves he and I raced forward to surprise three figures climbing over the bow. What a schemozzle! It was a hand to hand wrestling match which lasted for several minutes. Tom was big and strong and I'm not puny, so after a grand struggle we managed to force them over the rail into the water, and they swam off after their pal who had taken off in the canoe at the first sign of trouble aboard. Next day I asked the guard what would have happened if I had had a gun and shot them. 'Oh, we'd have had to take them to the cemetery,' he said wearily.

'Skipper, they're here again,' Tom whispered urgently in my ear as he awakened me the following night. Again we rushed forward with our staves to see black hands over the coaming as the bandidos balanced in their canoe. Bang! Bang! on those black knuckles, followed by screams of anguish—a very satisfying sound—as they let go, one falling into the water, then off they furiously paddled.

That must surely be the end of their visits—but no. One more and the worst—on Christmas Eve, and we didn't even know till the next morning. Tom, in the forepeak, called out: 'It isn't there.' 'What?' 'The front window!' Some time during the night the bandidos had got on board without the watchkeepers hearing—it being Christmas Eve we were not so vigilant, so Tom and I had dozed in the cockpit with a deck light on, but that hadn't deterred them. They had unscrewed the thirteen screws in the stainless steel surround holding the armour-plated glass window, taken out the glass and thrown it away or kept it, reached in, felt around the front bunks, taken a fishing line and some tins of food, then into their canoe and away without us hearing a sound! The glass was impossible to replace, being shaped and slightly concave to fit the curve of the cabin top, so Christmas Day was spent making a plywood and tin window and screwing and sealing it down; it sufficed all the way to England.

Norman ends.

After all that we reckoned we'd had enough of Cartagena. Although it had been a fascinating glimpse of an old world once so very powerful, our main memory of Colombia would always be the bandidos. We now headed West for the San Blas Islands. Bill Robinson, editor of the American magazine *Yachting*, whom we had met in the West Indies, had fired us with enthusiasm to visit this unusual chain of islands, stretching from the Colombian border 80 miles northwards to Cape San Blas, about 40 miles from Colon, Panama. These 365 islands, one for every day of the year, some inhabited, most not, are the home of the Cuna Indians, a short stocky people of simplicity and charm whose ancestors peopled the same area when Columbus landed.

We had heard the Isla Tigre was the most typical and this tiny speck on the chart was our objective. *Shebessa* rolled heavily through rough confused seas and cloudy weather until we picked up our landfall, Cayos Rotanus; then we followed the coastline, dodging the many shoals on which waves were breaking, to Conception Point, past Devil's Cays—a sinister name for a group of tiny islets—till a line of sticks with arrows led us through a narrow channel between reefs to anchor on Isla Tigre.

Before us lay a tiny strip of land one third of a mile long and 200 yards wide, on which were to be seen a cluster of native huts built of cane and thatched with palm leaves, closely packed together, and a scattering of palm and bread fruit trees. I wondered what sort of reception we should receive. We dressed carefully so as not to offend. I donned a skirt and the boys long pants.

We rowed ashore to the inquisitive yet impassive faces of scores of children and women shyly looking out from the doors of their homes, the women so strange and colourful, all wearing red headscarves patterned with fish and bird designs which, we were told, were made in Lancashire! They were flat-faced swarthy people with bronzed faces and high cheek bones. The women had long black charcoal lines drawn down their noses, and flashing in the sunlight each had a one inch diameter gold ring through the tip of the nose, hanging down to the top of the lips. Their blouses, called *molas*, were dazzlingly gay. The yoke and short sleeves were plain, but under the arms, back and front to the waist they had inserted rectangular pieces of embroidery, a reverse appliqué work, brilliantly patterned, portraying their interpretations of nature. I learned later that a woman often took as long as a year to finish a pair. Over their hips they had wrap-around skirts, varying in colour according to the island. On their arms and legs below the knee were bands of tiny multi-coloured beads, so tightly bound that their flesh bulged out between them; these were never removed unless the thread broke or they wore loose.

We wandered through the mud lanes dividing the huts, marvelling that 1,500 people lived in this small area that was so clean and orderly. We were eager to learn more about this Indian tribe, but had one big problem, the language barrier, knowing no words in Cuna. Somehow we managed to get the message over that we'd like to meet the old chief named Morris, but their signs gave us to believe he was in heaven. Instead we were taken to his son, Ramiro Morris, a pastor, who had been off the island but returned to his people to found a small mission, the Assemblies of God. He spoke reasonable English and became our guide, philosopher and friend.

He took us to visit the homes—one-roomed huts usually about 15 by 30 feet, built of cane with palm leaves for roofs with single and double hammocks slung between the upright posts, clothes and all worldly goods slung from the beams. Here the whole family—two or three generations and up to twenty people—lived in one room. Each family had two huts, one for living and one for cooking. By the waterside were a number of huts, each with a pig inside, and the loos were a row of huts built out over the sea, so they had no sewerage problems. They seemed happy people, always smiling.

On these islands living was communal in most ways with money not needed. Coconuts were the currency. Ramiro said 'Money is not necessary—the Lord will provide' and He did in Ramiro's case via his father-in-law! The men went off in their *cayacos* (canoes carved out of one tree) daily to the mainland about a couple of miles away to work, growing red rice, which grew like wheat, and coconuts, the staple diet; then they collected fresh water in drums from the Tangaw river, which meant paddling up it for four miles until they found the water pure, then paddling back, which was a hard chore. Some men went fishing but this didn't seem to be very successful. The coconuts and fish went into a central pool, the coconuts being sold to Colombian traders for from seven to fifteen to the dollar depending on the time of year. Coconuts were the staple means of support, the money being used to buy rice, sugar and outside commodities. The women formed themselves into groups to cook, taking it in turn to provide meals and make bread.

Although there were three Christian missionaries on Isla Tigre, a great many of the islanders still stuck to their pagan beliefs, worshipping small wooden idols in times of sickness which the witchdoctor made, imbuing them with mysterious healing powers. Despite so-called conversion to Christianity, this faith in idols was the pattern to be found in many islands we visited over the next few years. Uncertain what to believe, the islanders would hide their pagan objects away as an insurance to help them through in need.

The Cuna Indians believed in marriage but there was no ceremony as we know it. The father picked out a young man for his daughter, then if she agreed, he suggested a union or pressganged the prospective bridegroom into it. In either case the latter went into or was pushed into the family hut, where the daughter would be reclining in a hammock, and made to get into it with her for five minutes. He would depart and return next day or next week if he liked, but as Dad was always after him to finalise the union, he usually took the line of least resistance and returned to spend *ten* minutes with his girl. Same procedure next visit, where if he stayed *fifteen* minutes, he had the option of departing for good or else asking the father 'May I chop some wood for you?' This question meant he was committed to the daughter and also to working for the father all his life without reward—except the privilege of living in the father's house and being provided with food for himself, wife and children. The women had large families so they must have mastered the art of making love in a hammock in the same room as their entire family! This system made the elders all-powerful, and it was a poor man who had no daughters.

It was New Year's Eve. Ramiro had invited us to the council chamber at eight p.m. We wondered what festivities would take place on this island on the last night of 1971. The village was in total darkness as we threaded our way along the mud tracks, till we saw a glimmer of light as the door of the largest hut on the island was opened. We were ushered in to sit on a bench in a central position beside the chief, an old man lying in a hammock that swung from the rafters. The hut was crowded and in darkness save for two small Tilley lamps shining at each end of the chamber and the odd flickering kerosene light (made out of baby food jars) beside the women who were sewing their molas. They sat huddled together in their scarlet headscarves. One moved her head a little, the scarf fell and we were dazzled by the solid gold adornment, like a breast-plate, reaching to her waist that was caught in the flickering light. Then we noticed that some of them had hundreds of coins hanging from their throats, and now and again an earring the size of a saucer, solid gold, glinted in the darkness. Such riches! But where had the gold come from? Later we were told that Cuna women like to wear their wealth for all to see in the form of jewellery, many pieces being handed down from generation to generation. The older women sat back smoking their pipes. The men in their best suits sat together with expressionless faces, all wearing trilby hats!

It was a night for the elders to give an account of all the communal activities, and the missionaries harangued the assembled populace on the virtues of the so-called 'Tigre' way of life, simplicity of living, doing good to others, not going western. Included were warnings of disaster if this way of life was altered, for here as elsewhere, the young people were questioning their elders as to how to live. For four hours we sat on our hard seats, getting the general gist of what was said from Ramiro.

We met a middle-aged American couple on the small island of Pidertupo, keen shell collectors enjoying their vacation there. We rowed them to a nearby reef and all went shelling. Their knowledge, interest and excitement at finding certain specimens fired me with enthusiasm to become a collector too. Tom, while diving, found a beautiful tulip shell and the Americans came aboard and taught us how to clean it. Expert conchologists, in one afternoon they imparted a great deal of knowledge to me. Tom's tulip shell was the start of what eventually became my very large shell collection, and through this fascinating hobby, I was to meet and make friends with many people throughout the world as I exchanged shells. Later in our voyaging when finances were low, shells came to play an important part in our economy, shell-hunting became our chief activity, and we would sell shells to dealers in America, Australia and New Zealand.

We dropped anchor between Yantupu and Suatupu to take a look at these and other San Blas Islands before heading for Panama. The Indians here seemed more commercial, continually coming alongside to sell us shells and molas. Anchored near us was a yacht with an American couple, their ten-year-old daughter and grandpa on board. The girl had become a playmate of a little Indian girl, who was now and again asked to tea aboard the yacht. Children make wonderful ambassadors. One day the American asked her new-found friend to spend the night on the yacht, having gained permission from her Cuna mother. Returning her to her family next day, the Americans met with a chilly reception. 'She slept on your ship. She's no longer our child,' the woman said. 'Take her. She's yours.' Dumbfounded, the couple wondered what to do next. The child was now an outcast from the village and they felt responsible. She was finally adopted in Panama by this big-hearted American family. The ring was removed from her nose and stored in a special jewel box for her to look at whenever she wished, but not to wear. I've often wondered about this little girl brought up in a leaf hut, and whether she is now a normal American adolescent approaching adult life.

We sailed on for Panama, dodging floating logs and debris which seemed to be everywhere, the three of us awe-struck by the great amount of shipping about. The entrance to the Panama Canal at Cristobal was sighted. It was a proud moment. Little *Shebessa* had brought us safely all the way from England to the gateway to the Pacific. The 1,200 mile voyage Grenada-Cristobal had taken 35 days, with 17 stops.

Steve Doyle, who had answered our advertisement in the West Indies, joined us as crew. Steve had represented a drug company in Ontario. He wanted to sail to New Zealand where his two children were living. He arrived carrying a large Tupperware box of drugs 'for all ailments.' The contrast between him and Tom was marked—Tom with his mass of woolly hair and heavily patched jeans, always untidy; the older man polished-looking and immaculately dressed. In Grenada we had felt certain it was necessary to have four of us aboard for the long haul from Panama to Australia. Now we weren't so sure. Norman, Tom and I had managed well so far and rather grudged having a newcomer.

Would he be highly critical? Would he learn the idiosyncrasies of the cooker and loo and not put them out of action? Poor Steve—he had a cool reception.

4
Enchanted Seas—and Enchanted Isles

After a ten hour transit through the Panama Canal we found ourselves in Balboa among a medley of yachts all shapes and sizes, preparing for the big haul across the Pacific. Our plan was to reach Australia by early December, giving us ten months to explore the islands in between. Each of us was pretty strung up at the thought of a voyage longer than we had ever undertaken before, yet surmounting this uneasiness was bubbling excitement at the prospect of visiting the islands of Galapagos, the Marquesas and the 'dangerous Archipelago'—the Tuamotus, with all their treacherous reefs, before reaching Tahiti 4,500 miles away.

In December I had flown home to England from Grenada for a brief three weeks visit to see the family, and whilst there Norman had cabled me to buy a gun! I felt proud of the ·22 automatic pistol I bought. I had had to go to the Harrogate police to prove I needed one. Now, on the eve of our departure from Balboa, I couldn't help thinking of that police sergeant. 'Oh aye, Missus,' he said. 'We'll give you a licence. I reckon you'll need a gun if you're going to them sort of places.' Was it going to be so wild and dangerous?

But now I was fully convinced that *Shebessa* could and would take us anywhere. It was up to me to have enough food on board to carry us through any delays due to lack of wind or gales that might take us off course. Tahiti would be our next port of call to pick up large-scale supplies, but we had been warned prices were high there. Apart from fish and fruits from the islands ahead we would have to be self-sufficient.

We decided, before getting under way to Galapagos, to make a short call at the Las Perlas Islands, 42 miles from Panama, to follow up my new-found passion for shell-collecting. I had learned that this little group of islands was famed for its great variety of shells. We made an early start on January 22nd, 1972 and set course for the Islands, happy to be on the move again, as we were no longer used to the sticky heat, the noise, the bustle, the officialdom and endless frustrations of cities. Soon after noon we were at anchor on the south-west corner of Isla Trapische opposite a drying sandbank which joined this island to the main one, Pedro Gonzales. We wanted to search at low tide, so quickly dressed ourselves in protective gear. This was one of the moments when I wished I had another female to giggle with. I'd always fancied that I had a flair for dressing, yet here I was in the most incredible garb—a bikini, with a string around my waist with plastic bags for the shells attached to it, and on my feet—hockey boots! The boys had sneakers and we all had old fishing gloves to protect our hands.

In all tropical waters when walking on sand or rocks we wore this footgear, just in case. Stone fish, more prevalent in some areas than others, have a deadly sting that can kill you within an hour, and some cone shells also have a sting, a few being highly poisonous, making it necessary to wear a glove to grab them across the widest part, not end to end, when picking them up. It was just about low tide so we piled into the dinghy and rowed for the sandbank. In one foot of water I found myself staring at sand teeming with shells, beautiful Murex, so delicate and colourful, giant Olivia porphyris for which this area is famed, and many other types that took me weeks to identify.

Suddenly there was a piercing scream from Steve. He'd been stung in the ankle—but didn't know what by. A snake, a shell, not the dreaded stone fish? We rowed him back to *Shebessa* but he was beside himself with pain. We hadn't been to the village or seen much sign of life, but he needed help and fast, and perhaps local knowledge was the thing, so off we set for the beach, more or less carrying Steve to the huts where the village began. People suddenly appeared and by sign language guessed the trouble, guiding us into a small wooden hut. It seemed the entire population had turned out to watch the drama. The tiny room was crammed tight with bodies and it was a hot airless day. Steve was examined by a little man dressed only in dirty ragged shorts, who probed and squeezed, announcing that Steve must take a fast launch to San Miguel, another island twelve miles away where he could have an injection. 'There is a doctor there?' Norman asked in his best

Spanish. 'I am the doctor,' said the little man. 'Well, why not do it here?' 'I haven't the drug,' was the reply.

In the event the man found a syringe in an old jam jar, no boiling of instruments or disinfectant for him, and with this he proceeded to draw out the poison. Steve at this point all but fainted, the pain, the heat, what seemed hundreds of eyes watching him—and to add to it all this germ-laden syringe! The man finished attacking his ankle. 'Keep off alcohol,' he advised. After shaking hands with him and thanking him for his assistance we returned to *Shebessa*. The pain was less acute now, Steve looking more like his old self, but with that syringe uppermost in his mind he settled for a course of antibiotics from our medicine chest. We decided to relax for two more days to give him a chance to recover or cope if the ankle flared up; better here than way out in the ocean ahead. His ankle did heal eventually, but for five months it was a running sore and he was never free of dressings.

Tom had the urge for some strenuous exercise, as well as a thirst for coconut juice. We hadn't had any coconuts since the West Indies and rather missed them for our mid-morning drink, and the delicious cream squeezed out of the pulp that cooked so well with fish. The three of us went coconut hunting. Tom chose a suitable palm tree and like a born native scaled up it, cutting down four large nuts, Norman and I below ready to catch them as they fell. Precariously balanced between the branches, he started to fidget. 'Are you all right Tom?' I shouted, but no answer came. In a terrible hurry he slithered down that tree, then like a streak of lightning headed for the sea to fall headlong in. What on earth had happened to him? We collected the coconuts and made for the shore. Tom, now relaxed, was floating on the water and able to speak. The tree had been alive with ants! The hundreds that had penetrated his jeans were now dead and the water was soothing his bites.

Less attracted by the sandbank, we spent more time on board. We bought two large stalks of bananas from a passing canoe, lashing one to the mizzen stay and the other to the ratlines, covering them with towels to ensure they wouldn't ripen too quickly. I became absorbed with the shells we had collected, cleaning, identifying and packing them safely away.

Next stop Galapagos—860 miles West in the Doldrum area. In the old days there was no certainty one would ever get out of this area and many ships returned to Balboa after a hundred days at sea with food and water exhausted. It was time we moved on before our perishable stores were low.

We set sail, moving into the gulf in a freshening wind, and soon sped up to eight knots as the dolphins, our good luck omens, dived to and fro across the bow. Aware that our food stocks had to last a long time, we planned to catch fish whenever possible—and anyway canned food no longer had the same appeal as in the early days. We had had success with our fishing trailing a line, but at a cost. Our lures were the type with a metal head, plastic body and tentacles, an imitation squid, red, white and yellow being the favourite colours. If the fish didn't break the line, it invariably nibbled off most of the plastic. Our stock was low and it became an expensive pastime replacing them. We decided to experiment with a stronger line and a home-made lure. In Panama Norman had bought a strong cord almost as thick as a blind cord. I delved into our rag bag for suitable material. This I cut into strips, with many points like a harlequin dress, a small one in white and a larger one in red or yellow. These we wrapped round and lashed to the metal head of the lure, attached it to the cord, kissed it for luck and threw it overboard, streaming it out about 50 yards. The line was then wound two or three times round the sheet winch, from there to a shock cord on the guard rail and finally with lots of slack to a cleat. This way the noise of the winch whizzing round would alert us that a fish had taken the lure; there would be no sudden tug causing broken lines, the strain being taken up by the winch and shock cord before bringing gradual tension on the line.

Within minutes we had a strike. Tom grabbed the line and holding it taut, moved forward along the foredeck, and Norman grabbed the gaff as, thrashing the water, a gleaming fish came alongside. He bent over, gaffed it, and heaved 15 lbs of dorado aboard. This is an aristocrat of fish, with exquisite line and beauty, like a streak of solid gold bordered with vivid blue and green, but the colours fade quickly at death. It is a fish on a par with salmon, and we devoured this one over several delicious meals.

That night, with the wind still rising and rough seas, we settled down to our three hour night watches. At two a.m. I woke to hear Tom shouting 'Skipper—you have no steering!' What other words could frighten one more than those screamed into the saloon by a young helmsman at 0200 hours when you've been heavily asleep after a hard day's sailing, the first day out on the start of a long ocean passage?

We leapt out of our bunks and rushed up to the cockpit to find the wheel swinging idly, the wind blowing hard, and sails aback after a gybe! No time to find out why; we had to get the emergency tiller fitted and the sails off. We had had a beautiful day of reaching then running downwind with a strong NNW wind on the starboard quarter with full main, genoa and mizzen, surfing down the waves, congratulating ourselves on a wonderful start to our Doldrum voyage. Normally we reduced sail at night, but as the Gulf of Panama is notorious for calms and we were going so well, under control, we had kept full sail up for the night watches, trusting the helmsmen to avoid a broach. However, it had happened somehow, Tom had wrenched the wheel hard to avoid a gybe—then BANG, something had snapped in the steering system.

We clawed down all the sails except the mizzen and fitted the emergency tiller. Norman surveyed the situation. We were lying ahull with rather heavy seas breaking and slopping over the stern, even into the cockpit occasionally. The steering viewed from the engine room seemed OK, so the fault must be at the stern end, where the wire, chain and sprocket were boxed in within the stern locker. Opening the lid in these rough conditions, risking flooding the locker, was out of the question, so it was a matter of running downwind with the helmsman on the stern having a very unpleasant time, or lying ahull till morning. Norman chose the latter course, wedging me into my bunk, with leeboards, cushions, a rubber dinghy seat, all stuffed in beside me to stop me rolling. I slept fitfully, my mind continually jogging me back to consciousness with niggling questions. Should I have woken Norman on my eight to eleven watch? I had found *Shebessa* hard to hold, but being the female on board hadn't wanted to sound chicken and suggest reducing sail. Could Norman fix the steering? It was a repair he hadn't as yet had to tackle and what if he couldn't? We were 85 miles to leeward of any wind and current.

As dawn broke, we went up on deck to find *Shebessa* lying helpless, waves still looming over us. As we made our way to the stern the mountainous wall of water looked as if it would engulf us. I huddled up ready to be drenched, but somehow *Shebessa* rode these seas, and though terrifying to look at they never broke on board. This gave me confidence. I'd long ago fallen in love with our ship, but now without sail or engine she was really proving her worth.

The box around the steering was unscrewed and detached to survey the damage. The steering wire had snapped two feet from the chain around the sprocket, but luck was with us. Curling himself into a ball, Norman was fortunately able to see the broken end of the wire that had all but disappeared down its protecting tube, otherwise we should have had to remove the built-in lockers in the aft cabin to get at it. On one of those frustrating shopping days in Panama, Norman had bought a roll of 50 yards of plastic-covered stainless steel wire, thinking it might come in useful. How thankful we all were he'd visited that shop.

The problem was to thread the new wire, as well as an insurance line (in case it happened again), through the tube running the whole length of the engine room, then behind the built-in furniture of the aft cabin, through the bulkhead, around the six inch pulley, and thence to the chain.

It was an odd way to spend a day in the Pacific, with one man jammed in the locker, one in the engine room, one manipulating the tiller, while shouts of 'Pull'—'Wait'—'Push back' —'Stop'—'Have a rest'—'Have a beer' went on all day with endless cups of tea and coffee and trying to be encouraging when things looked bleak. We were all willing that wire to go through. By 1930 hours the new wire was finally secured and balanced and we were sailing once more. There was a warm close feeling aboard *Shebessa* that night. The wire breaking could have unnerved us all, but instead had drawn us together. We had tackled our first Pacific drama at sea and won.

Gradually the wind eased, the sun shone and the days melted into each other. We watched three dorado on our stern and tried catching them, but our speed was too slow. We didn't want to motor at this stage. Where would the next supply of diesel come from?

Whales were spouting on the horizon, sending jets of water shooting up into the air, and through the binoculars we caught the sight of an enormous tail disappearing into the waves. We were alerted by splashing noises near the ship; turtles were swimming around us. At dusk an incredible soft light hung over us, and the flat calm sea turned to the palest blue. We all experienced the same sensation of being detached from the world and a feeling of strange peace descended on us all. We were utterly alone and yet not lonely. Suppers were served in the cockpit as we watched the last dying rays of the sun. Birds circled us time and again, and one night on my watch a beautiful Royal Tern paid us a visit, soaring into the heavens, dipping and gliding in effortless flight. This speckled bird finally tried to land on the top of the mast, fluttering his wings, and was almost there—but he wasn't game to put his feet down. Was the movement too violent? Finally he darted into the cockpit and I ducked as he flew in, landing on the folds of the mainsail. He had found his resting spot for the night, preening his white feathers before nestling down to sleep. He looked an aristocrat of birds, with his orange bill and his black cap.

To be on watch for three hours while all the men were asleep was to me a very special time of the day. I loved the peace and needed it—as a female with three men on 42 foot of boat. For those three hours I was in charge, steering a compass course often by keeping a star or planet between the forestay rather than staring at the compass all the time. But there were so many distractions—a heaven full of stars, a moon shining down and all round a million twinkling lights in the water, dancing in an endless changing pattern in the froth and foam of the bow wave, phosphorescence caused by the abundance of plankton in the sea. Staring up at the maze of planets and constellations had a humiliating effect on me. We and our globe seemed absurdly small and unimportant. Were there people like us up there, plying the seas or rushing to catch the eight-thirty train, nations squabbling and fighting for wealth, land and power?

Shebessa began to shine again after morning cleaning, as we left the dirt of cities further and further behind us. We enjoyed the exercise too, in the idyllic working conditions, of keeping our home spick and span. There was one night of heavy rain when we experimented with water catching, tying buckets under the main and mizzen masts and topping up our tank; then drenched, we changed for supper, an unusual occurrence. Tom, not to be outdone in his sawn-off jeans, wore his best city tie on his bare neck and chest. These were days of simple pleasures, with all of us in harmony, at peace with ourselves and the life we were leading.

Alas, the twelve dozen eggs we had bought in Panama were a bad lot, and most were committed to the deep. At this stage I hadn't realised the importance of buying eggs unrefrigerated. Farm fresh eggs kept as long as two months, but eggs stored in a cool room or refrigerator lasted only a week or two. We kidded ourselves we were going to buy all kinds of exciting foods in Galapagos, juicy steaks, fresh vegetables and fruit, but we knew in our hearts it was all a dream.

Norman was usually on the dawn watch so that he could take his star sights and work out our position. Most mornings he brewed up tea and brought me a cup to the aft cabin. How I looked forward to that cuppa, and felt cheated if conditions were such that we missed out. To us it was like cracking the day off with a glass of champagne—a few precious moments alone together while the boys slept. The talk was usually trivial, the events of the night, the weather, the stars Norman had shot, the success of the voyage—but in those brief moments we were so close, silently reassuring each other. There was always a glowing feeling of well-being afterwards. What we were doing was right. We were in tune. We would laugh at the antics of our friends the long-tailed Bosun bird and his mate, which so often visited us at dawn, fishing for their breakfast and chattering to each other just as we did. We delighted in watching the ever-changing pattern of the sea, the waves rising to a crest, the colour changing from inky blue to the palest aquamarine, then at their height spewing over and making a million little white bubbles, froth and foam that chattered into the deep trough below. Life becomes very simple on the ocean. There are no pressures to wear you down and eat into you. You live for the day and keep yourself in trim to cope with whatever the old sea will bring you.

At eight a.m. each morning Norman put the radio on full blast to wake the boys and they fell out of bed, heavy-eyed, crumpled, dozy bearded creatures, staggering into the cockpit to say hello to the day and spend a penny on the stern. Breakfast was made by the boys, taking it in turn each day while I steered. Porridge was a must and the banter that went on each morning as to its quality was unbelievable, then if stocks were good came a boiled egg, or fish cakes when we had had a catch. Bread and jam, tea or coffee followed. Then the clearing up and the teeth round, the boys leaning over the side with a brush in one hand and a glass in the other. Work then commenced. At times we took it in turn to steer, at times *Shebessa* could steer herself with the wheel lashed. Occasionally when the batteries were well charged, Mr Pinta, our automatic pilot took over; but the drain on the batteries—up to nine amps when Pinta was working hard—had to be watched. On a fair day clothes and bedding were hung out to air, perhaps a rope that had chafed in the last port had to be spliced, rust appearing on the foredeck had to be treated, the bright work needed polishing, the tear in a sail sewn. There was the daily checking over of all perishable stores and equipment, anything worn or faulty receiving attention immediately. I prepared lunch and supper, making bread every few days and the odd cakes and pies.

At twelve noon the log would be read and the ship's run for the previous twenty-four hours calculated. Daily we gambled for a few cents on the ship's run, guessing the mileage for the next twenty-four hours, each having a scrap of paper on which we marked down our forecasts, and placing them in a screw top jar till the following noon. Competition was keen as the voyage progressed and there was much excitement and laughter as the figures on the scraps of paper were read out. We called this 'nerdling', why I'll never know, a word that one of us must have invented. 'Has everyone nerdled?' was a stock question uttered daily before the lid was screwed on the jar. The bar was then opened—if we had stocks. Lunches were usually cold, salad with meat or fish. A large cabbage would last as long as ten days, made into a coleslaw each morning with varied and sometimes odd additions.

In the afternoons we relaxed apart from a short watch on the wheel. As often as not we all had sleep to make up for the broken night, then we were free to dream or indulge in our hobbies, unless a sail change was necessary. The days were never long enough for me, as I tried to find time to write my diary and letters for posting at the next opportunity, clean shells and catalogue them, dream up a menu for the next day with the stocks available. The afternoon was a quiet time on board—unless fish were in the vicinity. At tea time conversation would pipe up again and round dusk we invariably collected in the cockpit to gaze at the sea and sky. Those wispy clouds, would they bring wind tonight? That dark mass to port, were we in for a storm or rain? This was the hour when Norman decided whether to retain our present rig or reduce sail for the night watches. Soon after sunset supper was served and at eight p.m. the night watches started with me taking the first one till eleven p.m.

The onions we had taken on from a wholesaler in Balboa looked damp as I checked them over. I put on my specs and studied them more closely, peeling off the outer skin of one. There looking at me were a family of cockroaches, Mum, Dad and umpteen babies! I shouted for Steve and quickly we emptied the plastic clothes basket holding the 20 odd pounds of onions into the cockpit. These onions were alive with the wretched beasties, nesting happily under the outer layers. I dug out my string shopping bags; we placed the onions in them, and leaning over the side dunked them in the sea. Then we hung them out to dry, checking they were cockroach-free before returning them to our store for'ard. But how many had left their nests to penetrate the ship? Time would tell.

Onion was a vegetable we couldn't live without, it was so handy to liven up a tinned diet. We ate vast quantities of them raw and cooked, convinced that the nourishment gained from onions kept us in constant good health.

On February 3rd at longitude 88°50', we crossed the equator. *Shebessa* was blessed with gin on her mast for her prowess in bringing us safely 9,000 miles. Land was only 50 miles away now. Tom and Steve started fingering their beards and actually cleaned the mirror so that they could see through it. Scissors and razors appeared and much titivating took place. We started reading up about albatrosses, boobies and sea lions. Never had we felt so carefree.

Living at sea, we found, had made us all super-sensitive to noise, so that any alien noise was checked immediately. That night strange plop-plop noises drew us all into the cockpit to stare at the dark red turbulent water surrounding us. Looking more closely, we found we were sailing through a sea alive and carpeted with tens of thousands of burgundy-coloured crabs with narrow bodies and very large claws, here in two thousand fathoms a rare, uncanny sight. Was this a harbinger of life on the islands ahead?

After an expectant night, at 0730 Tom let out a yell from the foredeck: 'Galapagos!', waving his arms with great glee. In high spirits I cooked up a celebration breakfast of bacon and eggs and the Skipper was duly congratulated on his good navigation, but the land was still 12 miles away, which was odd. We altered course to skirt the corner of Cristobal island which was 900 feet high—but the terrain we were viewing was low. Nothing quite added up. Norman took another sun sight to give a position line. Just east of Santa Cruz! The currents during the night had taken us 40 miles NNW in 17 hours, at over two knots an hour. The congratulations given to the navigator were hastily withdrawn, and there followed a flog back to windward against strong currents to make the port of entry, Wreck Bay on Cristobal, by sunset.

At last we were among the Enchanted Islands, not lush and green with the profusion of flowers we had seen in the West Indies, but volcanic, wild, primitive, with soft gentle colouring, rolling hills and white sandy beaches. Tired but thankful, we dropped anchor in the bay overlooking the small, ramshackle town of Cristobal with houses that looked as if they were tumbling into the sea. Beside us lay an Australian steel yawl, *Eclipse*, owned and skippered by Laurie LeGuay, a friend of Tom's from West Indies days, who wasted no time in diving in and swimming over to say hello and tell us some of the local gen. The Captain of the Port, Eduardo, and his secretary then boarded us and despite the fact that we had no visas, gave us a great welcome, offering us water, fuel, washing facilities, and repairs if necessary.

The next morning we inflated the dinghy and rowed ashore. Land felt strangely firm, my legs having difficulty carrying me as, with a rolling gait, I wandered through the town (I was never sea sick, but always land sick instead). Searching for the post office to dispose of our mail, we were led to a small wooden hut, with a man laid out on the floor of the verandah. The room was bare save for one chair, a table and a mountain of outgoing and incoming mail. Our sleeping friend on the verandah was the Post Master. Slowly he rose to his feet, informing us it was a part-time job. 'I've more to do than mess about with stamps!' he said. He had post cards for sale. Opening the desk drawer he handed me a pile, written, stamped and posted months before! In spite of all, we stamped our own letters and while talking Tom scouted round and found a mail bag to place them in, feeling they'd have more chance there than in the drawer.

The shops here were like the old village stores at home, selling a bit of everything, but one vital commodity was missing. There was no wrapping paper, no plastic bags, not even newspaper. Eggs were obtainable but how to carry them? Rice, flour and sugar were on sale too in enormous sacks. It was up to the customer to bring the necessary containers to carry them away. I looked upon my few plastic bags in a new light: these were precious commodities to be treasured like diamonds.

Soon we longed for the solitude of an uninhabited island, so sailed for Hood, the first to be visited by Darwin on the *Beagle,* a plateau of lava a few miles long, half a mile wide, with sheer cliffs to the South-West. The island is famous as the breeding ground of the Waved Albatross, which return annually to the high cliffs.

On anchoring we were greeted by scores of sea lions frolicking around *Shebessa* in crystal-clear water, with thousands of fish—angels, bass, groupers, grunts, and dozens of unknown types. The boys' eyes boggled at the sight and within seconds they were over the side for some real sport with their spearguns, although it was soon apparent the fish were so tame that it was no great achievement capturing them. Fish was on the menu for supper each night now. A few sharks were always swimming around but they didn't bother us—quite the reverse, for when Norman tried to spear them, they fled. The odd giant ray and an occasional Moray eel could be seen through the clearest water we had encountered since the Caribbean. Here was an island of solitude, just scrubland and lava, wild and barren land, you'd think unable to sustain any living creature—yet every yard of this rocky terrain was teeming with life from the smallest lizard to the giant tortoise.

On shore we lived with the local inhabitants, animals and birds, so tame that it seemed unnatural. Man so rarely comes to Hood Island that they have no fear of humans. We talked to the Blue-footed Boobies in their absurd blue wellington boots, and they let us touch their white fluffy chicks; Mocking birds followed us wherever we went, Oyster Catchers with scarlet beaks and pink legs wandered past us and we sighted herons, hawks and Frigate birds flying overhead. Iguanas up to two feet long clung like limpets to the rocks and we fed them with cactus flowers, ugly prehistoric-looking creatures, their colouring melting into the lava they clung to.

We lay on the sand with the sea lion cubs, their whiskers tickling our hands, till the bull, king of his cove, guarding his harem of women and babes, decided it was time we left and blundered towards us. Sea lions are enormous ungainly creatures on shore weighing round half a ton, heaving themselves along on their flippers, yet so agile in the water. Like human beings they enjoy the sea, not just for fishing, but delighting in the breakers that come in over the reefs, riding the waves towards the shore until the falling crest buries them and returning again and again like any dedicated surf rider. They delight in teasing too. They came towards us while we were swimming, and their vast hulk in close proximity was a frightening experience; then at the last second they would swerve away, making onk-onk noises as if chortling to themselves.

We were too early in the season to see many of the Waved Albatross, which breeds nowhere else on the globe but tiny Hood Island. The majority were still away roaming the oceans of the world. They are incredible birds, a little larger than a farmyard goose, their eight pounds gracefully born on a majestic eight foot wing spread. Most of their life is spent gliding and flapping over the endless sea, revelling in wind and helpless without it, travelling vast distances. Some have been sighted in Japanese waters. How these birds that roam thousands of miles manage to navigate to this pin-point on the globe is not yet fully understood, but navigate they do to land on one particular plateau where because of their high landing speed they often fall over, smacking the ground instead of floating down like a gull. It is said that broken legs are a common result of a bad landing and some occasionally have fatal injuries. I felt we had something in common with these birds, travelling long distances too, helpless without wind, and more at home at sea than on land.

One evening Norman and Tom finally speared a Moray and brought him on board. A Moray eel is a fearsome-looking creature, up to six feet long, having a huge mouth fitted with jaws of tremendous strength, which clamp like a vice on their victims with razor teeth. Three teeth are much longer than the others and exude a poison which paralyses the victim. I wasn't happy to have this creature aboard, but Norman bashed it hard on the head with a hatchet, then later skinned the slimy creature for supper, and to our surprise we found the white flesh a great delicacy to eat.

Days were spent roaming this beautiful wild unspoilt island. It was with great regret that we weighed anchor on February 12th for Floriana, 45 miles to the West, to a farewell onk-onk chorus from the sea lions. We set sail in the early morning before the sun had risen when the water was calm and its most delicate shade of blue, the horizon vague, the far sky and water pastel pink and blue, everything out of focus, *Shebessa* softly splashing in the unrealness. Then suddenly there were more splashings as hundreds of dawn fishing dolphin raced from all directions to reach us. We were surrounded by these magnificent creatures, swimming in pairs, diving then surfacing with extraordinary rhythmic grace, drawing in air through the hole on the top of their heads as they cleared the surface, sucking in and closing. Eight or ten were running immediately under our bow, some so deep that they were a pale blue shape, others so close that we could watch their eyes when they rolled slightly to look up at us, and see the long white scratches on their leathery skin where they had rubbed their backs against keels and other rough surfaces. They were like children. The ship was their funfair and they were enjoying every second of it, testing their skill and showing off. Some leaped out of the water as high as six feet, twisting in the air, then performing a perfect dive, others leaping and falling with a loud bellyflop. We could hear their chatter, which at first we thought was a high whistling in the rigging; scientists say they have a vocabulary of 32 different sounds.

We motored steadily on to the south tip of Floriana, then up the west coast to enter the anchorage at Black Beach, the home of a German woman called Mrs Wittmer. She and another family were the first settlers on this island 40 years previously, living for the first few years in a cave in the hills, then starting farming, which they still do today, growing potatoes, green vegetables, bananas and oranges and raising chickens. This plump friendly frau welcomed us to the small guest-house she now ran by the shore, selling us orange wine and German bread. Later we were to hear that there was more to this woman than met the eye.

We had planned to visit the Darwin Institute on Santa Cruz, making overnight stops at Barrington and Isles Plaza. At the latter, we anchored between the two small islands and went ashore to take photographs. The sea lions had monopolised the jetty and only grudgingly moved off amid many snorts. The island was a desolate strip of rock, scrub and cactus, rather like the moon. The sea lions were almost human, the older ones being jealous of the young having their photos taken and pushing to get into the picture, then rolling over on their backs, rubbing noses and nuzzling up together, their soulful, glazed eyes staring at us.

A few hours later we were in Academy Bay. Here at Santa Cruz was a varied assortment of cruising yachts in which couples were living, some travelling all over the world, mostly young and without any visible means of support, and yet they managed. A number of yachts had been here for many months and some would probably never leave. Galapagos is well termed 'the enchanted islands'.

We visited the Darwin Institute, which is engaged in the preservation of all fauna and flora of the islands, the whole area being now a national park. In particular they are trying to revive the famous giant Galapagos tortoise which grows up to six feet long. Once there were a great many throughout the islands but they were practically exterminated by the seamen, traders and pirates who carried them away in their thousands for food aboard; they kept well as a tortoise can live for months without food and water. Then goats, dogs and rats destroyed most of the young. There were only a few giant tortoises left when the Darwin Institute started the work of salvation and revival some years ago. In a pavilion on the edge of the reserve we gazed at numerous babies receiving special care, tiny creatures three to six inches long, that given a chance would one day grow to the size of their parents and live for hundreds of years.

One morning word went round the yachts in Academy Bay that a beast was being slaughtered; just the thought of it set the saliva going in our mouths. Juicy steaks danced before our eyes—we all had a craving for fresh meat. Jumping into our rubber dinghy we rowed ashore. A queue had already formed outside a small shed which I presumed was the abattoir cum butcher's shop. I joined the line. The stench was overpowering, and I was nauseated by the bloody sight before me. On a large wooden table, stained and dripping with blood, the remains of the beast were laid out. It was first come first served, no joints, fillet or stewing steak was all the same price. When it came to my turn there was little but the liver left, so I settled for that and the dripping wet mass was put into my hands as the flies buzzed over it. In my haste I'd forgotten the all-important plastic bag. At this moment I would have gladly dropped the liver—but it was fresh meat. I made a beeline for the dinghy, thankfully dropped it into the calabash we used for baling and rinsed my blood-stained hands in the salt water.

On Santa Cruz we met the Angermeyer colony from pre-war Germany. Originally there were four brothers who had come to the island over 40 years before. It wasn't the rich fertile land they had hoped to find, yet they had remained there living the simple life off the land and the sea. One died, leaving Gus, known as King, Carl the Duke, and Fritz, who all married and built homes on the low cliffs out of surf-worn lava stones and boats using local timber. They seemed an integral part of this land they had adopted, learning to be self-sufficient without any modern aids. The supply boat from Ecuador called once in nine months if then; it was an erratic service not to be depended on. Without school or doctor their children thrived, some speaking four to six languages, and were by no means backward.

Gus had a rowing boat known as the Royal Barge, and it was up to us in our dinghies always to give him right of way. He and his brothers were all fine-looking men with big hands and feet, their toes in a straight line and widespread because they had gone shoeless for most of their life. Carl had built himself a beautiful home on the point of Embassy Bay with water lapping on three sides. Here he and his wife Margot lived, sharing their home with many of the local creatures. Their patio was covered with red crabs; iguanas wandered in and out of the lounge. Margot had a pet sea lion which slept under the dining room table. Carl expressed himself through his painting and has now become a famous artist. He was able to obtain paint but not brushes. 'I tried donkey tail and goat tail,' he told us, 'no good,' and he shook his head. He held out his large powerful hands. 'These fingers of mine are better. Now I use these.'

Margot was a petite gentle person, whose looks belied her. Inside that tiny body of hers there must have been a steel-like quality to cope with the life she had led. Sitting in our cockpit one evening she told me in her broken English how she managed to provide for her family. Bread was made by grating unripe bananas and plantains as flour, and yeast from sweet potato peelings, lemon or coconut. Cakes were made with turtle eggs, and the turtle, apart from providing meat and eggs, gave oil to nourish the skin. 'Why rush?' she concluded. 'We have learned to take care and don't have accidents and that goes for the children too.' Dear Margot, she gave me that added confidence I needed for our own Robinson Crusoe way of living, teaching me to improvise and tread carefully. Had this family, despite the hardship of the early days, found paradise?

It was hard to tear ourselves away, but the longer we stayed the less time for the islands ahead. We had to reach Australia before the hurricane season started in December. Were we physically and mentally adjusted for the long voyage ahead across 3,000 miles of wide blank ocean?

Unlike the owners of racing yachts, which have the advantage of a strong and numerous young crew and all modern means of communication, able to ring up and receive advice on how to deal with anything from appendicitis to a broken mast, we had come to realise how alone we were on these passages. Our telephone range was 150 miles; we were dependent entirely on our own resources and knowledge to cope with any emergency or crisis that might befall us. We were a team in each other's hands with the heaviest responsibility on the skipper's shoulders. He and he alone could navigate us to the lands ahead. We had learned to plan and provision to cover most situations that might occur, but the most important thing we had discovered was to train our minds to think positive. This mattered enormously, and carried us through many a bad patch—an attitude of mind dispelling all fears. By now, too, I was convinced there was an other-worldly Being guiding and protecting us. I no longer worried about myself and became a fatalist ready to live to the full till my number was up. Physically, Norman and I were in good trim. Steve, despite his ankle which niggled him, was now relaxed and enjoying himself. He had lost the paunch he arrived with in Panama, had fallen into shipboard life and no longer felt queasy in rough seas.

In this world where there was little inter-island communication it was difficult for us to dissect fact from fantasy. The farm at Floriana was our best bet for stocking up with meat, fruits and vegetables, but we had heard strange stories of the untimely deaths and disappearances of many men living there. Was it in each case an accident or was there a murderer or murderess abroad? There was a compelling fascination to return to this island again.

As dark fell, we anchored off the black beach and stared at the cottage in darkness. Was it worth the risk of landing? Leaving Tom in charge of the anchorage we launched the dinghy and surfed in on the rollers, landing in a wet heap on the black sand; then the three of us stood there trying to wipe off the tiny black particles and make ourselves look vaguely respectable. From nowhere two men appeared, startling us and wanting to see our papers. Norman fobbed them off by telling them we would produce the necessary papers next day. Sodden and cold, feeling our way in the darkness with the sound of the waves crashing in our ears, I began to feel afraid, thinking of all those stories.

Wishing we had never come, we made our way to the door and knocked. The door opened and there was the German frau, candle in hand. I nearly jumped at the sight of her again after the dark thoughts that had run through my mind on the way from the beach. She was surprised to have such late visitors but ushered us into her back parlour. In the flickering light, the room looked cosy; a table lamp was lit and I was drawn to the shade. I had never seen one like it before, parchment in colour but softer with tiny lines running through it. We told her we were setting sail for a month and wanted to buy any meat, fruit or vegetables she had available. She retired to the kitchen to check her stores. You could have cut the atmosphere with a knife. Nervous as I was, I had to draw Norman's attention to the strange lampshade. He took one look. 'Made of human skin,' he said in a loud voice. (Norman was a little bit deaf and didn't realise at times how loud he spoke.) 'That's done it,' said Steve. 'We'll be lucky to get out of this place alive.' Within minutes the woman came back, seemingly oblivious of our conversation, with an armful of goodies—not quite what we expected: three pounds of goat, two bottles of orange wine and some jars of cucumber pickle, but we gladly paid for them, trying to weigh her up as the money changed hands. This rosy-cheeked mature lady had been courteous and kind to us. We shook hands and returned to the beach to make a wet dinghy ride back to the ship and a thankful Tom.

5
To the Marquesas

On February 29th, 1972 we set sail for the big hop across the great empty wastes of the Pacific to the Marquesas, for thirty days at least in a world completely our own. It was as if the Enchanted Islands had cast a spell on us; the ocean seemed so silent, our ears having been attuned to the continual onk-onk noises of the sea lions twenty-four hours a day.

It was hot and sunny with barely enough wind to puff us along. At night we motored South in search of the trade winds. At times we were stationary, so flopped over the side two at a time for a swim and a freshen-up. Swimming in the ocean out of sight of land for me was an experience all its own. My emotions were so mixed up—I had the intense joy of the clear deep blue water enveloping my body, the fascination of looking down into the unfathomable depths below, yet always the feeling that we were so far from anywhere, so alone except for *Shebessa*.

On the third day out with only a zephyr of wind from the South, then nothing, there was a restive feeling aboard. Were we to wait like the old sailing ships or should we consume a little more of our precious diesel in hopes of finding wind? As we were having our supper that night, the curtain over the cooker on the port side began to flutter. There was a sudden silence as all eyes were drawn towards the galley; even the clatter of knives and forks against Melaware ceased. The curtain continued to billow out. Wind! Abandoning the meal we all rushed up into the cockpit to find a reasonable breeze, but from the South-South-West. It was all sails up as we beat into it. But it didn't last long. During the next few days the breeze blew intermittently from many points of the compass, causing much sail-changing. We even chased black clouds, hoping for wind only to find rain. Where were the trades? After a week the wind veered to the South-East—the trade wind at last. With the genoa and yankee, full main and mizzen the steady wind on the quarter pushed us along and we relaxed and settled down to our sea life routine.

Norman and I had kept amazingly fit since leaving home, but now our feet ached. Was it something to do with being barefoot so long and standing on teak decks? I dipped my feet in a bucket of salt water, then stood on the deck studying the wet impression. Our arches were falling! We both had a picture in our minds of a flat-footed gardener we had once employed who walked like a duck in his sand-shoes. Was this to be our fate? We did exercises daily, walking round the cockpit on the sides of our feet, even picking up pencils with our toes. After a week the pain left us, and the exercises were forgotten. We accepted the fact that we were suffering from an occupational hazard, feeling disgustingly healthy in every other way.

One night around dusk I noticed some little brown creatures scurrying around the saloon, some no bigger than a pinhead. Those cockroaches we had taken on in Panama had been breeding and now we had a large family aboard. It was time we learned more about them. Steve found a screwtop jar and in it placed a match for them to clamber over, a speck of loo paper and a few crumbs. Tom caught three nice specimens. Two of them had a furious fight, and in the morning we had one dead cockroach, whose remains soon disappeared—cockroaches are cannibals. We assumed the remaining two were male and female, and we christened them Cuthbert and Chloe. They settled down in, sure enough, marital bliss, Chloe soon becoming pregnant. We watched her pod grow larger each day, quite unperturbed by the jar bouncing around in rough weather and the lack of air and food. Three weeks later Chloe gave birth to sixteen young. We decided to give the family its freedom when we reached Fatu Hiva, the first of the Marquesas.

Our feelings towards Cuthbert and Chloe were quite unaffected by our routine cockroach hunts; we often chalked up fifty dead a night, as the ship seemed suddenly overrun with them. These incredibly hardy creatures were very partial to the colour orange. Our orange plastic bowl was always full of them, our orange rubber mat their playground. Only later in the trip did I discover that Baygon powder sprinkled in their favourite haunts soon annihilated them. Dy-Roach also proved an excellent spray.

I always encouraged crew coming aboard to bring with them any special comfort they needed, that little something that kept one ticking over, the reward to oneself after a hard day. Tom had a passion for peanut butter and Smuckers strawberry jam. With regular intakes of these, he was as happy as a king. Norman had a secret store of sweets which I occasionally raided. I had a precious jar of Marmite, difficult to buy after leaving the West Indies. I kept it hidden under my pillow. After a sail change in the early hours of the morning, when I would always be at a low ebb, I would sink back into my bunk and soothe myself with Marmite, sticking the tip of my finger into the delicious brown substance.

Rows at sea were comparatively few. We were all too dependent on each other to cause upsets. Steve and Tom sparred at times but nothing serious. Steve received a lot of ribbing at first, not used to being wet and unable to wash regularly in fresh water, but he rode it all quite good-humouredly. One rough night when we were all rushing up to make a fast sail change, Steve was coming down blocking the stairs. 'You're going the wrong way!' shouted Tom. 'My pants are wet,' said Steve. 'Turn around and get out there,' said Tom, pushing him back into the cockpit.

Tom would often tease us and make us laugh. He was the world's best fish filleter, dissecting with a surgeon's skill, always removing the heart. Once he called out: 'Look Skip, it's still beating and the fish has been dead five minutes', as he held out a tiny red heart for us to study.

Norman and I were too busy to be bored or have time to find fault. We had little to grouse about, anyway: the sun was warm on our backs; the trade winds were pulling us along at a hundred-odd miles a day; we had time to sit, think about things, and assess our lives.

Norman was a tower of strength at sea in all conditions except lack of wind, when he would become edgy and restless. He always spoke his mind, occasionally causing upsets till people got to know him better. He never asked anyone to do a job he wouldn't do himself, and through his training, care and seamanship not one of the crew we took on, many of them novices, fell overboard or came to any harm, despite some diabolical conditions. Many a night he'd be woken up time and again to come on deck but preferred this to having the crew cope with a problem they weren't experienced enough to handle at the risk of our lives and the ship. People often think of yaching as a world of bawdy language and rough living. In times of stress Norman shouted his orders, but never swore, nor did he allow any man on board to do so. Norman and I were making the sort of world we wanted to live in, a world of peace, at times uncomfortable, but never crude or rough.

There was never any real friction between us at sea. The longer we sailed together the closer we became, often not speaking for hours on end, each involved with the job on hand yet completely in tune, and a telepathy grew up between us, Norman reading my thoughts and I his. So often after hours of silence we'd both start talking and ask exactly the same question or make the same remark. It was uncanny. We had one hundred per cent trust in each other, and I feel sure that there lay our incredible strength despite our mature ages. Problems between us were ironed out in ports, never on the oceans. It takes strain and a great challenge for people to find their true selves, and at sea I was learning a great deal about my husband that I'd never discovered in the first twenty-eight years of our married life. His courage and tenacious drive to keep going and win through, against sometimes considerable odds, were on occasion to leave me dumbfounded. To us both our voyaging was truly the zenith of living.

The trades continued to blow and freshen after two weeks at sea, yet *Shebessa*'s speed slackened. Once when we were well heeled Norman took a look at the hull on the windward side and gave a gasp. Masses of goose barnacles covered our antifouling! They were jelly-like creatures in the shape of fingers, one to two inches long, firmly stuck on our hull. We should take a long time to reach land unless these were removed, so we hove to, and the boys dived over the side with snorkels and masks and their knives to rid us of these pests, as hard on as if they'd been stuck with Bostik. Norman, Steve and Tom were weary from their labours, but were soon elated as with full sail we glided through the water at six knots.

As the wind strengthened, cooking on board became more difficult with the ship tossing and pitching and the floor moving under me. Our gimballed stove swung out, the base about to bash me in the shins if I didn't dodge back. It was rather like going through a strenuous dance routine, with every muscle of the body in action—two quick stirs, then two steps back, then forward again to stir the pot. Preparing a cake or a pudding was even crazier, the bowl and ingredients tossing to and fro. It was a game of chance and to win I needed more than two hands, so brought the rest of my body into action. Sitting down I would wedge the bowl between my knees, not an elegant position but safe. My feet held the milk bowl, hands were then free to grab the ingredients and do the mixing. Measuring out was a dicey business, a lurch here and there altering the quantities. Recipes became far more imaginative. It was rare to have even half the required ingredients on board, so I substituted with what was available; some were dismal failures, some gourmet's delight, all were eaten. I laughed to myself when I thought of those little vibrating machines that we had found on our bedside tables in hotels on business trips to Canada and America—place a coin in the machine and the bed vibrates you to sleep. Here in the Pacific we were being vibrated twenty-four hours a day.

Our fresh water tank held 160 gallons. This water was carefully conserved, used only for drinking and cooking. Eggs were always boiled in salt water and vegetables half fresh, half salt. We were mean with our water supply, but a good stock gave us confidence. With enough food to keep us alive for many months and plenty of water we had no worries of any kind. *Shebessa* would never let us down. When the heavens opened with tropical rain it was all go. Buckets were tied under the main and mizzen boom and the decks lined with every receptacle we could find from the washing-up bowl to empty tins of dried milk. I had carried from England a canister of pills to place in the tank to keep our supply pure but had never used them and in fact never did, having been told it spoilt the taste of tea. We preferred to catch rain rather than risk a water supply that might be doubtful and we never had any problems.

One night on my watch I saw a white light on the horizon—a ship! In a state of excitement I woke up the boys. Tom was up in a flash, waving his arms on the foredeck, shouting at the top of his voice: 'Come on over and join us. We'll have a party!' The light grew bigger and higher ... It was Venus ascending.

That same night the pants of my bikini were blown off the guard rail—an old friend and a sad blow. Our possessions were so few that we got absurdly attached to them. What we had on board had to do us for many a long day and we'd all learned to take the greatest care of everything; little went overboard. Screwtop jars were kept for storing food and equipment, tins for paint and varnish, large ones for catching water, plastic bags were washed time and again and stowed. Steve unpacked some engine spares one day, overjoyed because they were wrapped in newspaper, which we flattened carefully and all sat down to read the *Daily Express*, unperturbed that it was over a year old.

On the twenty-eighth day out, with only a few hundred miles still to go to the Marquesas, I decided to catch up on my neglected pile of sewing. The boys had been airing their shore clothes, only to find the zips of their pants had seized up. Run a pencil or rub a candle down the zip and you'll be trouble-free, I'd been told, but this was a job that had been forgotten. I sewed in strips of Velcro, noisy when the pieces were pulled apart, but at least it didn't corrode. The boys couldn't all arrive at the Marquesas with their flys open!

As we came nearer land, with less squally weather and clear skies, Norman made a habit of taking a dawn position by star sights, usually of Vega, Altair and Jupiter, to check on the current, remembering our experience approaching Galapagos when we had been pushed NNW of our DR position. At dawn on March 29th he took careful sights on Vega, Altair and Jupiter, the bearing lines on the chart forming a beautiful 'cocked hat' of only one mile which put us well north and west of our estimated position, so we changed course to sight Fatu Hiva on the bow at 0930 hours next day. Again we had experienced a very strong current in the vicinity of islands. The Marquesas at last! Bubbling over with excitement we prepared for our landfall, tidying up the ship, running up the Q flag and making out crew lists in readiness. As yet the island was in cloud, only the odd jagged peak standing out through a cotton wool blur. How strange it would be to talk to someone else besides Norman, Tom and Steve—and in French too!

We dropped anchor in five fathoms in the Baie des Vierges, surrounded on three sides by majestic mountains. There was a canyon cut through the peaks of basalt rock, forming extraordinary shapes. Down this the wind whistled in violent gusts to a rocky shore where the surf broke like thunder. This would be an uneasy anchorage, however beautiful. We feasted our eyes on the green vegetation. A bull was eyeing us from the heights above; goats were feeding on the steep tracks below. An elderly islander came alongside in his dugout canoe with outriggers, depositing some fifty bananas on our deck as a welcoming gift, talking to us in pidgin French.

In this group of islands the bite of the dreaded no-no mosquitos, although they are not malaria-carrying, causes a fiendish itch, and the bites soon become infected, turning into nasty sores that take a long time to heal, often leaving scars for life. Determined to be free of these pests, we dressed in long trousers and long-sleeved shirts, putting elastic bands at our wrists and ankles despite the heat. We rowed ashore, surfing up a welcome ramp to step on land after a month at sea. Small children appeared from behind bushes and undergrowth, all wanting to hold my hand, shyly presenting me with wild flowers they had picked and kept hidden behind their backs. Chattering in their local languages they led us up a mud track lined with trees laden with grapefruit the size of footballs and oranges and lemons in profusion. We walked past homes made of wood with tin roofs; the islanders were no longer allowed to live in their traditional leaf huts. The French Government seemed to have imposed quite a few bans here. The boys had long been looking forward to being tattooed in the Marquesas, carefully pondering designs and the best spots for them; but we were told this practice too had been banned—probably because of the risk of infection. We stopped to read the village notice-board, pinned to a tree. It was written in French, informing the community that meat would be on sale on Saturday, and it was listed as horse, goat and dog!

There was sickness on the island. These beautiful children's arms and legs were a mass of scars and open sores from no-no mosquito bites. In one home we visited, two tiny mites lay on the mud floor, running a high fever, not having stirred for days. We helped all we could by handing out dressings, iodine and Disprin. The islanders blamed the sickness on the fish which they felt had been poisoned by the fall-out from the atomic bombs set off regularly each year in the Tuamotus. We felt it was much more likely that the poisoning was caused by fish kept too long before cooking in a fly-ridden area. We ate all we caught immediately and stayed healthy.

On Easter Saturday we sailed three miles to Omoa, another bay on Fatu Hiva with a wild rugged beauty all its own. I watched the huge heavy rollers sweeping in to crash on the sand beach. Would we ever get ashore? A large canoe, holding two men and fifteen women and children, appeared and paused close to where we were anchored. Quietly all its occupants sat there crossing themselves as if asking for divine help to get them ashore safely, biding their time for a break in the rollers lashing the shore. Suddenly they were off, the two men paddling for all they were worth, arriving safely on the beach. It seemed to be all a question of timing. We decided to have a go, rowing the dinghy rather than using the outboard in case we were tipped. Patiently we waited a good 50 yards from the shore, while the huge waves rolled under us, lifting the dinghy high in the air. Three large ones had crashed on the beach. This must be the lull. Steve rowed hard for the shore: 25 yards off I looked behind and gasped at the sight of a towering wall of water about to crash over us. A second later we were all flung out as the dinghy pitchpoled. The roller bashed us under, then dumped us and the dinghy on the beach like pieces of flotsam. Three very bedraggled creatures staggered along the grass-covered track to the village amid much giggling from the islanders. We stopped to read the notice outside the small church. It was April Fools' Day!

From Fatu Hiva we visited the island of Tahuata. This looked less primitive: a motor bike was leaning against a wall, a lorry stood outside a house. A very large man with a withered arm who spoke a little English welcomed us ashore. 'You engineers?' he said, turning to the boys. 'You mend motor bike, truck?' The boys had a look at the vehicles. They hadn't run for years and needed many parts renewing, parts their owners couldn't obtain or afford. They weren't unduly worried, at least they owned them as status symbols. By the shore there were row upon row of racks and on these were hundreds of bananas sliced longways drying in the sun. Women were busy packing the dried slithers into bundles of fourteen, wrapping them neatly in banana leaves then tying them with fibre and hanging them up in the store for export to Tahiti on the next trading boat. We were presented with two bundles. They were very sweet, not unlike crystallised fruit, the bundles keeping indefinitely if not opened. The women were dressed in rags. They kept asking me for scent. Food, clothes, cigarettes I could have understood, but surely scent was low priority among people who had so little? I learned later they drank it!

On Hiva Oa we entered the Marquesas officially, a gendarme meeting us as we leapt ashore in a heavy swell onto a small landing stage, not in the least perturbed that we had visited two other islands first. The town looked like the main street in a western, with rickety old wooden buildings with balconies and balustrades where horses were tethered while the owners shopped. There were a handful of stores selling the basics. Eggs weren't sold in the stores: the hens ran wild—if you wanted eggs, you went on a hunt through the bushes.

At the main island of Nuku Hiva we anchored in the scenic bay opposite the town amid a scattering of other cruising yachts. The French atomic frigate *Amiral Charnier* steamed in on a courtesy visit. It was party time, the islanders entertaining the officers and crew as well as the yachties to a do on shore with displays of local dancing, with much hip-swinging to the beat of the drums. The captain was kindness itself, supplying us with new rigging wire for the steering and arranging for our portable Honda generator, which was not charging, to be repaired for nothing. We were invited to a cocktail party aboard, where we revelled in the exciting company and—oh the luxury of it!—champagne, caviare and smoked salmon.

6
Atoll Paradise

Between us and Tahiti lay the dangerous Tuamotu archipelago, a group of 78 islands, almost all of them atolls. (An atoll is made up of one or more small coral islands of low elevation, completely flat except for coconut palms, somehow perched on a solid mass of coral reef welling up from the ocean floor in the form of a ring surrounding a central lagoon. Usually there is only one pass, a narrow break in the encircling reef, through which all the water in the lagoon rushes as the tide comes in and goes out, thereby creating strong currents.) We had been told in Galapagos and here in the Marquesas about these isolated islands, including the southerly Muroroa where the French explode their nuclear bombs each year. We had heard varied reports of the area—'the clearest water in the world for spearfishing'—'abounding in beautiful shells'—and on the other hand 'If you value your ship, keep away from those waters.' Norman and Tom were eager to have this chance of a lifetime to dive and spearfish in these waters, I couldn't wait to go shelling on the reefs, Steve, whose main goal was to reach Tahiti, was neither averse nor enthusiastic. Norman as usual was landed with the decision. 'We'll go,' he said, 'and take the risk.'

Course was laid for Takaroa, an atoll at the north of the group, with a good South-East trade wind carrying us along. Up forward, the ship looked like a fruiterer's shop. Dozens of huge grapefruit were piled there, presented to us by the kind people of Nuku Hiva—no need for vitamin C tablets any more. On the second day out Norman caught a 16 lb tuna on his early morning watch, a firm stocky fish silvery blue in colour, and hung it up on the guard rail to drain—treated this way tuna flesh is lighter in colour and more palatable. All this fresh food—there never were such days! For lunch I cooked the tuna as if it were veal. It tasted very similar. Supper was curried tuna; tuna fishcakes were made for breakfast.

The Admiralty pilot made very gloomy reading about navigating in this area, and we were acutely aware of the dangers and the toll these islands had taken in the past of large and small ships alike as well as yachts, owing mostly to the uncertain direction and strength of the currents to the east of the area and between the atolls. Norman found it comforting each day to take dawn, morning, evening and sometimes night sights, if the moon was up, to establish our exact position. The fifth day required special care but dawn sights of Vega, Formulhaut and Deneb put us 37 miles out, just right for a noon arrival if we hurried. Noon is the ideal time to approach an atoll from the East, as the sun is high and behind, so one can easily see the reefs in the clear water. Course was altered for the north end of Takaroa for our landfall, to be sure we would not be carried too far South. We set sail and charged confidently along at maximum speed.

Steve, while performing his morning ritual of brushing his teeth on the deck, was the first to sight Takaroa, and shouted. On the horizon we could see what looked like palm trees growing straight

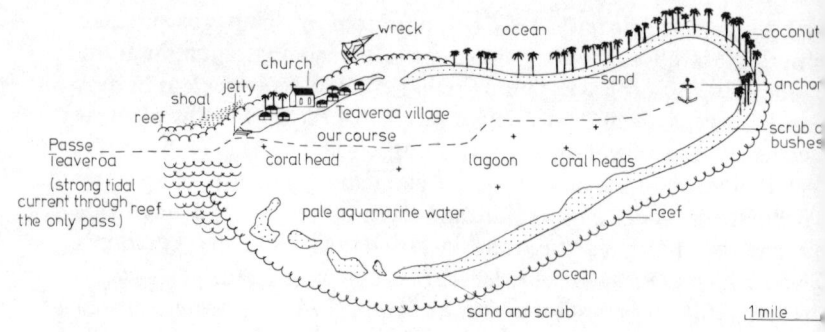

Takaroa atoll

out of the sea. As we closed in, a narrow strip of sand eight to ten miles long became visible, rising only a few feet above the ocean, so flat you would swear a big sea would roll over it. On this strip was a sprinkling of palms, and beyond, glimpses of pale aquamarine water in the lagoon. On the south-west corner of the atoll we saw an isolated patch of land on which ramshackle wooden huts with tin roofs were clustered together with one large building, probably the Roman Catholic church, marking the entrance to the pass. With engine at full bore to stem the six knot current rushing out of the lagoon, and with Norman up the ratlines signalling directions while Steve and Tom kept a lookout on the bow, I nervously steered *Shebessa* through the pass, the jagged reef with water spewing over it all too close. It was a relief to tie up to the little stone jetty at the village of Teaveroa.

I looked around to see a crowd of smiling faces greeting us, Polynesians speaking a language peculiar to their island but also pidgin French. They gazed at our yacht. Apart from the copra boats that called spasmodically to collect the dried coconuts and supply boats, visitors were rare here. Rows of tiny grinning children looked hungrily at our stalk of bananas. Tom handed them around but the grown-ups refused. 'For the children,' they said. It was good to watch the expressions on their faces as they bit into the first fruit they had tasted for many a day.

Norman and I took a walk down the sandy tracks to explore the village. At first sight it looked in a bad way—sadly neglected homes with paint peeling off and yawning holes where the wood had rotted. The only greenery was the line of palm trees bent over by the constant South-East trade winds. Yet when we looked closer, we saw that despite the lack of wood and paint, each family had decorated their home with the one thing they had plenty of—shells. Shell leis hung from balconies, shell ornaments adorned walls. Men, women and children rushed out of their homes to greet us, enormous mammas weighing all of 20 stone, wrapped only in a length of calico which rippled and wobbled like jelly as their smiles turned to gurgles of laughter. They hugged and kissed us on both cheeks, placed beautiful shell leis round our necks, shook hands and crowned us both with head bands of shells. In Hawaii, visitors arriving or leaving are invested with flower leis. Here it was the same, only shells were used instead. Moneta cowries—the kind used long ago as money by Polynesians—and many other similar species were pierced with a stiletto and threaded into necklaces and head bands of many designs. Agasp at these people's spontaneous friendliness and generosity, we returned to *Shebessa*, bursting with laughter as we stared at each other. What a sight we were—Norman with his lean figure striding along in his old bathers, his bare chest covered with leis, his shell crown clamping down his hair above his flowing beard, and myself looking just as crazy with numerous adornments dangling down my old shirt. It was as if we were off to a fancy dress ball.

When school was over the children again descended on the ship, masses of little ragamuffins scrambling and clambering all over her, good children, not grabbing or dishonest, just terribly curious. We were their movie show, their television, entertainment they would remember for months to come. Supper time came and they were still there, though no longer below; through every porthole big brown eyes stared down at us.

As the evening drew on a crowd gathered, squatting on the stone slabs of the jetty, the women nursing their babies, the men playing their home-made guitars, serenading us with their music and songs long into the night. Norman cracked a bottle of rum and handed it round. Dusky bare-footed young girls appeared, strikingly beautiful, their thick glossy black hair falling to their waists, with only a gay-coloured length of calico wrapped round their slender forms. Tom and Steve, starved for months of young female company, jostled in the saloon in a mad rush to find clean shirts and pants with zips that worked. Then, smarter than I had seen them look for months, they chatted up these girls and disappeared into the night.

This little group of eighty Polynesians had no stimulants, not even tea or coffee. Their only diet was rice, fish and coconuts, occasionally dog! These dogs were not domestic pets but lived wild, mongrels fending for themselves. At low tide they would stand on the edge of the reef, staring into the clear water below; then all at once they would dive in, shaking themselves as they came out with a large fish wriggling between their jaws, and hungrily devour every morsel. They were the best fishermen we had ever seen. The men, when they had a mind to, worked the copra on the other side of the lagoon, chopping the coconuts in half, then laying them out to dry in the sun. At night, if the moon was high, they would collect shells. (Most shells shun the sun, burying themselves in the day time in the sand or under rocks; cowries are particularly active in night feeding, and for some obscure reason move more as the moon rises and are easier to collect in moonlight.) Otherwise these men would spend their time playing with their outboard engines, which rarely sparked into life through the familiar lack of spare parts that could neither be bought nor afforded. The women did most of the fishing, being almost as adept as the dogs. Wearing only a strip of cotton round their more than ample figures, they would wade into the water up to their waists, a bucket hanging from the left arm, a cane fishing rod in the right hand. Using shell fish for bait, within half an hour they would have their buckets spilling over with a variety of highly coloured reef fish. Heuri, a nine-year-old who haunted us from dawn to dusk, making himself thoroughly at home, told us he had two fish for breakfast, three for lunch and four for supper!

These were halycon days and nights, but after a while we needed a breather away from people. We were no longer used to being with a crowd. For twelve hours a day the islanders were around and on the ship, watching our every move. The continual stares became unnerving, although they were charming, but privacy was at a premium. Even going to the loo was an exhibition. It was time to move *Shebessa* to explore the lagoon. But we were not to be allowed to go alone. 'Too dangerous,' said a Takaroan called Ellis, the island's leading singer who also played the guitar. It was true: the many coral heads dotted all over the lagoon would be likely to trap the unwary. 'I will guide you,' said Ellis.

The next morning he arrived with two friends in his outboard-powered boat to guide us the seven miles to the head of the lagoon. He tied his boat to our stern and the three came aboard.

In happy mood we threaded our way through the coral heads, some awash while others lay a few feet under the surface, brownish shapes clearly visible in this purest aquamarine water imaginable. We arrived at the top of the lagoon, anchoring close to a sandy beach. Ellis and his pals indulged in some of our whisky, then singing at the tops of their voices, clambered into their motor boat for the journey back to the village. The engine wouldn't start—pull after pull—no go. 'Don't worry, we'll start it,' called Ellis. They were used to the engine's idiosyncrasies and remained unperturbed. They hauled out a box from the cabin, broke it up and laid the sticks on the wooden deck. Now it was our turn to stand and stare. What would these crazy wonderful people do next? Ellis poured petrol over the wood, setting it alight. We waited breathless and tense for that boat to go up in flames. But no, Ellis, still singing, removed the plugs from the engine and threw them into the blaze, lolling back as they cooked. The plugs were then extracted, the fire swept into the sea, the plugs replaced, the cord pulled and bang! they were off amid much shouting and laughter. We were alone at last, away from staring eyes, and settled down to a peaceful spaghetti supper.

Tom was up at dawn swimming and diving for shells. He came back with a hoard of cones he had spied scurrying in the shallow water to bury themselves in the sand before the sun rose. Norman and I confidently set out for the sea across the narrow strip of atoll; but what a walk it turned out to be—three-quarters of a mile of dense scrub with clearings here and there, the ground dry and cracked with deep crevasses, then pools of water with thousands of crab holes around the perimeter, and further dried up scrub and plants. Dripping with sweat, suddenly through the brush we saw the rocky beach and felt the breeze on our faces. We rested on a large boulder, lazily watching the water bashing into the rocks, gushing and foaming up every crevasse, spraying over us as we sat there. It was the exhilaration we needed after the stillness of the lagoon.

After a day or two of relaxation on *Shebessa*, we returned to the village, this time alone, to say our farewells to these kindly people. More presents of necklaces and shells were showered on us as with long waves and alohas we cast off, the tears rolling down my cheeks. We would never forget these people. In their simple way they had given us all strength and renewed our faith in human nature.

It was a quiet moonlight night, and *Shebessa* sailed steadily along at three knots. Shortly after dawn Manihi came into view. More confident now than we had been when approaching Takaroa, we motored up the pass, again with current against us, to tie up at the stone wharf. Here there were three yachts to welcome us in, two British and one French. This atoll had more vegetation than most, flowers blooming in abundance near the shore. Close to the wharf was a man-made pool holding eight sharks and four turtles. We should have to watch our step at night, I thought as I watched those evil-looking monsters with their wide gaping mouths, frightening even in captivity. Were they stored for food or for the entertainment of passers-by, like goldfish? We never did find out.

Norman and Steve went spearfishing, while Tom and I stayed on board. Then the local trading boat approached. *Shebessa* had to be moved, and with help from the other yachts Tom and I led her forward, tying up against the French yacht. We went onto the jetty to join the throng while the trader tied up. I wish we hadn't, as lying aft covered in a blanket was a local man who had been ravaged by a shark, losing most of his leg. He and his pals had been spearfishing, tying their catch on a line trailing behind them. The smell of blood had alerted the sharks and before the man could reach safety, he was savagely attacked. We turned away, sick at heart. A mercy ship was on its way to pick him up and take him to hospital in Tahiti, where he would get all possible aid and treatment, but it still wouldn't give him back his leg. The boys took even more care after this.

The second chief of the island, named Huri, thrilled at the rare occurrence of four yachts visiting at once, came to see us, and arranged to take Norman and Steve night fishing. He led them to a stretch of beach near the village as darkness fell, collected green drinking nuts from the coconut grove skirting the sand, cut them open and handed them round. Then he lay down. 'What about the fishing?' said Norman. 'Not yet,' said Huri. 'We must wait for Venus to sink below the horizon, only then do the shells come out of the sea and the reef fish sleep.' He pointed to the heavens: 'Look, Orion's twinkling. We'll have strong North-East winds in two or three days.' We had read about the Polynesians' ability to forecast the weather by the stars. In a few days we would know if Huri's prediction was right. As Venus disappeared below the horizon, fishing began. Wading in a line in the shallow water the party moved forward, catching glimpses of fish as they drove them forward to a previously built corral. This was no sport but was the means of obtaining basic food needed to feed the village. Within half an hour they had two bucketsful of grouper, chub and Moray eel, quite a haul for one night.

Next day we moved into the lagoon, anchoring close to a coral beach. For a few magic days we roamed the shores in search of shells, fanning the tiny tracks in the sand to find olive and cones, new species we had never set eyes on before; turning over rocks to find cowries, all sizes and colours, marvelling at their beauty. We lay on the fine coral sand, idly picking it up and feeling it run through our fingers as we stared up at the palm fronds gently swaying above our heads. For hours at a time we would swim and snorkel, fascinated by the marine world below us. We dreamed of paradise no longer: we were in it.

The weather broke. It was time to move on. In squally rain with strong North-East winds we headed for our last Tuamotu atoll, Apataki, going well with only the mizzen and yankee. Huri had predicted this weather. These Polynesians spent a great deal of time studying the heavens; they knew their weather indeed.

At mid-morning we entered the straight short deep pass leading to Niutaha village. Here was the strangest spectacle we had seen yet on these atolls. On the left side of the channel the sea was rushing out of the lagoon, yet on the right side it was rushing in, sweeping us along at a great pace, even with the engine in reverse, the boys having to jump ashore fast and tie up before we shot past the stone wharf. The chief's son and others welcomed us, and with the usual hordes of children led us down a tree-lined avenue to the village store, where we stocked up on canned baked beans and peas. The owner of the shop, Victor, presented us with a huge turtle shell, insisting on varnishing it there and then. His wife Elaina stood behind the counter, a very large gentle person spilling out of a black bra many sizes too small, with a gay cotton wrapped round her bulging hips. Lillia, their ten-year-old adopted daughter, came forward and took my hand.

As we made our way back to *Shebessa*, the young girls shyly stared at us, but mostly at Tom and Steve. They had such natural beauty—till their smiles broadened into a toothless grin. Dental treatment in this region was rare and very expensive. Only Elaina, who had been to Tahiti, had dentures. She and her husband and three children, one a babe in arms, came on board for drinks. The rain fell heavily so it was necessary to go below. But there was a problem. Elaina was a little wider than the companionway! Unperturbed and laughing, she struggled to get through, finally turning sideways to squeeze her flesh in as she held her breath. She won the battle.

Our last night on Apataki, Victor and Elaina asked us to join them in a simple fish supper. We all happily accepted their kind invitation. What a feast this proved to be. Through the back of their store we entered their home, clean and simply furnished, to see a table beautifully set for dinner—a table-cloth, napkins, posies of flowers. Lillia was in her best party dress. The dinner that night seemed finer than any served in the best restaurants in the world. For starters we had tiny cubes of raw fish marinated in lemon juice and garnished with greenery (not parsley!) and French dressing, followed by cold lobster. Elaina had cooked ten of these from Victor's stock of a hundred and fifty which he kept in his fish corral. We ate and ate, thinking this was the main course, but then came stew—New Zealand cornbeef cooked in a delicious sauce, followed by fruit salad and a cake with slices of pineapple at the bottom. They had dug deep into their precious stores to dine us so well. Overwhelmed by their generosity to us, with bursting tummies, we prepared to leave. At the door I slipped my beloved Grecian ring on Lillia's finger. It hadn't great value, but I knew she admired it and I'll never forget the ecstatic look on her little face as she held out her hand to stare at it.

Tahiti was now calling us. It was time to move on, especially as our basic stocks of food were perilously low and our last calor gas bottle almost empty. We hadn't had mail for months, so were hungry for news of family, friends, and home. On May 14th, 1972 we set sail, sadly saying farewell to our friends on our last Tuamotu atoll.

As dawn broke on the 16th, the island of Tahiti loomed up ahead of us, shrouded in mist, a great hazy mass, and as we sailed on the astonishing mountains and gorges grew larger, clearer and more spectacular. Our excitement increased. Civilisation was near. I would even be able to buy needles and not have to sandpaper each one before sewing! The very word Tahiti conjured up in our minds romance, an ecstatic way of life, the scent of flowers, the beauty of dusky maidens bubbling over with joie de vivre.

7
The Land of the Frangipani

Tahiti is entirely surrounded by a barrier reef which lies anywhere from a few yards to half a mile or so from the shore, upon which the sea always breaks heavily. There are passes here and there which vessels may enter, but because of the strong currents it is necessary to take the greatest care. Identifying the main pass, we ran in with the thunder of the surf ringing in our ears. Once inside we made a sharp turn to the East, the town of Papeete unfolding before us with its famous waterfront. The harbour was packed, dominated by warships, freighters and fishing boats jostling together; a large liner was tied up at the wharf, and along the promenade dozens of yachts were anchored stern to the promenade. We joined them, waited for customs to clear us, and then rushed ashore to the bank to collect our letters, tearing them open there and then to hear news of home.

Happy to know that all was well with our family, we strode along the waterfront, acclimatising ourselves to civilisation. It isn't easy to explain the feeling you get after five months at sea, visiting only way-out islands, to be suddenly confronted with the land of plenty, green trees, exotic flowers in abundance, traffic—the hustle and bustle of a thriving city. Being at sea accentuates living, our senses had become intensified; there was so much to assimilate and enjoy on this first day ashore. Though deafened by the noise of cars and dithering about crossing the road, we immediately grasped the atmosphere of gaiety and relaxation; the warm sun beating down, the unlined faces of the big mammas, some out shopping, some sitting behind their stalls selling shells, shell necklaces, and sharks' teeth; young girls in the miniest of mini dresses, Tiare Tahiti or Frangipani flowers tucked behind one ear, singing and laughing as they strode by. On the wharf the fishing boats were unloading their catch, huge tuna, the pungent smell mixing with the scent of the flowers. I gazed at the well stocked shops, full of colourful, exquisitely tailored French clothes, dazzling after the faded togs we had grown accustomed to living in. Then we came upon the market packed with stalls, each one piled high with mountains of avocado pears, tomatoes, papaya, peaches, apricots, plums, pineapple—even coconut cream was for sale in beer bottles. Just now and again in life you get moments of ecstatic happiness. My mouth watered at the sight of it all; we had not had so much as a blade of lettuce since January.

It was Norman's sixty-first birthday, so dinner out was a must. We settled for a small restaurant less than 200 yards from our ship, to have our first steak and salad for five months. Just a straight grilled steak—but I doubted if we would ever enjoy and remember one so good again. Tom and Steve had been talking for weeks about ice cold milk and ice creams with gooey chocolate and fudge sauce running in rivulets down the sides; they settled in at the nearest milk bar.

We were among a big ocean-going fraternity, old friends we hadn't seen since Panama or Galapagos, and many new ones we now made, sailing folk of all ages tramping the seas, but happy to relax for a while on this lush green island. We visited and had continual visitors, at all times. A knock on the hull: 'May I come aboard?' 'Come right in!' whatever we were doing. Cruising yachtsmen don't come to be impressed or expect to be entertained in style. They come to swap experiences, knowledge and know-how, to lend and borrow tools and charts, sometimes flags.

There were a young Australian couple, Nancy and Clive, with their two-year-old daughter Carole, who had sailed their 24 foot sloop across the ocean like a dinghy, Nancy swearing Clive had glue on his feet to make him adhere to the deck. Carole was born to shipboard living, sure-footed, hanging on with her tiny hands to a stay when the swell rocked the boat. Children weaned on this sort of life seem to have a built-in self-preservation system, rarely falling overboard and, if they do, paddling like a dog till helped. Carole's chief pastime ashore was pulling the chain of the public loos at regular intervals to watch the water gush in and out, a toy she had never set eyes on before. The loo she had known on board was a bucket with a lid, known as the honey pot. I was lost in admiration for this Australian girl Nancy, used to all the comforts of living at home, yet happily making a success of living in very cramped quarters with no mod cons.

In a central position along the promenade was the 28 foot American sloop *Salty*. All Papeete knew *Salty*, skippered by Chip Anderton with John Olsen, another American, and Ted Cully, a Canadian, on board, young men full of fun and kindness despite what seemed like insurmountable problems. *Salty*, through some error of navigation combined with unknown currents, had run up on a reef at night on one of the atolls of the Tuamotus, hard on, high and dry, helpless until a passing French naval vessel hauled her off and towed her back to Tahiti, where repairs were undertaken to make her seaworthy again. But how to pay the bills? Her crew hadn't enough money and they weren't allowed to work. They weren't allowed to leave. The thought of having an enforced stay on this island didn't dismay them. Something would turn up, the Tahitians making sure they didn't go short of food or wine. It was always party time on *Salty*, starting as early as ten a.m., the little cockpit overflowing with people, well-wishers carrying on various bottles of booze, all poured into their one bucket, making a weird diabolically strong sort of punch, that was handed out all day.

Papeete was full of excitement and dramas. Cruise ships came and went, packing the streets with tourists for a few hours. At breakfast time one morning, a great shadow fell over *Shebessa* and we raced up to the cockpit to see thousands of tons of liner looming over us, perilously close. She had had a complete power failure entering port, dropping her anchors just in time to save us yachts from being squashed to pulp.

A retired English bank manager who had sailed from England en route to New Zealand had suffered the terrible loss of his friend overboard on the long voyage to the Marquesas. He was now looking for crew. Steve, who had been with us now for five months, decided to join him. As Steve's and Norman's personalities were so different, and they had been getting on each other's nerves more than ever lately, it was a cordial parting on both sides.

Time was running out for Tom, who had to return to Yale. We decided to tour the Society Islands, returning to Papeete for the July 14th celebrations before he flew home to America. The three of us headed out for Bora Bora, a stiff thirty-six hours' sail away.

We fought the wind and the current to anchor before dusk in the lagoon. The island was a windy one, dominated by high mountains and peaks, the wind funnelling down the gorges and valleys, the land near the shores abounding in lush vegetation, orderly and well cared for, soft white sand beaches stretching for miles round the shores with endless reefs to explore.

We stared unashamed at the shapely young girls, their faces with such fine bone structure, their honey-coloured skin. All of them had big brown soulful eyes which invariably captivated any male on sight, and went bare-footed, completely natural, their sheeny black hair swinging gently above their hips as they strode along, proud and poised. No wonder the Society Islands are the end of the road for many a yachtsman, like Bernard Moitessier who gave up the Single Handed Round the World race to return to paradise.

Polynesians are such happy people, never dwelling on problems, loving dancing, music and song. The mammas—all of 20 stone, proud of their size, their straw hats shading their plump serene faces as they swing along on Sundays and fête days in their full-length frilled cotton dresses—have very large families, obviously thriving on it. Their maternal instincts are strong, and not only for their own brood, for they are happy to bring up a few they haven't given birth to as well. No child is ever neglected here. Homosexuals are treated with the same respect as any other members of the community, no sly glances or backchat. Nowhere in the world had we met such tolerant, contented people, whose motto seemed to be that life is for loving, living and above all enjoying.

On June 26th the wind blew hard and we were bumping about. Our anchorage was no longer a sheltered one. We decided to take a look outside the pass and head for the island of Raiatea, only a day's sail away. Well heeled, doing seven to eight knots, we tacked our way to the pass, awe-struck at the sight of the spray shooting 50 feet high off the reef, deep blue water turning to aquamarine, then a glorious mass of white bubbles, froth and foam as it was flung into the heavens. Just now and again in life you can be lucky enough to gaze at something so beautiful it makes your spine tingle. I was spellbound, trying to imprint the sight on my memory forever. I found it hard to concentrate on the turbulent sea between the reefs as I steered *Shebessa* through the pass. At dusk we tied up to the wharf at Uturoa. Tired and intoxicated with the intense joy the sea had given us, we had supper and went to bed.

I woke to the cries and noises of a small bustling town. We were surrounded by pirogues—dug-out canoes—coming and going, people from neighbouring islands who had paddled over to buy stores. We mingled with the throng and went shopping for bread, fresh fruit and vegetables. Strangers stuck out like a sore thumb in a small town like this. Madame Jolier, the wife of the Governor of the northern group of Society Islands, befriended us, taking us out in her car to view the island, then inviting us to her home for dinner. There was the usual mad scuffle aboard, trying to find presentable clothes to wear, as well as trying to brush up our French. I had almost forgotten what a real home was like, walking on soft carpets and gazing at the dinner table beautifully laid out with crystal glasses and fine china; we had stepped into another world. Sustaining a conversation in French we found difficult, but managed to converse somehow, delighting in all the comforts, sinking into a chair and sipping champagne, then partaking of a delicious dinner served with all the trimmings we had to forgo on board; it was all too much.

At dawn we had to leave for the island of Moorea. Just as we were about to cast off the last warp, Monsieur and Madame Jolier and their three children arrived on the quay to give us a Polynesian farewell, placing shell leis around our necks, specially chosen to please each one of us. Where else in the world would you find a whole family rising before dawn to say goodbye to a small yacht, not their nationality, with people aboard they had met only the day before? We were deeply touched.

We had arranged to slip *Shebessa* at a small yard on Moorea, the last Society Island to be visited, to antifoul and paint her. We stared and stared at the sky-line as an island of breathtaking beauty came into view. Could it be natural? It looked unreal, such fragile-looking peaks, the whole scene like an exquisitely intricate piece of carving fashioned by a master craftsman. The slip was a rickety old railway line leading from land over the reef to the sea; boats could be pulled out only in calm water. Our hearts sank. It didn't look very safe; but then slowly, slowly, we were pulled out of the water across the reef, then the road, and deposited on a patch of grass surrounded by palm trees. Could anyone wish for a lovelier location to work on a yacht?

Each day from dawn till dusk we laboured, the sea only a few yards away to fall into at intervals to cool off. We looked like clowns with paint daubed on our heads and striped bodies. The first night, Tom, who slept in the saloon, woke to strange noises. He switched on the light to see rats sitting on the dresser, devouring our bananas, and flung a pillow at them to chase them out. The following night we removed all scaffolding and drew the ladder up on the deck to stop any more visitors, but still they came, climbing up the vertical steel girders of the cage. After that we slept with every porthole hatch and door closed despite the heat—rather like having an eight hour turkish bath. Next night, unable to eat bananas, the rats made a meal of the plastic cockpit cushions instead, gnawing holes in every one.

After five days *Shebessa* looked spanking new, and we sailed a few miles up the coast to a picturesque spot called Robinson's Cove. One morning a little Tahitian girl swam out and clambered on board, making herself at home in the cockpit. Celina, aged eleven, had come for a friendly chat. 'Mummy's having a baby soon,' she told me. 'Well, that's nice,' I said. 'How many brothers and sisters have you?' 'There are twenty of us,' she replied. 'Twenty is all right, but twenty-one is too many—I'm glad I'm not old enough to have babies,' and she gurgled with laughter.

Bastille Day, July 14th, was the start of a seven day fête in Tahiti. To see these fun-loving people celebrating was a must. We returned to Papeete to find the town bursting at the seams. Polynesians from the outer islands had all converged to compete in the dance spectacles; outrigger races, with up to sixteen men or women in one canoe, with canoe, paddles and loincloths all matching in colour; javelin throwing, copra cutting competitions; basket making—mammas with nimble fingers turning palm fronds into baskets of varying shapes and sizes in a matter of minutes. The town was throbbing and the atmosphere electric, the sound of drums beating everywhere, groups practising in their own back yards. We were caught up and swept along by the fever. The music of the famous Tahitian dance known as the Tamare stirred the girls into the most energetic display of hip-oscillating we had ever seen, the pace ever faster and faster, their bodies vibrating, twisting and shaking to the rhythm of the drums. Even the tiny children were adept at this, being taught at school and loving every minute of it. Fire dancers pushed a beacon of flame into their open mouths, parades with girls carried on litters showered flower petals to the crowds and family groups, majestic mammas in full-length white cotton frilly dresses and straw hats proudly led their families into their dance routine.

Salty was still in residence, as resilient as ever. Her crew had finally sorted out their problems with the various Government offices and had been given permission to leave, paying off their debt to the French Navy at a future date when they had found work. The students of Tahiti weren't going to see them sail away without food. They had a whip-round and with the francs collected, provisioned the ship. It never pays to worry!

At the end of the celebrations Tom had to leave us to fly home to America. He was ill at ease at the thought of going back to conventional living again, and we were sad to say goodbye to this fine young man, who had become one of us, and had contributed so much to make our voyage a success. Over the last seven months, Tom and I had often played rummy at sea and he had won hands down. His prize was a bottle of champagne. In the early dawn before he left, after filling him up with a plate of porridge we cracked the bottle, all feeling at a dismally low ebb. It helped as we said our farewells. There was a void on *Shebessa* after he had gone and we still miss him.

It was time to get organised for the next hop to the Cook Islands, then on to Tonga, Fiji and Australia. We pinned a large notice on the stern 'Crew wanted'. It was incredible, the number of young men there were available to sail on a yacht with the money to pay their way. A steady stream visited us, most, we felt, wanting a cheap ride as passengers rather than crew. A few yachts up from us was a delightful Frenchman, Bernard Polter on his sloop *L'Affranchi*, who had been a lone sailor up to the West Indies—apart from his beloved dog Whisky—from there had taken on a twenty-one-year-old German boy as crew, and now no longer needed him. I was interested to meet this Munich lad, who had left home with a few marks in his pocket to hitch-hike to South Africa to join his married sister. Finding it was impossible to get visas to travel through Africa, he had crossed on a yacht to the West Indies, there joining the Frenchman, still determined to reach South Africa somehow. He came to visit us, a wiry, emaciated youth with wispy unkempt hair to his shoulders, his eyes sunken with dark shadows below. To keep body and soul together he had become a welder in Papeete (a skill he had never tried before) and had held the job. He looked the least suitable of all our applicants and yet there was something about this boy. He had proved already he had guts to battle on despite his lack of money. We signed on Frank Roedel and with the few dollars he had left he bought some clothes and had a hair cut, so short there was only a quarter of an inch of blond fuzz all over his head. At the same time we took on an American, Ken from Chicago, assured and confident. 'I've sailed on Lake Michigan for years,' he said, 'the ocean will be peanuts to me.'

In a freak storm with blinding rain we set off, waving our farewells to the boys on *Salty* and many other friends on their yachts. It was a rugged sail to Rarotonga, with lumpy seas and plenty of wind. Frank was soon a changed man, happy to be at sea again, alert, competent, a natural on deck in the worst conditions. Ken on the other hand had lost all his bounce and was suffering from seasickness, but this was a common occurrence the first day or two out; with time we felt he'd adjust. He didn't. Afraid to go below or eat in case he was sick, he lay in a heap in the cockpit twenty-four hours a day, wrapped in his space blanket, a body we clambered and fell over while adjusting and changing sails. It wasn't an easy voyage. Frank so eager to please was always a few jumps ahead, but his English was poor, and there were many misunderstandings. 'Ease the sheet, Frank', and like lightning he'd pull it hard in. Norman would be in the cockpit cogitating whether to reduce sail, talking to himself, 'Might be about time we got the genoa off and put on the number two', then he'd go below to get a time signal and come up to find the job being done, the genoa down and the number two ready. Many times the cry went up: 'Wait Frank!'—'Not yet!'—'Take it easy boy!'

On the sixth day we sighted Rarotonga, and our black lump of space blanket stirred and came to life. Ken perked up and started eating. We arrived in a heavy swell at Avatiu harbour, which was packed with craft. Where to moor? *Salty* had arrived a few hours before us and there was John on the quay waving his arms, signalling us to tie up stern to against the wall not far from them. This we did, adjusting our gang-plank for the hazardous walk ashore. Then a pair of customs officers came aboard white-faced and shaken at the perilous walking of the plank. Here they were worried about the beetle that was doing so much damage to the coconut palms around Tahiti. The agricultural officer asked me to produce all fresh fruit and vegetables. It had to be burnt! We didn't know then that Rarotonga abounded in citrus fruits.

Ashore we saw trees overladen with oranges, grapefruits and tangerines, more than the islanders could handle; they were rotting on the trees. We were in the heart of the Cook Islands, and gaped at this lush land with its mountains rising from the green coastal belt below, islands administered by New Zealand, as a local told us with a great grin on his face—'New Zealand supplies us with money and we spend it.'

Ken took a teaching job at one of the island schools. He was a changed man on land, happy and confident. We wished him well as we said goodbye, but here was another crew man we weren't sorry to see go.

A hundred odd miles north of Rarotonga was the small island of Aitutaki, entered through a passage half a mile long, extremely narrow and skirted by reefs, only deep enough to negotiate at high tide. As it was reputed to be a good fishing ground we decided to go there. We beat into heavy seas, Norman and Frank continually reducing sail till we were down to storm jib only. The huge waves banged our sides like shot guns going off.

At dawn we motored through the pass at a snail's pace, Norman up the ratlines wearing his polaroid specs—a godsend in reef country, the coral below the surface being clearly visible through these glasses—and Frank on the bow, all four eyes studying the crystal clear water with brown coral uncomfortably near the surface. Following their directions, twisting and turning, I steered our girl through. At last we tied up a few yards from the pier, laying an anchor out on our starboard side to hold us off. We had been told about the shelf at the jetty to be avoided and the nasty winds that whipped up in this area.

We weren't alone. There was a catamaran beside us with a Swede on board. He had sailed from Rarotonga with a girl-friend who had never been to sea before. Battling with the heavy seas, this boy had fallen overboard while under full sail. The girl was panic-stricken, not having the least idea how to drop the sails or rescue her boy-friend. He was swimming like crazy, but had no chance of catching up unless she acted fast. She had seen a pair of bolt cutters in one of the lockers, and with these she cut all the halyards. The sails collapsed, and the forward motion of the boat was effectively stopped. The boy had a hard swim but caught up and clambered aboard, horrified to see his halyards cut. It was the end of the romance—yet this little girl in her own way had saved his life. Later that day *Salty* limped in looking decidedly the worse for wear, her main halyard broken and half the guard rail washed away by the heavy seas.

We had been told that this island was a paradise for men, the girls coming down to the quay and embracing each boy as he stepped ashore. Sure enough, adjusting the last warp, I looked up to see Frank leaping onto the jetty and into the arms of a local girl—no shyness here. We didn't see much of Frank after that.

Each morning he'd turn up around eight to make breakfast, feeling duty-bound to put in an appearance at that hour, not co-ordinating too well. Tired and with a dreamy look on his face he would endeavour to boil us an egg, only to disappear again for the rest of the day and night. Norman and I became the night watchmen for the other yachts, rarely seeing our young friends unless they returned for rest and sleep.

Women here were starved of male company. The young men left the island to seek work in New Zealand, few returning, while most of the young women stayed at home. While a great many women in the world go to great lengths to avoid being pregnant, the main desire of these girls was to conceive a child. It was fascinating to study the toddlers around the town. What a hotch-potch they were, blond-haired with dark skins, dark-haired with fair skins, but all happy, well fed and cared for. It was a feather in a girl's cap to have a white baby and her family would encourage her. I couldn't help thinking how fascinating it would be to return in two years' time and look at the new batch of toddlers and try and decide who had fathered whom! There was a local woman nicknamed Sea Wife who had a home by the lagoon, and there the young couples collected for the nightly revelries. I never did find out why this woman opened her home to the youngsters, whether she like to see the young things enjoying themselves or whether she had dedicated her life to improving the strain of the island's population.

Our next stop was Tonga, the only remaining Polynesian kingdom. It took us four days, five by the calendar, to reach Vavau, the main island in the northern group. On Friday September 15th we crossed the international date line. It was our lost day. We and *Shebessa* had sailed half way round the world. But these were four miserable days of torrential rain, gusty winds and crashing seas. Watches seemed endless as we took it in turn to steer in our oilskin tops, rain trickling down our necks and our legs as we sat in pools of water. At last the sun fought its way through the clouds and we were relieved and happy to sight land, dry out our clothes and sail into the sheltered waters leading up to the harbour of Neiafu. Here we met many yachts, like us traversing the Pacific.

Two huge Tongans representing customs soon cleared us, then

we went ashore. The Tongans, unlike the Tahitians, took a little time to get to know us, appearing aloof and shy at first. The older men and women wore black skirts called *valas*, the traditional Tongan dress for both sexes, short for the men, ankle-length for the women. The younger girls wore two or three dresses one on top of the other, not liking to be seen in only a mini. They swam and played in the sea but always fully clothed. The few shops in the town were poorly stocked, the people having little money to spend. Here I couldn't even buy a needle, and cigarettes were sold singly. Norman and I took a walk along the shore to see the big project for the island, the Port of Refuge Hotel, then in the process of construction, a complex of thirty *fale* (Tongan hut) units—wood walls with thatched roofs tastefully designed in Polynesian style. An airfield for tourists was also being constructed.

Though lacking in many comforts that go with civilisation, these well-mannered people seemed happy and proud of their heritage. Each Tongan-born man reaching the age of seventeen is entitled to a piece of land from the King, his for his life-time, as long as he pays a small yearly tax. On this he builds his home, planting and growing enough food to support his family. He is a land-owner. Medical and dental attention are free; education is also free and compulsory up to the age of fourteen, so illiterates are few on the Tongan isles.

Johnny, a Tongan who had befriended us, rowed out to invite us to a feast at his home to take place after church on Sunday. Among the many churches, the Wesleyan, to which the Royal Family belongs, has the largest following in Tonga; but as a little man in the market told me, 'We always go to church on Sunday—but not always ours. You see missus, sometimes other churches give away clothes and books—then we go there.'

Together with a couple from another yacht we rowed across the bay and climbed the hill to a small wooden hut where Johnny lived with his wife and eight children. The hut was empty save for a beautifully woven straw mat covering the floor, and in the centre a flat piece of wood covered by a cloth. On this was placed the Bible, and Norman was asked to sit in front of it. Was he going to be asked to give a sermon or read the lesson? We sat down cross-legged. The Bible was never opened or mentioned; perhaps it was just put there to remind us all it was Sunday. Johnny's wife and the children remained outside. Lemon drinks were served in coconut shells, followed by yams carried in on a leaf and placed on the mat, each of us hacking off what we fancied. Later a large leaf package appeared, being opened to reveal a sort of pudding made out of coconut, taro root and unknown vegetables with a small amount of fish. We all dug in with our fingers, enjoying the change of diet. Sitting cross-legged for so long proved a strain. Our haunches weren't as well padded as the Tongans'. Norman leaned back in the hope of getting some support for his back from the wall of the hut, but went through it! The wood was ancient and frail.

Amid rain and squalls we sailed to Nuku'alofa, the Tongan capital on the island of Tongatapu, anchoring in the tiny harbour of Fauua. *Salty* had arrived a few days ahead of us. John came over to welcome us. He and his two crew had run into bad weather from Aitutaki and had kept going rather than visit more Cook Islands. They had decided to put into Nuku'alofa although they had no chart. 'Blazed a trail right through the reef,' said John. 'Now this island has a new pass!' Exhausted and damp from the continuous rain, thankful to be on land again, they had tied up quickly to the jetty and made a beeline for the local hotel for a skinful of beer. They had omitted to notice a ledge a few feet under water at the side of the wharf. Their thirst quenched, they had returned to *Salty* at low tide to find her lying at a precarious angle. John, a little unsteady, looked carefully at the yacht and smiled. 'My God, they brew a strong beer in Tonga!' he said in wonderment. The three of them rolled into their bunks. Only next day did they realise they really were aground with a 20 degree list to port. At high tide they moved out, laying another anchor to hold them away from the shelf. There was something very refreshing about *Salty*; no matter what they always came up smiling.

We felt at ease among the Tongans. The local stores were well stocked and full of English brands of food, Fray Bentos pies, canned kippers; they even had haggis and an abundance of fruit and vegetables. I stocked up with box-loads of stores, then stood outside the shop wondering how I'd get them to the dinghy. The Tongan women simply picked up their boxes of stores, balanced them on their heads and strode off erect, flashing me a smile as they went. I felt very inadequate. After a while a lorry-driver took pity on me and carted my load to the jetty where our dinghy had tied. Tonga is the only free port in the Pacific between Panama and Australia, so Norman got busy ordering booze and cigarettes.

Sunday here was like a Sunday in Scotland, the entire populace turning out to church, and the strict Sabbath rules were adhered to by all, no sport, no fishing, no boating; it was even illegal to collect shells. Norman asked a young girl in an office how she spent her day of rest. She smiled and said 'I just sit and think about God.'

HMCS *Gatineau*, the Canadian 24,000 ton destroyer, arrived in Nuku'alofa on a courtesy visit. We and Frank were invited to their cocktail party aboard. It was fun to have a reason to get dressed up, even though our gear was a bit the worse for wear. It was a chance for us to meet a number of Tongan ministers and their wives. Later we were asked to join the Captain's dinner party of eight to meet the Crown Prince of Tonga. I was sandwiched between the Prince and another guest who was fidgeting in a desperate attempt to hide a very large hole in one of his socks. 'Those damned cockroaches,' he said, 'look what they've done—eaten half my sock away.' I gazed down at Norman's bare ankles and thongs. 'You're one up on my husband,' I said. 'He couldn't find a pair to wear.'

The Prince was a tall, well built young man of around 15 stone, growing to be like his father King Taufa'ahau IV, a man of 20 odd stone who liked two chairs to sit on, one for each cheek. The Prince, utterly relaxed, spoke in a quiet very English voice and had the knack of making us all feel at ease, politely ignoring the fact that some of us were erratically dressed from the waist down. He spoke nostalgically of his Army days at Sandhurst, and told us how on his last visit to England he had gone to Chelsea Barracks to look up his old sergeant-major. He was led to the parade ground; an NCO went over to the sergeant-major to tell him he had a visitor, and pointing to the Prince said: 'Do you know this man?' 'Naa. 'oo is 'e? Wot's 'e floggin'?' The NCO tried again. 'He says he knows you.' The sergeant-major looked more closely. 'Corblimey,' he said. 'It's Mr Prince.'

With the crew of *Salty* we took a tour of the island in a truck, bouncing along the bumpy roads with a local driver who explained Tongan life to us. Queen Salote, who died in 1965, was still loved, revered and talked of in this land. In her lifetime she had done so much for her people. In large areas of the islands she had arranged for the planting of Faa bushes, a tree with a great variety of uses, so that her subjects would never be in need. No one is allowed to cut down the trees; they are there for the benefit of all. The leaves are used for basket making and mats, being cut, folded and soaked in water to make them more pliable; the older leaves are used for roofing. The fruit of the Faa tree ripens like a red pineapple and is taken home for the scent. Many of the roots we saw were above the ground, some stumps ending in a nipple shape. Young babies that are born with a constriction in their throats and can't suck properly are brought to these trees. The nipple stump is cut off and mashed up, and the juice poured into the babies' mouths, while the throat and face are rubbed with it. The story goes that many are cured. Some of the root ends are cut off and dried for use as brushes to paint tapa cloth.

Tapa cloth is a big industry in Tonga. Yards of this cloth are made from the beaten out bark of the Paper Bark Mulberry tree, and decorated by the Tongans with geometrical and floral designs, using reddish black and brown dye from the sap of the Koka tree. The cloth is used to make blankets, wall decorations, mats, even calendars. I bought a calendar, every inch of it hand-made, but November and December were missing. The craftsman had grown tired of making figures by the end of the year!

We passed family groups burying their dear ones at the side of the road. Upturned beer bottles encircled many a grave, and other flotsam washed up by the sea and carefully stored. Some graves looked as if they had the name emblazoned on top like a neon sign. On closer inspection it turned out to be glass or tin cut with the name of the person who had died, the sunlight making it glint.

The villages reminded me of rural England, with their leaf cottage-like huts, tidy and cared for, surrounded by green grass and gentle hills. In one village we saw flying foxes hanging on trees fast asleep, weird-looking creatures, making strange noises; the trees in this particular village seemed to be their haunt. These animals, flying high and only at night, were protected by custom, to be hunted and eaten only by members of the Royal Family.

8
Hurricane Bebe

It was time for *Shebessa* to sail to the Fiji Islands. The capital, Suva, lay 430 miles West, but the islands of the Lau group lay nearer, about 200 miles from Tonga. The Fijis, now an independent Dominion and member of the Commonwealth, consist of no less than 300 islands, about a quarter of them inhabited; their closest contacts, in trade and tourism, are with Australia and New Zealand. We had heard that the islands of the Lau group were as yet unspoiled by western civilisation, so we had a great desire to visit them. The only snag was that the powers that be in Suva said that Suva was the port of entry for the Fijis and that one must not go anywhere without first calling at Suva. Sailing 230 miles there, then 230 miles back to the Lau group, then later back to Suva, required unlimited time, which we didn't have, so we had to find a way round the problem.

Norman had read in the *Seven Seas Cruising Bulletin* of a yacht that had visited Vatoa, the most eastern island of the group, and had had a wonderful time. It was just a dot on the chart so probably it did not have any Government officials. We decided to make for that and worry about the permission later.

We left Nuku'alofa on the afternoon of October 2nd, 1972. The seas seemed to be particularly nasty that night; with the ship rolling badly and drizzly rain we started to worry about finding Vatoa. We had heard that yachts had missed it altogether. Although this would be our hundred and forty-ninth anchorage, Norman was always concerned about the possibility of running into a low island or atoll at night because of unknown currents—the Pacific is littered with wrecks of vessels that have done just that—so always aimed to be at least 20 miles off any landfall at dawn, to take star sights, then adjust course to arrive around noon when the sun would be high and it would be easier to see the pass, reefs and coral heads. However, calamity struck near noon next day when the sextant, during a particularly violent lurch, fell from Norman's hand into some sea water on deck. Even after it had been carefully dried with loo paper, we could not be certain that it would still give an accurate reading, and this doubt was to overhang all navigational calculations until we reached Fiji. Visibility deteriorated during the afternoon, no evening star sights were possible either, and so we had to rely on DR. It was cloudy and *cold*, definitely not Pacific cruising weather!

Luckily the sky cleared somewhat at dawn the following day, and Norman got quick sights of Canopus, Achenar and Venus, the resultant fix putting us 22 miles ENE of the northern tip of the island where we had to enter. That was about right—if the sextant was all right. We expected to see land on the bow and to port, but after 20 miles there was nothing to be seen. Then at 1015 land appeared on the *starboard* beam, about ten miles off, and *North-West*! How on earth had we got down there? The sextant tested not much out, so it had to be because of the strong SW current.

We had no chart of Vatoa, only a small drawing a couple of inches long in the *Seven Seas Bulletin*, but it did show the pass behind the reef at the north end. This looked rather frightening as we approached in a strong wind and high seas, but glimpses of a calm lagoon beyond heartened us; somehow we had to find the narrow pass. But as we approached the far end of the reef there was no pass to be seen. 'Sails down, Frankie, and let's have a quiet search.' We hadn't seen an approach like this before. A curving above-water reef extended a mile offshore to a point, then stopped. Behind it, where we now were, it was quite calm; certainly there wasn't any breaking water on each side of the pass, which was the usual approach to any atoll, but we could now see there was a reef underwater. After a couple of approaches and recces down the reef from the ratlines Norman reckoned he could see a track. We decided to go in but very slowly.

Suddenly we saw a canoe paddling towards us from the shore and two men came alongside. The elder one, a handsome man of about thirty-five, extended a huge hand and with a great smile and flashing teeth said: 'Welcome to Vatoa. I am Kolionis and this is Luka. Would you like me to guide you through the entrance?' 'Not half,' sighed Norman. 'Thank you very much. Come aboard.' We tied their boat, a crazy, battered, boxlike arrangement with an outrigger full of leaks and nailed up with bits of deal, to our stern, then the two of them came aboard. Under their guidance I steered *Shebessa* over the reef, twisting and turning to avoid the many coral heads showing under the surface; I wondered about coming out. 'I have my plantation on shore and come out to guide any boats in,' explained Kolionis. 'This is my island, I'm sure you will enjoy it.'

'Kolynos,' said Norman—the name of the toothpaste was easier to pronounce. 'We haven't a clearance from Suva and we've got Frank here sick. Is there any medical assistance on the island?' (We reckoned a tropical ulcer that Frank had suddenly developed on his forehead—a large hard lump not unlike a boil that had grown from a small infected cut—was as good an excuse as any for coming in.) 'Don't worry, no problem. Anna will fix Frank up in no time.' Kolynos wanted to return to his copra, so handed us over to eighteen-year-old Luka. 'Luka will arrange everything with the chief.' We sailed with care about two miles along the south-west coast, at last fetching up opposite a few leaf huts.

A couple of rums for Luka, then we all went ashore in our dinghy to be met with welcoming smiles from the populace, most of whom were gathered on the beach. Anna, an amazing person aged about forty, had been looking after the health of the island—300 people—for the last twenty years, with no drugs, just a scalpel, a pair of forceps and six bottles of mysterious different-coloured liquids on her shelf. She also had six kids of her own, but no sign of a husband. She bathed Frank's ulcer with liquid from one bottle, stuck a plaster on and said 'He'll be all right now.' And he was.

Then to meet the chief in his hut with his wife, two sisters and five grandchildren. He was a very thin, wizened old chap of seventy-three with Parkinson's disease. We all sat on the floor cross-legged for a while, feeding him cigarettes and smiling away, while Luka explained our situation, the chief nodding and smiling

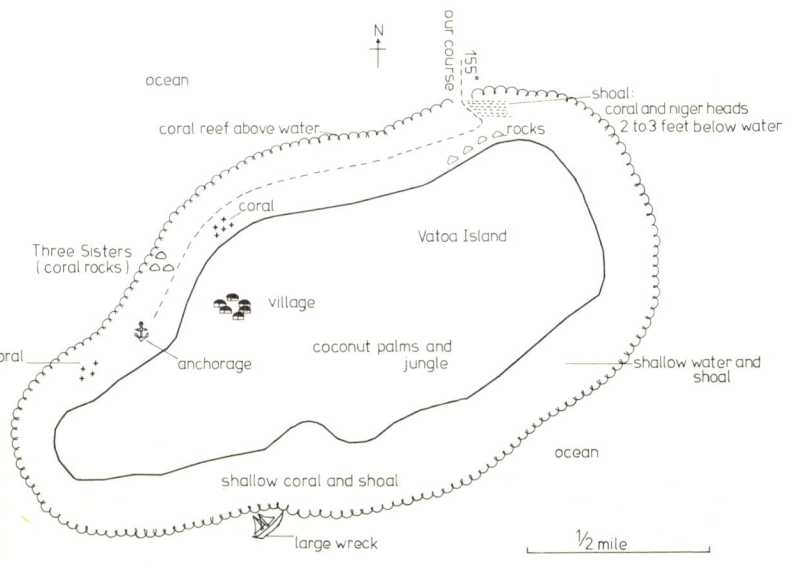

Vatoa Island

at us; he spoke no English. Through Luka he invited us to a special kava ceremony that night at seven o'clock, so we wandered back to the ship for a spell of rest until then. However, we were interrupted by the arrival of the Government official to see our papers! We explained about Frank and the sextant problem and apologised profusely about the lack of papers, the discussion being frequently interrupted with glasses of rum. In the end our stay was blessed—until Saturday when the official would have to report us to Suva by radio. Apparently all the outer islands were in contact with Suva daily by radio. We hadn't thought of that.

Ashore that evening we were met by Moses the large, happy, frizzy-headed island schoolmaster, speaking good English, who conducted us to the chief's hut. On the way he asked for the kava. Of course we had none. We didn't even know what it was. Moses explained that as visitors we had to present some to the chief as a sign of friendship and respect, so Luka was despatched to get the storekeeper to open up to buy some at 50 cents a pound. We sat on the floor with the chief until it arrived, then as Norman offered it to the chief, Moses delivered a long speech about us, where we were from, how we hoped to stay on the island, etc, etc. The chief responded by accepting the kava and ordered the making of the potion. Kava is the root of a species of pepper plant which grows on most Fijian islands—except Vatoa, and it is made into a concoction which only the men have (I was to be excepted from this rule as an honoured guest) as a ceremonial or celebratory drink. It has a sedative effect after an initial lifting of the spirit, and takes the place of alcohol on the outer Fijian islands.

Luka hammered the roots into dust, then poured the dust into a canvas bag. He then poured about four gallons of cold water into a huge wooden bowl, intricately carved, standing on four legs about six inches above the ground. Tied to this was a string with a large white Ovula ovum cowrie shell at the end, pointing at the chief. It was taboo to pass across or even reach across this string. Into the water went the bag, then Luka kneaded it for ages while a horrible-looking muddy concoction developed. When it was the right consistency the ceremony began. Luka filled a special half coconut shell with the potion and handed it to the chief, who clapped hands once, took it and swigged it down in one gulp. Everyone clapped three times. Now it was Norman's turn. He clapped once, forced it down in one gulp, and everyone clapped three times. I followed suit. The drink had a strange astringent taste, was rather heavy and a little sickly. Then to Frank, and thence around the assembled company which now numbered fifteen, as elders of the tribe kept coming in, squatting in a large circle to pay their respects to the chief and to us as visitors. Then a second round: it tasted better this time.

We learned from Moses that this custom had been carried on for hundreds of years, the basic idea being that if kava is drunk together, then all is well between the drinkers. But the bowl had to be emptied in one sitting. Norman had ten quaffs without losing control, but some of the old men, after a few, keeled over, had a little sleep, woke up, then carried on. However, it was not for guests to give up before the chief did and we didn't. I had special dispensations as a woman. The ceremony broke up dizzily at 2300 hours with some of the elders out for the count. But the chief kept all his faculties about him, and formally granted us the freedom of the island until Saturday.

We invited the chief on board for tea and cake the next day. He turned up on the beach at 0900! How were we going to get this doddery old fellow into our rubber dinghy, out to *Shebessa*, up the side and on board without some accident? We realised that if anything happened to the old chief through our fault, the islanders could easily get the cooking pots out for us. However, the boarding went well, Frank rowing him over from the shore carefully placed deep in the middle of the dinghy, and we got him on board without incident. The dear old chief was interested in everything. We showed him charts and a map of our route, opened the lockers, and showed him how everything worked, all with sign language and smiles, and gave him tea for which he had a passion. When we offered a cigarette, he indicated he wanted newspaper which we produced whereupon he unrolled our cigarette, emptied the tobacco into a piece of newspaper, rolled it and smoked that. Later we found that everyone here always rolled their baccy in the *Fiji Times*! The chief's hour-long visit was all too short.

Moses too spent time on board, telling us of life on the island. His philosophy was that life on Vatoa could not be bettered anywhere. 'Where else in the world,' he asked, 'could I live like a millionaire without being one?' He showed off by sailing past us in his crazy hollowed-out log 'canoe' with a small lateen sail made of flour bags full of holes. Each day he or one of the elders came out to tell us we were breaking the law by staying without a permit and that they might get into trouble for allowing us to stay, but a drop of

Scotch always smoothed things over. At last Saturday came and we had to go.

The 230 miles to Suva proved to be a worrying as well as a wet passage. With the North-West wind we had to beat to windward, which we hadn't done for some time, towards Toyota island with its old volcano 115 miles West and a good mark for the course. This we successfully passed. But as we approached Suva the proximity of Nasalai reef on which many ships had come to grief gave us concern.

As dawn broke we could see what looked like the reef with low flat country to the East of it, then a lighthouse. But which one? It was a round tower with red bands about a hundred feet high, whereas the one mentioned in the Admiralty List of Lights was a square tower 14 feet high—very strange indeed. But there was nothing else we could do except to keep motoring West, keeping within sight of the reef extending right along the coast, hoping to see Makuluva and Nukulau islands about ten miles further along. Visibility was only about half a mile. We were most thankful to pick these islands up after only a couple more hours. We were safe now, as it was only a case of following the reef until the pass into Suva harbour showed up, which it eventually did. Despite a heavy swell and mist we slipped safely through into the calm water of the large harbour.

Suva was a busy, bustling city. The shops were filled with goods from all over the world—all at duty-free prices. There were large supermarkets and lots of banks and hotels—what a contrast with simple, unhurried Vatoa. Everyone seemed to have plenty of money to spend, and spend it they did, much of it on beer. The pubs were full all the time, the Fijians also, but they were friendly souls, wearing a great grin on their faces if they staggered into you as they frequently did on the pavement.

It was very hot and humid—not conducive to work, and very wet. On Suva and the eastern half of Viti Levu it rained every day for about half a day, so an umbrella was part of the standard dress. But the anchorage off the Royal Suva Yacht Club was comfortable, and the Club itself was pleasant, with lots of other yachties to yarn to, many of whom we had met on our way across either the Atlantic or the Pacific. Suva is a crossroads for yachts and yachties, for one can sail from there South to New Zealand,

Left: Shebessa sails North from Bequia, West Indies

Below: Splendour in poverty – Cuna Islanders

The author talking to sea lions on Hood Island, Galapagos

With Tom in party mood, Tuamotu style

... the Bay of Islands, Suva, Fiji, we await our fate as Hurricane Bebe
... aches us

... orman (centre) on the Yarra, Melbourne, with his erstwhile rowing rival
... an Jacobson, with Noel Wilkinson in the cox's seat

Loyalty Island mother, wearing traditional Mother Hubbard dress, with her children, Uvéa

Lopevi volcano, near Epi, New Hebrides

Malaita, Solomons.
Left: Norman trading with islanders

Below left: Shells for sale

Bottom: Are Are Lagoon

At anchor off the Cosmoledos. Big Mike and Little Mike display their trophies of the sea

The author with the priest and a student at the Roman Catholic Mission on Garove Island, off New Britain

The moon-like landscape of the Atlantic island of Trindade

New Year fertility ceremony of the Incwala, Valley of Heaven, Swaziland. The King's warriors cross the arena at speed

North Atlantic passage

South-West to Australia, or West to the New Hebrides and Papua New Guinea, all fairly long passages—or one can just stay put. In the wet and humid atmosphere, unless one has a driving ambition to go to a particular place as we had, one just defers a decision. Some yachts had been there for years.

We reckoned on sailing round to the western side of the island which was said to be very beautiful, and then setting off for Australia before there was any chance of getting caught in the hurricane season which extended from late November to April, although there hadn't been a hurricane in this area for some time. There was plenty of time—it was only October—so we decided to repaint the top and sides of our fore and aft cabins to make them smart for arrival in Australia as there we knew we would not have time for work. We engaged two local painters to help us do the job one weekend towards the end of October, and by Sunday lunchtime we were finished—undercoat and topcoat of gleaming white, and handrails, hatches and windscreen revarnished—a beautiful job. But quite a bit had been happening while we'd been painting.

On the Friday afternoon the weather report had mentioned a low pressure area well north of Rotuma, a small island 400 miles North-West of Viti Levu, with strong winds moving South-West. Next day the low pressure area had been promoted into the hurricane category and named 'Bebe'. This name will forever stick in our minds. But it was forecast to move South-West. People in Suva started to talk about the course of Bebe, but were not worried. 'We haven't had a hurricane for twenty years so why should we worry?' was the attitude. Some yachts however moved from the Yacht Club anchorage in the open Suva harbour to the Trade Winds Hotel in the Bay of Islands, the accepted 'hurricane hole' of Suva, being protected behind Snake and Mosquito islands. Others went up the shallow Kumbuna Creek on the west side of the Bay which was completely safe.

Sunday brought a full hurricane warning for Rotuma but again its course was to be South-West away from Suva. More yachts left but we had to let the paint dry! On Monday we were practically alone at the Club. We drove around to the Trade Winds anchorage to see what room there was, but found it full of yachts and small island vessels coming in from all over the coast, making it very crowded for everyone; it certainly looked a sheltered place. We spoke to the hotel manager, who said that if the hurricane did come

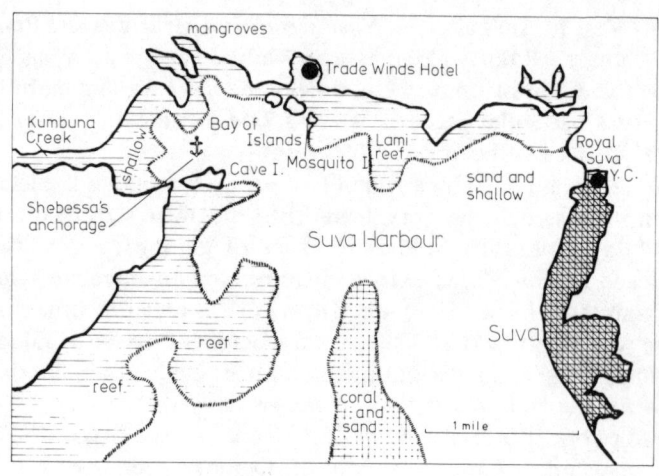

Suva Harbour

it would be chaos at the anchorage with boats charging around, dragging and crashing into each other; he advised us to go across and anchor in the bay just north-east of Cave Island where there was plenty of room. Already there were a couple of freighters and two barges there—but it looked very exposed. The Lloyds surveyor who then turned up agreed it was good holding ground and suggested we should tie up to one of the barges. With some misgivings we hurried back to move, with a preliminary hurricane warning for Suva ringing in our ears. Hurricane! A dreaded word among sailing folk, and for those who have not experienced one, like ourselves, bringing a spine-chilling fear of the unknown.

We collected Frank from the bar at the Club, rowed out to *Shebessa* and got under way with the wind stronger from the East, motoring across to the Bay of Islands to find our 'safe' hurricane hole. Where to anchor? Finally we dropped our starboard anchor with 30 fathoms of three-eighth inch chain to lie between the two big barges 60 yards apart, one of which was tied to a huge mooring buoy and the other anchored. We dug our starboard anchor well in and surveyed the situation.

Sayonara, a 105 foot charter steamer which took tourists around the Fiji group, was astern and to port; *Alwyn*, a 26 foot Bowman sloop sailed single-handed by Al, a sixty-year-old from Bristol, was to port of her; a friend, Bobby on *Falasia* was astern of the barge at anchor; two freighters were well to starboard, with some small freighters and a large schooner far ahead of them. All very nice and open—in fact, too open; we seemed to be completely exposed to the full force of the wind and sea from the East. As they had said at the hotel, there was certainly plenty of swinging room. But—what was this? A glass-bottomed boat with high superstructure had anchored only 50 yards ahead of us! Not so good—she seemed to have only a warp and was already sheering about, and her crew had gone off in a motorboat leaving her unattended. We shackled on 15 fathoms of chain and 15 fathoms of one inch diameter nylon warp to our port anchor, and in the dinghy with the Seagull got it out near the stern of the glass-bottomed boat. We got our remaining two anchors ready and made other preparations.

The East wind was much stronger now, and rain started to lash down. We were plunging about, the barometer was a few points down, and then the full hurricane warning for Suva which we were hoping wouldn't come was heard over the radio, now on continuously. Rotuma was directly in the path of Bebe, which had curved South-East, putting Suva right in line. We'd got two 45 lb CQR anchors down, both well antichafed, a 30 lb Danforth with all our mooring warps—about 35 fathoms—in reserve in case we dragged, a 20 lb CQR kedge with 20 fathoms of half inch terylene warp to back it up, decks cleared, everything on the stern securely lashed down, sail covers on and lashed, storm canopy up, dinghy on two painters sitting tight behind the transom—what more could we do now except sit tight and await our fate at the hands of Nature?

We seemed to be holding well as the wind rose still more, unlike the glass-bottomed boat ahead of us which was charging about from side to side like a mad thing—she surely couldn't last the course. Shops and businesses were already closing, and schools, banks and Government offices were also to close next day so that everyone could look after their homes. Rotuma was now getting the full force of the hurricane; the Yasawas would be next, poor devils; then it might well be our turn.

At 0400 hours I saw a light through the aft cabin starboard window and close! Up on deck Norman rushed to see *Falasia* charging about trying to get her anchor up. Bobby motored back and forth then disappeared astern. Later we heard the starboard barge had dragged back over one of his anchors so he had to slip it to get out of the way. The glass-bottomed boat was still charging around, all boats were fully lit and most sheering about, but we were steady. We had just lain down again when crash! on our bow. Norman and Frank struggled forward to find the glass-bottomed boat close abeam. She had crashed into our bowsprit and was now out of control alongside. Then we saw her anchor—a tiny Danforth, right there on our bowsprit! It must have been dragged, picked up our chain, run up it and then along the warp to finish up right there on our deck. Somehow we managed to release it to hurl it to port, and off she went. I thought then of the hotel manager's words. We must be mad to be out here among other vessels in this, but nothing we could do about it now.

Dawn brought quite a sight—still terrific rain, wind very strong, visibility poor, sea rough and muddy, breaking over our bow as we pitched up and down. All other craft were present except *Alwyn* and *Falasia*. I hoped they hadn't dragged ashore. The radio was telling tales of flooding, people homeless, houses damaged and some blown down, much damage in Rotuma and the Yasawas. Around us the waves were only five feet high but very short, bursting under the bow of the barge to starboard to make her pitch like crazy. She had a heavy anchor no doubt, but it must be under a lot of stress—we wondered fearfully about that one.

The barometer dropped quickly now from the normal 1013 millibars. By 1000 hours it was 994—19 mb down. The book said a hurricane was coming if it dropped 5 mb! And so it continued all day: 1100 hours, 991; 1230 hours, 990; 1530 hours, 985; 1630 hours, 984—29 points down. Already seven points lower than Robinson had on *Svaap* in his Tongan hurricane which came through Fiji in 1929! Our Ventimeter blew up at 54 knots—that was 71 knots at mast level! It was beginning to get hectic. But we were holding OK. The radio said Bebe would be over Nandi 70 miles West, at 1800 hours, and West of Suva at midnight—but how far West? It is amazing how everything bad at sea always seems to happen at night.

The three of us sat looking at each other, thinking our own thoughts of what might happen, all of us jumpy but trying to make light of it, tired and silent, listening for any sound other than the rain lashing down and the wind screaming in the rigging. The radio said the wind was 120 knots in the centre of the hurricane—50 more than we had now. Would we survive if we got that? We decided to have a good meal whilst there was time. I made a cheesecake for the first time in my life—anything to keep my mind occupied.

Although we had been told to tie up to one of the barges, they looked none too safe, especially the one to starboard, which was taking a pounding, so we reckoned we were better off on our own resources of two anchors—we would stick it out as we were. The dinghy sometimes turned over, then righted itself. Perhaps we should take it in, but how? It was riding nicely in our lee now—where would we put it on board?

Nandi radio was now out of action and Wellington Radio, New Zealand rebroadcast the hurricane news. Bebe was centred 30 miles East of Nandi and moving South-East at 15 knots towards us! The barometer was still dropping—980 at 1900 hours. Wind and rain had become fantastic; Met office Suva reported the wind here at 80 knots—quite enough please! Norman and Frank crawled forward to look at the anchors but couldn't really see in the blinding rain. We still seemed to be holding. *Sayonara* was still in the same position astern. There was terrific spume being torn from the tops of the waves, making the sea look practically smooth—and the wind was actually getting stronger!

2100 hours—and this is IT. Three terrific gusts hit us, sending us sheering from side to side. 'We're dragging!' from Frank. Heaven help us if we are. But how else to explain *Sayonara* on our port beam? Astern there's no sign of the starboard barge but it's hard to see clearly with the spray and the rain. We motor into the violent gusts which keep coming, to relieve the strain on our anchors as we sheer beam on to the wind. *Sayonara* starts to fall back astern and slowly disappears. We stop motoring to check if we've dragged, but reckon we haven't. Probably we're safer to let the anchors take the strain steadily, instead of perhaps wrenching them out when motoring.

It surely can't get worse than this? We're all now plain terrified, with the mighty gusts, a sky full of flares from ships in distress, always wondering—how much more can we stand? Will we be here in the morning? And if not where? And still the barometer dropping—972! Worse to come!

The large schooner which was anchored 400 yards ahead suddenly appears, gradually dragging back onto the freighter *Uniwai* which has to power out of the way while the schooner just keeps going astern and disappears—where she's gone God alone knows. No sign of the anchored barge either. That's three large vessels gone. Will we be next to go? We hear on 2182, the distress frequency, of two fishing vessels going aground on reefs on the north coast of Viti Levu and calling for assistance—but who can help them?

This wind. I've never felt or heard wind of this intensity before and I sincerely trust I never will again. The hurricane's centre must surely be close now—the barometer is down to 970. Radio reports extensive flooding, power shut down, everything closed, Nandi and Lautoka badly hit, Nawau River bridge down, the Yasawas devastated. The monster Bebe is flattening the Fijian Islands, causing devastation, chaos and death.

As each violent gust hits us we wonder if it's stronger than the last or less. One's sense of perception is dulled now with the incessant howling of the wind, the screaming tone in the rigging rising higher and higher in the gusts, the torrential rain lashing down, waves bursting over the bow and rushing along the deck—what would we do without our storm canopy? Radio gives wind as 90 knots here.

Radio says two yachts are on the reefs: dragged out of the Yacht Club anchorage—poor yachties. Who can help them? Only *Solmar* and *Negati*, the two gallant local tugs which are out. Both glass-bottomed boats gone—no wonder.

2245 hours: barometer has steadied at 970. Is the wind any less? Yes, it's slackening—and suddenly, calm! Good or bad? The lull means the eye must be close or over us and that means, according to the book, increased wind from the opposite direction. What a prospect! What about swinging room then? *Uniwai* looks close and Cave Island is to leeward if the wind changes. Norman says if this is the calm before the final onslaught, there's time to do something—reanchor in a better position. Forward to find only one anchor—the starboard one on chain. Warp on port side is hanging limp in the water, a 45 lb CQR, 15 fathoms of chain and 15 fathoms of warp gone. The glass-bottomed boat's Danforth sliding up the warp must have cut it, so that it later parted. How long have we been hanging on only one anchor? What a great job it's done—and didn't like coming up either.

The rain stops, the stars have come out, the air has cleared, and it's completely still as we reanchor with the one CQR and our reserve Danforth. An incredible sensation, unreal and impossible. Wait for the second instalment . . .

From the West, here it comes—

But not bad, never more than 40 knots for the rest of the night. Barometer 971—was it over? 0130 hours, 975; 0530 hours, 984 ... We and *Shebessa* had survived.

Dawn brought an amazing sight. We were alone except for *Uniwai*. The big schooner *Sayonara*, *Alwyn*, the two glass-bottomed boats and one barge were all on the shore. Queen Salote's old royal barge, now a charter schooner, was lying on her side on a reef, a few motor boats were on other reefs. The rescue tug *Solmar* was rushing around. For us it was a hearty breakfast then cleaning up and drying out, then to bed for a few hours as suddenly we felt very, very weary.

In retrospect we were glad, in a strange sort of way, that we had been through this experience, in spite of all the worry and terror, and later, back in the Trade Winds Hotel, we felt just a little smug about it all. Nonetheless, we realised how lucky we had been. The crew on *Solmar* said that at the peak we had been pitching like mad with the whole of the fore cabin disappearing under the waves. *Shebessa* had taken a terrible bashing. The new paint and varnish was all gone—completely skinned off by the lashing rain, the waves and the wind. The most important lesson we had learnt was that one cannot have enough anchor chain on board—warp is useless in a hurricane or in any strong wind for that matter. Later in Suva we bought another 30 fathoms of chain ready for the next time.

We spent the first day after the hurricane lazing in the sunshine and receiving visitors. *Camdella,* owned by a young New Zealand couple, John and Diana Barraclough, came to anchor near us. They had had a terrible time at the hands of Bebe. Anchored with warp only behind Mosquito Island, near the Trade Winds, they had dragged out and right across the Bay in spite of motoring flat out in the opposite direction, towards the reef around Shark Island which was to starboard and ahead of us. They were certain they would be wrecked, but as they passed a small freighter near the reef, the skipper threw them a line to hold them to him and off the reef.

Bobby in *Falasia* came over. He had gone up Kumbuna Creek early on Tuesday morning after slipping his anchor from under the barge, and had been safe, but now he had come to look for his anchor and chain. We lent him our trusty dinghy and Seagull with its small anchor to drag back and forth hoping to pick it up, but he had no luck. The next morning we did the same for ours, but had no luck either.

We decided to go over to the Trade Winds Hotel as now there would be room. But the Danforth snagged on some obstruction, and only slowly came up as we used the full power of our electric winch. We had picked up a buoy mooring chain, we thought. But that chain around the stock looked familiar, with its three-eighth inch links—it could be ours, the one we had lost? Excitedly we payed it in ... and sure enough came to the warp, our warp with its frayed end. How about that for luck? But we couldn't understand the location. We started to get the chain and anchor on board—but the chain wouldn't budge even when we tried to motor it out. John in *Camdella*, seeing the struggle, suggested he would dive with his Scuba to try to find the snag. His offer was gratefully accepted. He took down our high pressure deck wash hose driven by the bilge pump motor to dig the anchor out of the mud. With us winching too, after fifteen minutes the faithful CQR surfaced. The anchor had sunk more than six feet in the mud—some holding ground! The hotel manager had been right after all. We had a drink to him.

Then to the Trade Winds to tie up stern to for a few days' rest and to listen to the tales of the other yachts in their respective havens. Those in the basin and up the creek were all right, but *Valhalla*, a 65 foot schooner, had dragged out from near the Trade Winds, dragging her 100 lb Fisherman anchor and 50 fathoms of half inch chain. She had been rescued by *Solmar* to reanchor behind Mosquito Island and then at the peak of the hurricane had dragged out again to a shoal in the Bay where she secured to the beacon marking the shoal. Poor *Alwyn* anchored near us on warp had dragged out on the first night and finished up in a clearing in the mangroves. Al had been quite happy there until the big barge which had been to starboard of us followed him across on the second night, grounding right across the entrance to Al's clearing and locking him in, where he stayed until *Solmar*, attending to *Sayonara*, found him two days later! The two yachts from the Club on the reef were also salvaged by *Solmar*. She did well with salvage charges, but was very fair to the yachts: A$6,000 for *Sayonara*, A$350 for *Valhalla*. Hearing all this we decided to celebrate our luck with a 'hurricane holiday'—while Frank threw a 'hurricane party' on board with his special brew.

We spent three luxurious days at the Fijian Hotel near Yanuca Island about 60 miles west of Suva. Travelling there by road we were appalled at the devastation everywhere. The villages had their buildings and homes smashed down, fields were flooded, crops ruined, banana and coconut trees uprooted—whole areas were laid waste. A barge type of cable ferry had been rigged up to carry the traffic over the Navua River in place of the bridge that had been carried away, and it was hair-raising crossing on this structure, which appeared none too safe with muddy floodwater swirling underneath.

At the Fijian Hotel we became professional beachcombers on a snug sandy beach and forgot all about hurricanes—blissfully sunbathing, snorkelling, waterskiing, and eating all manner of local Fijian dishes.

On our return we heard about Frank's party—the party of the year. Apparently the brew had been left to ferment just a little too long. People had fallen overboard, dinghies were capsized, the noise was terrific and the heads next morning were terrific. All agreed it was a fitting end to Hurricane Bebe.

9
Australian Homecoming

In a week we were ready for the last hop before fulfilling Norman's ambition to sail to his home town of Melbourne. Ted Cully, the Canadian who had crewed on *Salty*, joined us—*Salty* was going to remain in Fiji over the entire hurricane period. Ted was a tall easy-going man and unshakable; he brought with him the famous happy-go-lucky atmosphere of *Salty*, and he and Frank became good friends.

Our voyage to Australia took twenty-one days, the first week dream sailing with the wind on the quarter pushing us along through calm seas. We caught plenty of tuna, which we salted. First we filleted the fish, then cut it into thin strips, which we laid out on the table. We all worked in the rock salt, rubbing it into the flesh with our fingers, and strung the strips up on to the ratlines to bake in the hot sun, leaving them there for almost a week till they shrivelled and became hard. Then we stowed them away to use later in the voyage when we weren't so lucky with our fishing. Soaked for twenty-four hours to remove the salt, the fillets made many a fish pie and kedgeree. Frank seemed to have blossomed and filled out with regular food, and thought of *Shebessa* as his first home. One day I made a chocolate cake and was about to ice it. 'Oh, you mustn't use a knife,' he said, 'my mother always used a brush.' 'Have a go then Frank,' I said and left him to it. He did a great job and the icing shone like glass. Funny, mine never had that sheen. Only when we ate it did we realise why. The varnish brush had been used for the job!

Because he couldn't contribute funds for his keep, Frank insisted on doing all the washing up and serving the food. He laid a cornbeef stew on our plate as if it were beef stroganoff, and somehow every dish tasted better when Frank served it. He had left Germany half way through his training to be an industrial chemist. He would have made a superb waiter in any of the most exclusive restaurants of the world.

The second week there was practically no wind. We motored on but for some reason our engine suddenly started gobbling oil until we had no more to cope with her thirst. Keeping our last can for emergencies, it was sail only from now to Australia. Becalmed in what seemed to us an endless ocean, we sent up a prayer for wind. A day or two later it came at last—but from Australia, right on the nose. Any wind was better than none, so with yankee, main and mizzen we bashed into it, water cascading over the foredeck day after day.

We had been unable to obtain a chart of Sydney harbour in Fiji, but had been lent a road map. This and the pilot book would have to bring us safely to Norman's home shores. We weren't keen on tackling Sydney harbour without an engine, with the thousands of craft sailing there. Charging our batteries, using the Honda generator, Norman called Radio Brisbane to ask permission to take on oil at Byron Bay, our nearest landfall and stated in the pilot as a port of entry for vessels from New Zealand. It was put up to Canberra and later a cheerful voice came through informing us we could land for fuel only and that customs would meet us. Ted and Frank decided bread was fuel—not to mention a few beers too. Spirits rose.

In the early morning of December 5th Australia was sighted, and within hours we dropped anchor a few hundred yards from the shores of Byron Bay, our gaiety slightly dampened by the sight of the huge surf rollers crashing on the beach. With our Q flag up we waited for customs. An hour passed but no one came, no sign of life except for the surf riders on their boards—so near and yet so far. Surf or no, we were going ashore.

We got into the dinghy and Frank rowed hard, pausing to watch the wave patterns as we neared the shore; often there were three or four big dumpers and then a quiet spell. Picking the moment, we surfed into Australia intact and dry. No welcoming committee came to meet us. The bodies of the surf riders lying on the beach didn't move; perhaps they were used to yachts—anyway it was siesta time. Norman, who had lived on my side of the world for nearly forty years, was at last in his own land again. We all sensed the emotion welling up inside him as he stepped ashore, sank to his knees and kissed Australia.

Shakily we staggered to the town. Here Norman bought the oil we needed, while I loaded up with bread, oranges and apples. Then we all met up at the local pub for an ice-cold beer, so strong and freezing we could hardly drink it. Here we met the local doctor, who looked us over. Assured of our good health, he was kindness itself, advising us to reanchor further from shore, knowing his bay well.

As dawn broke we set sail for Sydney, but didn't get far. A high-powered speedboat raced towards us, just as we hit the heavy swell at the edge of the bay. Then two men with great difficulty boarded us, as we all fended off the speedboat that was being tossed against our topsides. How thankful we were for the car tyres we had on board that saved *Shebessa* many a bang. 'Customs,' the men barked, as they clambered breathlessly on board in T shirts and shorts. 'We want to search your ship.' We told them to carry on and search to their hearts' content. Should we turn back and anchor in calmer waters or just stay wallowing in this heavy swell? We decided on the latter. There's a mean streak in everyone at times. No wonder these men weren't friendly. They had been sent down from Brisbane at short notice to spend the night patrolling the beach, in hopes of catching us unloading drugs, and they had had to borrow a speedboat and clothes to board us. They never did search us. One of them turned green within minutes, retching his heart out in the cockpit, while stoically the other saw through the entry formalities, trying hard to adjust to the violent motion, mopping the sweat that was pouring from his face, going up at intervals for air. We were a mixture of nationalities, one German, one Canadian and two British, yet I had never seen forms filled in so fast. Those wretched, tired, sea-sick men couldn't get off the ship fast enough. Only later did we find out that Byron Bay was notorious for drug smuggling.

As soon as the customs men had gone, Norman announced that he would start the engine. He had filled her up with the new oil. The engine burst into life—but clouds of smoke enveloped us! Engine off. We'd have to stick to sailing.

We covered the 300 miles to Sydney in three days with the help of the friendly South-going current of about 40 miles per day. The weather on this coast was very variable, the wind changing direction and strength all the time, so we had a busy three days constantly sail changing—reefing, dereefing, booms up, booms down, gybing and tacking with thunderstorms, heavy rain and brilliant sunshine.

It was thrilling to arrive at Sydney Heads on a sunny Saturday afternoon to see thousands of boats of all shapes and sizes, some racing, some cruising, ferry boats and the odd freighter all filling lovely Sydney harbour. We threaded our way through all these with no engine and no chart, past all the beaches and snug coves on each side, with the famous harbour bridge and the new opera house in the background, searching for the entrance to Rushcutters Bay where we had arranged to moor.

At last we sailed in to tie up at the Cruising Yacht Club of Australia, affectionately known as the CYC, where we were met by the press and TV and radio in a stupendous welcome. We had scores of visitors, some old friends but mostly complete strangers who had read in the newspapers of our voyage, who inundated us with invitations for touring, meals and accommodation ashore. Even in the busy streets and shops we were stopped by people who had seen our photographs. A couple of friends from our hurricane holiday at the Fijian Hotel invited us for three gorgeous days at their bungalow at McMaster's Beach some miles north of Sydney. Peter Campbell, editor of *Modern Boating*, who had published some of our articles, wanted more, and he gave us a spin in his speedboat around the harbour. Someone lent us a car. The CYC gave us tremendous help and hospitality, with free berthing, although they were full with yachts competing in the One Ton Cup and later in the Sydney to Hobart Race starting on Boxing Day. The CYC must be the ultimate for any yachtie—a safe mooring, a shop 50 yards away with all basic supplies, a lovely swish clubhouse with every comfort imaginable.

Our engine trouble was diagnosed as 'cylinder glazing', caused by our inability to obtain the correct high detergent oil in the Pacific. We refilled and hoped it was cured.

In Sydney we said farewell to Frank, who had been with us for five months. Goodbyes, though part of our life, were always difficult, boys living on board often so quickly becoming one of the family as we got to know each other through and through as one never would on land, our likes, our hates, our dreams. Norman and I, having been through World War Two, still deep down harboured prejudice against our war-time enemies. Frank had dissolved those bitter feelings, making us realise more than ever that it is only politicians who cause so much upset and turmoil in the world. Older people can so easily get set and bigoted, so it did us good to have young people aboard. Ted and Frank took a flat, found jobs and reckoned they would stay in Sydney forever.

The weeks rushed by with all the hospitality, interspersed with visits to the great bustling city only a short bus ride from the Club. Sydney gave one the impression of thriving, thrusting purpose, of confidence in its ability to keep expanding and developing. One could not fail to be impressed with the faith of its people, of all nationalities under the sun, in their own future and that of Australia generally. The standard of living here was higher than we had seen anywhere else, everyone seemed prosperous and above all enjoying life. As the saying goes, Australia's future can only get better with such vast natural resources and plenty of space to develop them. Where else in the world is this now the case?

I had lived with an Australian for 32 years, but this hadn't in the least prepared me for the impact now made by this down to earth nation of forthright extroverts. To me it seemed very much a man's country, with the men free to enjoy their clubs and meet their mates over a few beers while their wives stayed at home with the children. It's an unwritten law in Australia that if you meet your mate at a bar for a beer and bring along friends, each man has to 'shout', and none leaves till all have done so. It's not uncommon for twelve to fourteen mates to get together over some beers, with the evening meal often being a very late session and husbands rolling home with a great many unexpected guests. The wives seem to have grown accustomed to this and cope beautifully, keeping their fridges bulging with meat, salad and beer.

Sitters-in charge astronomical sums, expecting an evening meal and television thrown in, so children, often out of necessity, will be taken out with their parents. It's strange to dine at a smart restaurant in the evening and see little ones running around in pyjamas and dressing gowns, some having to prop their eyes open to keep awake.

Grog, as they call it, flows freely, beer, wine and every spirit imaginable. The town seemed to me at first over-provided with filling stations—till I looked more closely and found they were drive-in bottle stores, with crates of beer and flagons of wine in place of petrol pumps—you place your order and it's put into the boot, you pay up and drive away.

I took time to get tuned in to Australian English, with its slang and very different words for everyday things. 'Toiking a sicky todoiy mate?'—'Are you taking a day off sick mate?' 'Have a bonza crissy'—'Have a good Christmas.' I asked someone at the Club where I could find a hose pipe to replenish our water supplies. 'It's on the noiture strip,' he said. 'Where's that?' I asked. He gave me a funny look. 'Loidy,' he said, 'even a boiby knows where the noiture strip is.' Oh well, I'd learn in time. Obviously something to do with bathing, I thought, and searched the showers, but had no luck. The nature strip was the grass border to the footpath—and there I found my hose, installed for watering the grass. I asked a woman in the street where the nearest greengrocer was. 'Never heard of it,' she said, shaking her head. 'We don't have anything like that here.' 'But surely—' I said. 'Where do you buy your fruit and vegetables?' 'Oh,' she said, 'you want the fruitologist.'

Barbecues are highly popular in Australia, an easy way of feeding large numbers, and have become very sophisticated. On my first visit to Australia in 1959, I well remember Sunday lunch in the garden being cooked on a grid on a wheelbarrow packed with rolled up newspaper as fuel. Now each home has its own barbecue with gas jets and bottle. Australia is certainly changing rapidly in many ways, with the vast and growing body of immigrants settling on her shores making for cosmopolitan living; sentiment is drifting away from the traditional loyalty to England and the English way of life.

I was continually asked at interviews: 'Why do you do it, drama after drama, uncomfortable living—what for? Don't you get bored? Aren't long passages tedious?' In the early stages I'd asked myself the same questions. It wasn't possible to give a pat answer.

As the months went by I had found a deep contentment living at sea, a peace out there beyond all man's understanding on land—space—silence—freedom; a life so full of contrasts, with a chance to experience every emotion; intensifying living. The ocean was an ever-changing pattern and rhythm that in time seeped into our souls; the endless waves in continual motion, the effortless gliding of the albatross skimming the waves then soaring into the heavens, the rhythmic movement of the dolphins surfacing in pairs as if one. On our 42 foot of boat in a vast ocean, we were a tiny speck in a world of sea and sky, cut off from the rest of the universe, entirely dependent on ourselves and the resources on board. Life came into perspective and our middle-aged set ideas took a severe jolt as we looked at the world through new eyes. We were like kids starting afresh, in a second youth with all the zoomph and energy of seventeen-year-olds.

No, life at sea was never dull or tedious. At times it was extremely uncomfortable—but how can one experience the ultimate in living without light and shade? I found that to dare and do things I never dreamed I could was stimulating and rewarding enough. I even began to like myself a bit more.

I couldn't hope ever to put into words the feeling I had out on the ocean, just Norman and myself, on those pitch-dark nights in storms. I had long since given up trying to understand myself—I just didn't make sense. At heart I was a frightened sparrow who got hot and had palpitations at the thought of catching a bus in a big city, but at sea when all hell was let loose and when I knew I was incapable of sailing *Shebessa* or navigating without Norman, I had a wonderful, inexplicable calm inside me. No panic, no daggers in my stomach. It was as if some heavenly body was carrying us along and calming my soul.

It was hard to leave Sydney, with its great natural playground for all aquatic sports, its baking weather, its marvellous beaches, and the company at CYC—but Norman was yearning to get to his home port of Melbourne, the climax of our voyage, to see his deceased brother's children, Neil, Bruce and Cherylle, with their own families. So we slipped *Shebessa* at CYC—the cheapest and best haul out we had ever had, A$30 up and down—to paint her bottom and make her even more beautiful for arrival in Melbourne. Neil came up from Melbourne to meet us, and to sail down there with us. I think he was as delighted as we were to be with family again. Despite all the kindness and hospitality we had received, Christmas had seemed flat on our own. Neil and his brother and sister, after the tragic death of Norman's brother and his wife in a car accident in 1962, were short of older relations. Neil welcomed us with open arms. He was enthralled with our ship and the bubbling excitement shone in his eyes as he checked over each piece of equipment and learned how to use it. At this stage he was a dinghy sailor, but plans were already formulating in his mind to have a larger craft. He proved a wonderful help on the passage from Sydney to Melbourne.

On January 20th, 1973, after six glorious weeks in Sydney, we three Martins took off for Melbourne 600 miles South. There has always been and still is a very strong feeling of rivalry between Melbourne and Sydney, each deprecating the attractions of the other, so it was natural that everyone at CYC tried to put us off this voyage with talk of 'incessant gales, head winds in Bass Strait and poor visibility', not to mention the 'dreadful' harbour and anchorages in Port Phillip Bay.

The boys at CYC proved accurate about the voyage: we had all kinds of weather, winds up to force seven, mist, and brilliant hot sunshine. On watch the first night out I saw a blaze of light before me. Norman had said we should be sailing past the naval town of Jervis Bay, so I wasn't unduly worried—but we still had to weave our way through all those ships. I had a look through the binoculars. They weren't ships. It was land and quite close! No time to wake Norman or worry about sails: I swung the wheel hard over to port, and chaos reigned aboard.

We sailed on determinedly for Port Phillip Heads, the entrance to the Bay of Melbourne. It was important to be at the Heads at slack water or at the start of the flood, as on the ebb the tide rushes out of the narrow channel at anything from four to eight knots, kicking up quite large waves because of the shallow, rocky bottom. We were an hour early so tacked around outside until the right moment arrived, signalled to us by the keeper on the Port Lonsdale lighthouse at the entrance telling us to go NOW, so we charged through under twin booms and mizzen without the engine at five knots—thrilling, especially as the pilot was very gloomy about what could happen here. It was late in the afternoon, so we anchored off Portsea jetty for the night. Neil went off to alert everyone of our intended arrival next day at Sandringham Yacht

Club, 25 miles across the Bay—the climax of our voyage, to which we had been looking forward for months. Norman fidgeted nervously about, tidying the ropes, putting things straight on deck; everything had to be perfect for his homecoming.

Norman: My thoughts were mixed about our arrival in Melbourne; I had been worrying quite a bit about it. How would I be received after my long absence? Would I be disappointed in Melbourne after Sydney? Would I feel rather alone after the loss of my mother and my only brother and his wife? Would many of my old pals be left? Would it be rough on *Shebessa* and ourselves living on board at SYC for a few months? We had been warned there would be no good anchorages round Melbourne. The southerly buster, a vicious wind often reaching up to hurricane strength, was to be expected in the summer months. Melbourne was noted for its sudden changes of temperature, three seasons in one day being not uncommon.

In lovely warm sunshine and no wind we motored across Port Phillip Bay to Sandringham Yacht Club where we tied up to the main jetty. What a tumultuous welcome followed from Neil's wife Irene, their three boys, Neil's brother Bruce with his wife Jeannie and their three boys, old friends and many members of the Club. I was overjoyed to see Ken Crossley, my oldest rowing pal with whom I had raced many times in the Thirties. The champagne corks popped, the beer flowed, TV, radio and press interviews followed, then to Neil's house. It was a strange sensation that night to sit watching ourselves and *Shebessa* on TV sailing into Sandringham Yacht Club to the welcome of the crowds. The celebration family dinner that night saw the completion of the first half of our circumnavigation—18,000 miles in two years.

Now came weeks of sheer pleasure. *Shebessa* was inundated with visitors, old friends and strangers, who showered us with invitations night after night so we were never lonely. Our mooring at SYC proved comfortable and convenient with the officers and members doing all they could to smooth our way, and all for free! We had trips into the mountains, some racing, barbecues, and rowing on the Yarra River at Banks Rowing Club, my old club, in the centre of Melbourne with some of my rowing pals of the Thirties. What memories this brought back. The Rowing Club was exactly as I had left it in 1937—rowing clubs seldom change. As we carried the boat down to the water I pictured the races down the

Henley mile—the packed crowds, the cheers, the competition—sometimes winning, sometimes losing, the comradeship, the conviviality and friendship among all oarsmen. What memories these were, highlighted by the still recognisable faces of a few of my contemporaries from those days with whom I swapped yarns and reminiscences around the barrel in the Clubhouse. Everyone wanted to hear more of our way of life, many wanted to emulate it. It was here that we first had the idea of writing this book.

In 1935/6/7 I had stroked the National Bank eight and four in the Interbanks regatta on the Yarra, rowing against all the other banks, but in particular against the Commercial Banking Co. of Sydney as one or the other of us always won. One day Ray Todd, the rowing reporter on the *Herald*, Melbourne's evening paper, phoned and suggested: 'Why don't you have a row with Alan Jacobson for old time's sake? He was your rival in the stroke seat of the CBC and you're the only two of that era still rowing. The public would be interested to read of you two rowing not in opposition but together now after all these years.' It sounded a great idea. Alan was now the national rowing coach. Noel Wilkinson, one of our few remaining contemporaries and now a leading administrator in Australian rowing, offered to cox, so one Saturday afternoon Alan and I with Wilkie, as he was affectionately called, took to the river again in a racing pair under the eyes of Ray and his photographer and many onlookers. We had a very happy row.

This was just one of the ways the years rolled back for me as I gradually picked up with those old friends of mine that remained—until I felt as if I had never left. One day I took Sheila to see my birthplace in South Melbourne. As in most of the suburbs of Melbourne the old weatherboard houses with their tin roofs were still standing and occupied. Such a one was 20 Napier Street, exactly as I remembered it from more than half a century back. The grocer's shop where I had worked delivering groceries was still on the corner. The bent lamp-post around which I had wrapped my father's car while kissing my favourite girl had still not been replaced! A couple of kids were fighting on the pavement giving each other hell—they could have been my dead brother and myself. I could almost hear the voice of our neighbour—'Carlton and South are at it again!' (Carlton and South Melbourne were, and still are, great rival football clubs.)

I did some consultative accountancy work to recoup funds. I

was delighted to see how Neil and Bruce had made a great success of their family builder's merchant business and hire service, much regretting I never seemd to have time to do anything much to help them to repay the love, understanding and hospitality they insisted on showering upon us.

The weeks flew by even faster than they had in Sydney, bringing our April departure date for South Africa nearer far too quickly. With winter approaching we were getting restive—yet still didn't want to leave. 'Poppy,' I said one day. 'What about spending this year in the Pacific visiting the islands we've missed—New Caledonia, New Hebrides, Solomons and Papua New Guinea—then coming back to see some of the north coast of Australia?' Sheila quickly agreed, so preparations started. We would return to Sydney, and take off for the French islands of New Caledonia from there. John Preston, an eager youngster from Queensland, and Rob Allen, a short bouncy man passionately fond of sailing and a member of the SYC, asked to join us.

So on March 8th, 1973 all our family and friends old and new gathered at SYC to give us a rousing send-off to Sydney. It was a fitting end to one of the happiest periods of my life. I wondered, as Melbourne receded astern, if I was seeing my home town for the last time.

Norman ends.

10
'Missus, we don't eat people no more!'

We all felt hollow inside after saying so many goodbyes—but gradually our spirits rose with the exciting prospect of the months of voyaging ahead. Passing Wilson's Promontory, we woke to a beautiful sunny morning, soft rolling hills to stare at and the radio playing that haunting Scottish melody *The Tangle of the Isles*. 'Fish!' Norman shouted, but as we drew closer we gazed on a mass of furry penguins frolicking in the water, popping up, swimming under the surface, while others relaxed flat on their backs with their flippers waggling above the waves.

The next day, while cooking, I heard water sloshing around below me and opened the bilges, horrified to find they were half full of water, our brand new cans and their labels sodden. The pipe from the sink had come apart and the water, instead of draining into the dirty water tank, had poured into the bilges. At Rushcutters Bay we covered the foredeck with our hundreds of cans to dry out in the sun. 'A supermarket at the jetty—not a bad idea,' said a passing yachtsman. 'But where are the price tags?'

On April 23rd we left Sydney, heading North-West for New Caledonia with a spanking south-westerly force four just abaft the beam, giving us five knots in a calm sea and warm sunshine. The log entry was 'perfect sailing' and it was. But only for twenty-four hours. Our arrival and departure from Lord Howe, a tiny bit of Australia set in the Tasman sea—a dependency of New South Wales—took place in rough conditions. Thirty-six hours out from Lord Howe, although we had had no forecast of strong winds, a real Tasman Sea force nine hit us. First it blew out two panels in the mizzen, the first sail we had lost in *Shebessa*, so we hove to all night, but the combination of wind and strong current forced us right back so that after a day and a half we were south of where we had started. It was a salutary experience, proving even more forcibly than we already knew that one should be extremely pessimistic about one's position when at the mercy of wind and current within 50 miles of any Pacific island. It took us four more days to cover the 700 miles to Nouméa, the capital of New Caledonia.

The south-east coast of Nouméa had an evil reputation because of its tremendously long barrier reef practically encircling the island at its south-east end and extending up to 15 miles out from the coast, on which many vessels had come to grief. At first sight at dawn the whole vista of high ground ahead was such that we couldn't pick out any definite mountain—it all seemed the same, which didn't help us in fixing our position. Also the current was very strong in the area. Floating beacons at Dumbéa passage showed a wide entrance to the lagoon, so we took this way in to find the Circle Nautique Club tucked into the south-east corner of the harbour. The French, Australian and New Zealand members preparing for the first Nouméa-Vila ocean race welcomed us in.

Nouméa, with some good French and Vietnamese restaurants, and shops full of goodies from France, was very expensive—most goods double Australian prices, and that was saying a lot. The great nickel mine gave the locals a very high standard of living—far above poor yachties'! It was a good place to celebrate Norman's sixty-second birthday. We found, when leaving, that the lagoon was very tricky to navigate with its many currents and dangerous reefs and shoals. Later we heard that the Commodore of the Club, when returning after the start of the race, had run up on a reef and lost his boat!

The voyage to Lifou, an island in the Loyalty group, dependencies of New Caledonia, 60 miles away to the North-East, was a queer one with the current overnight setting us 14 miles North-East, whereas it was North-West approaching Nouméa. It

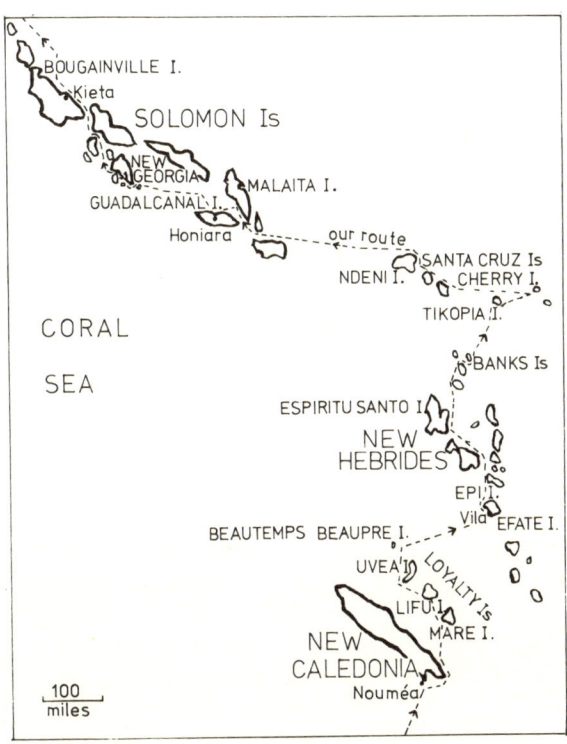

Shebessa's course through New Caledonia, the New Hebrides and Solomons

was on the adjacent island of Maré that Bernard in *L'Affranchi* had lost his boat because of this current, so we were watching out for this. *Shebessa* was the first yacht at Lifou for a year, and the village in Bay Iatio gave us a great welcome—even the gendarme, who had never entered a foreign yacht before. We were taken to the chief's house and given presents of paw paw, chinese cabbage, yams, watermelons, limes and many other things. The island was completely flat, and boasted a new airstrip for local traffic to Nouméa. The wife of the airline rep prepared a banquet for us—but first they had to dress us up. I was presented with a beautiful hand-made embroidered dress in the Mother Hubbard style, worn by the island women. 'The slit goes to the back,' I was told. 'When you're feeding your baby put it to the front.' I felt flattered indeed. Norman had a hand-printed parae wrapped round him and was given an old war club, a casse-tête, making him look more like a caveman than ever.

We were told of the two atolls to the North-West of Lifou—Uvéa, well populated with wonderful beaches and fishing, and the mysterious Beautemps Beaupré, spoken of with awe in Nouméa—uninhabited, practically all reef, said to be bewitched, and it was strictly taboo for any female to land on it. This sounded very tempting for finding shells for my ever-growing collection; even if I had to stay on board *Shebessa* I would go there!

Uvéa was a real South Sea paradise, with 27 miles of wide golden beach inside the giant lagoon and wonderful fishing—tuna, mackerel, bass, kingfish there for the taking. *Shebessa* became a commercial fishing boat for a day as we landed 40 kilos of fish which we sold to the local hotel for 75 francs a kilo: a nice change for money to come rattling in instead of always out. One day we were asked to take six locals to an island for a fishing picnic for two days, with two local boats to lead the way across the lagoon. We said OK, but in the morning were boarded by sixteen women, with 21-gallon jars of water, bedding, tents, luggage, loads of other junk and no men or local boats. 'What about navigation?' said Norman. 'Oh, she'll do it,' said one of the women, pointing to an old woman lying already asleep on top of the cabin. We ourselves kept a good look-out to miss the reefs near the isle of Gui, our destination, anchoring a hundred yards out in the narrow passage. Then we had to ferry all of them ashore, plus their gear, in our four man inflatable across the drying reef. It took the rest of the day with Rob and John becoming exhausted with rowing; I strained my back lifting the junk and we spent an uncomfortable night in the fast flowing stream. We swore we'd never again transport local islanders—but we did.

We sought out the chief to obtain a permit to visit Beautemps Beaupré. He was a venerable gentleman who after a few packets of cigarettes was happy to give permission, saying it was taboo only for single women. It seemed that long ago the population had moved to Uvéa because of lack of food, except one old lady, the witch, who was disgusted at the desertion especially by the young women, so she put a curse on any single woman ever setting foot on the island again, and on the vessel that brought her there.

After a fast 23 mile sail we anchored off a sandy beach in the clearest water imaginable, with the most beautiful reef I had ever seen nearby. Every type of coral and sea vegetation was there, with hundreds of reef-fish of all species. And shells! Augers and shiny olives buried in the sand, countless tiny coloured clams scattered over the beach, and we took a rich haul of cowrie and cone shells. We caught crayfish, dug up coconut crabs, swam, and speared fish for a blissful couple of days, glad that the place had been taboo for so long.

Our next stop was Vila on the island of Efate, capital of the New Hebrides. This South Seas trading post is the seat of two governments, in fact they have two of everything: a gendarme and a policeman, a French court of law and an English court of law, Australian dollars and New Hebridean francs, even two hospitals side by side, French and English. With one government the bureaucratic wheels take time to turn—but here with two life moved even more slowly than usual. Immediately we hit shore we met traditional French hospitality, being met by a complete stranger who picked us up in his car and showed us the town. We enjoyed its French informality and cuisine, its English efficiency, and its Chinese shops.

John decided to leave us here and we were sorry to see him go. He had become progressively worried about his girl in Queensland, having received no mail from her since Melbourne, so made tracks for home.

Skirting the coast of Epi island north of Vila, amongst miles of wild wooded country we suddenly came upon a clearing with row upon row of wooden huts surrounded by well kept lawns, a football pitch and crowds of children. We were in Lomuda Bay opposite a British boarding school for children from neighbouring islands catering for boys and girls up to the age of seventeen. We rowed ashore to be welcomed by hundreds of laughing faces. The headmaster, Frank Haskins, was playing football with the boys, but interrupted the game to come over and welcome us. There was a wonderful atmosphere here, the children all happy and busily occupied with various tasks, the huts well kept and orderly, surrounded by newly cut lawns, an oasis after days of viewing nothing but jungle. Frank told us his school was run on a very small grant from the Government, but he had made it nearly self-sufficient. The children grew most of the food, and in groups did the cooking. I couldn't help remarking on the lawns. 'All done by the boys,' Frank said. They went out before breakfast and cut them and the football pitch with their jackknives! Teaching, he said, was a pleasure, the children had a thirst for knowledge and being among the very few islanders to have a chance of this education, they used every moment to benefit by it, proud of their school and often not even wanting to return home for holidays. The one problem was that at night the children would shut themselves in their huts, afraid of evil spirits, and sometimes there were screams in the night.

I now wrote a letter home to my mother.

Dearest Mum,
We've been spending a few weeks touring the islands of the New Hebrides, really beautiful scenery reminding me of Scotland, except for the climate. We anchor each night and go ashore to meet little groups of people, sometimes just two families living in a world of their own, often 30 odd miles from their neighbours with nothing but jungle in between and no transport save their legs or their pirogues. At least they understand English and are kindly but shy. We had a weird-looking old chap called Samuel on board last night for tea. To soothe my worried look, he turned to me and said 'Don't worry missus, we don't eat people no more!!' The next day his friend called; his name was Donation. 'Off now,' he said, 'catchem fruit for you', and he returned later with grapefruit, lemons and mandarins. There's even talk of a chicken tomorrow. I said I'd like it dead! We scoop oysters off the rocks for supper.

Sunday July 1st. We've arrived at Santo, a funny little country town, mud streets and a few shops. They sport a restaurant though, Vietnamese. We had a rather strange meal but it was nice not to have to cook it. The sea here is very rough. We go ashore in next to nothing and get dressed on the beach. What an odd way of living!

In Santo, the post office, hearing we were heading North to the Banks Islands, asked us to deliver the mail to the mission station on the north of the island of Saint Maria. 'Ships don't call there any more since the hurricane last year,' they told us, 'and this pile of letters has been sitting here for over nine months.' We know how much mail means to us, so gladly accepted the package.

Our next mail address will be C/o ANZ Bank, Honiara, Guadalcanal. Hope to be there early August.

All love,

Sheila

In Santo we heard a strange story of a court case that had been heard this year involving a plantation-owner, half English and half New Hebridean, who had married a New Hebridean woman and had a baby. His wife was told by the Archdeacon that as their baby had not been baptised he would grow up evil and if he died go to hell. The woman was very frightened and became hysterical. To calm her, her husband Roger agreed to the baptism. Beasts were slaughtered and friends and relations gathered for the ceremony and the feast. The baby was duly baptised but Roger had the last word. In front of the assembled company he insisted on the Archdeacon giving him a written guarantee that the baby would grow up pure and stay healthy for one year. Grudgingly the guarantee was given. 'Now,' said Roger, 'leave my plantation and don't you ever return. It's private property and I don't like trespassers.' He hated the man for upsetting his wife. There came a day when the Archdeacon and his colleague did visit the plantation. There was talk of an airstrip being built on the island, Roger's plantation was a likely spot and the church had a finger in this pie. Roger was returning from hunting with his gun when he sighted the Archdeacon and his colleague in a jeep. It was like a red rag to a bull. He fired ahead of the jeep. It stopped and the occupants crawled underneath. Roger kept firing time and again round the jeep, then in no uncertain terms told the two to go; they were so shaken it took them all of five minutes to clamber back and get the engine going.

Shortly afterwards Roger was accused of attempted murder and ordered to attend court. Nobody was less worried than Roger. On the morning of the trial he put a few bullets into his pockets and sauntered into the court room for the cross-examination. The judge opened the case. 'You tried to kill the Archdeacon and his colleague?' 'No,' said Roger, 'if I want to kill him, he be dead.' 'You shot at them?' 'No,' said Roger, 'I shot near them.' Roger saw his gun, exhibit A, lying on the table. He left the dock and coolly walked to the far end of the court-room where he pinned up a small card, then walked back, picked up his gun and loaded it. There wasn't a sound in that court-room, just a line of tense faces. He fired three times at the card, each time a bull's eye. 'Now you know,' he said, turning to the judge: 'If I want to kill him he be dead.' Roger was acquitted.

We headed for the Banks Islands, sighting Gava at dawn after a bumpy night at sea. Running along the west coast we were seen by a man in his pirogue who paddled for all he was worth to reach us. He came aboard, streamed his boat astern, then directed us to an anchorage near his village, a few huts just visible in the jungle on the rise of a hill. Other men soon appeared, excited to see a boat at last and new people. They all had a beer and a smoke, the first they had had for many a month. Hurricane Wendy had turned their lush island grey overnight till not a sprig of green was to be seen. The coconut palms, their only means of making money, were ruined. The trading boat used to call once a month to collect the copra and on board there was a shop with good supplies and a bank. 'But they don't come any more,' said Nelson, the man who had first come aboard. 'There's no copra to collect, no money to deposit and no money to buy goods.' These tough islanders were resigned to their lot, making do with what they had—fish if they could catch them; they had no hooks or lines but speared them from their pirogues with hand-made wooden spears as they paddled over the reefs.

In driving rain we went ashore, climbing the slippery wet mud track to the village, which comprised four weatherbeaten leaf huts, one of which was the church. We went inside. A rough-hewn wooden cross rested on logs; the altar table and bible stand were inlaid with beautiful shells. Behind these were four logs on which the congregation sat. These people were afraid not to have a church, afraid of what might happen to them if they didn't sit there on Sundays. Would another disaster hit them if they didn't? I felt it was small wonder they still clung to the beliefs of their fathers, their wooden idols and stone images, no longer in evidence but buried in the bush. I only saw a fleeting glimpse of the women hidden in their huts peeping out through the tattered leaves. Nelson produced some small wooden sticks, carved and painted at one end with heads, dead man's batons for the dance of death—the ceremonial dance performed around the body before burial—then a taboo stick, a black stick with a rough carving at one end: point the head at anyone and they became sick! We handled it with care.

Norman was now led into the jungle; Rob and I were told to wait. In the jungle, Norman told me afterwards, they unearthed a piece of wood five feet high and about eight inches wide, one end carved into a man's face and tall head-dress, garishly coloured. It was Nelson's dead father's figurehead, meant to have been buried with him but instead hidden in the bush. Desperately short of the most basic commodities, he offered this precious object for sale, and Norman agreed to buy it. Nelson's father had been the customs chief, and at each corner of his leaf hut, now owned by his son, he had placed two large stone heads as corner stones to keep away evil spirits, callers having to touch each and kneel before entering; Nelson wanted to sell these too. Norman offered Nelson Australian dollars. 'No good,' he said. Cockroaches ate them. So these strange objects and one of the stone heads were traded for a bottle of gin, four tins of tuna and luncheon meat, some hooks and fishing line. (When we got back to England we gave the stone head to the British Museum.) We carefully loaded up the dinghy—hoping our purchases weren't bringing evil spirits with them!—then in now calm seas motored North-East to our first Solomon island, Tikopia.

11
The Ways of the Solomon Islanders

Faraway Tikopia, way out in the Pacific, 200 miles north-east of the New Hebrides, most isolated of the British Solomon Islands, just a tiny dot on the Pacific chart, inhabited by light-skinned Polynesians—unlike the larger Solomon Islands whose population is mostly Melanesian—with a language all their own, was an epic stop on our circumnavigation.

We felt a strange feeling of excitement and anticipation of finding something different as the island appeared on the bow of *Shebessa*, gradually getting bigger and bigger as we sailed in the lovely warm sunshine on the bluest ocean possible that only the tropics can provide, with the old volcano gradually taking shape. Tikopia looked beautiful from the sea, a lush, green island seemingly covered with coconut trees, fringed by white sand, with waves breaking gently on the surrounding reef and grass huts peeping out from the tree-lined shores.

As we dropped anchor 200 yards offshore, scores of small children swam out to us or floated on logs waving and laughing, excitedly diving for the sweets we threw to them in the crystal-clear water. Then men in pirogues paddled out bringing coconuts and shells as presents, plying us with questions in pidgin English. We were the first visitors they had seen in over a year.

Ashore, naked children—clothes seemed very scarce on this island—surrounded our inflatable dinghy, the first they had ever seen, and carried it shoulder high above high water mark. Then, vying with each other to hold our hands, they escorted us along the shore path among the houses to meet Edward, eldest son and heir of the number two chief. On the way groups of topless women and girls dressed only in brief skirts of home-made tapa cloth gazed curiously as we passed by. Some had shaven heads and this we later learned denoted they were married. Edward was English-speaking, teaching at the mission school—now without a missionary. The island had four chiefs, who were each absolute rulers in their own villages, controlling behaviour and responsible for the preservation of their old customs and beliefs. The number one chief was overall bossman.

The house of Ariki Tafua, Edward's father, number two chief, was typical—a 40 by 15 foot rectangle, soundly built with solid trees as rafters and posts, a 15 foot roof sloping down to within two feet of the ground, covered solidly with pandanus leaves to make it completely waterproof, with entrances on three sides. The doors gave us a real surprise—they were only three feet high and wide. The idea was to enter on hands and knees, never stand but sit cross-legged on the palm-matted floor, and on leaving, back out on hands and knees—all as a mark of respect to the chief. Visitors were expected, of course, to give some sort of present to the chief.

We sat in a line facing Ariki and Edward as they smoked our cigarettes—a great change from their home-grown baccy. We drank milk from freshly cut coconuts of which there was an unending supply, answering and asking questions through Edward as his father spoke only Tikopian. Later we were invited to the kitchen, a separate large hut where all food was prepared and cooked. The main occupation of all the islanders was the cultivation and preparation of food, as there was no industry or craft here of any kind.

During the mornings the women went up to the high ground where the gardens were, to bring back taro, yams, sweet potatoes, tapioca and bananas. The men and young boys gathered the coconuts. The vegetables were cooked among hot stones, then placed in large wooden bowls shaped from trees. Bananas were added, then the whole lot was pounded for hours by the whole family—even Ariki had a go—to make a 'pudding'. To the whole mass was added burnt coconut milk, then it was kneaded by hand to a consistency like dough. It was then divided into parcels, carefully wrapped in taro leaves and taken to the main hut.

Before us, the chief and Edward—the chief's wife and daughters sitting on the side out of the party—the parcels were ceremoniously opened. With none too clean fingers we each dug into our puddings, with yams and breadfruit on the side washed down with more coconut milk. The women later ate what was left by the men. These puddings served for every meal—one made with tapioca or fish was a variant. One custom was that if anyone was sick or hurt, all friends took gifts of this food. The search for, cultivation, carrying, preparation and cooking of food took up most of the day. In between, everyone sat around smoking home-grown baccy, passing the pipe around the family and chewing the inevitable betel nut taken with ground limestone. The betel nut was a real drug here. Astringent to our taste, it acted as a mild sedative, making the teeth black and the lips a bright red. Mouths were not a pretty sight but it is said by Western dentists that betel nuts prevent decay.

The Tikopian men wore an extraordinary garment, a string of bark beaten out into tapa cloth, around the waist with a bit hanging down in front, then passed between the legs and buttocks and back to the waist. So we had the extraordinary sight of women with bare tops and men with bare bottoms!

Christianity came to this island only in the early Sixties, much later than on previous island groups we had visited. The Archdeacon, making one of his rare visits, had been shocked to see his women converts topless. He felt it showed a lack of respect in church. On returning to Honiara, Guadalcanal, capital of the Solomon Islands, he bought a load of T shirts for the Tikopian women and despatched them on the next Government vessel to call there. The women were overjoyed to own a garment; cloth they had never set eyes on before. When Sunday came they struggled to get into their shirts. They were all too small. The Archdeacon had omitted to notice the size of the women's busts. Undeterred, they cut two holes in the front of each T shirt, donned them and proudly marched to church!

Edward and lots of our children friends conducted us on a walk across the island to the 'other side' to meet the number one chief—a special honour. On the way we passed through two smaller villages where again all the inhabitants turned out to see these strange visitors, welcoming us with smiles and showing us some of their treasures, ancient bows and arrows, fish hooks made from turtle shell, home-made rope, wooden pillows, and their canoes, hand-made, cut out from trees, fashioned with the ancient *adze* (a kind of hand-axe cum chisel) with the outrigger fitted and bound with the home-made pandanus string. They had no other tools or nails. The canoes used to be used for long voyages to the other Solomon Islands—the nearest one to Tikopia being 200 miles away! The navigators used their own methods of navigation, without instruments, simply with their traditional knowledge of the sun, stars, currents, swell, shape of the waves, etc. Long voyages are now forbidden by the Solomon Islands Government—too many canoes never came back.

The number one chief was a majestic figure, with long flowing white hair, a kind of woven grass mat wrapped as a skirt around his waist, adorned with a leaf in his hair, arm and leg bands and an ornate belt. He had been thus dressed when meeting the Queen on her last visit. He represented Tikopia at all official gatherings or conferences, which usually took place at Honiara. Near his village was the old volcano, its water-filled crater making a delightful lake with fresh water, placid, clear and blue, in which people bathed. This, with the brilliant green trees surrounding it and view of the hills beyond, was a breathtaking sight.

With no machinery of any kind, not even an outboard, the islanders couldn't fish for the big stuff, so we were very popular when we suggested a fishing expedition. With the chief, Edward and his brother aboard, we motored up and down in the open sea to catch six large tuna, providing a feast for the village, with the surplus salted and dried for future use.

A few years ago a cyclone had struck Tikopia, tearing down houses and coconut trees and destroying the gardens, and for a time food had been very short. Now there were holes dug where, in the cyclone season, food such as puddings was stored, and changed often so that there was always food in stock in case the 'big wind' came again.

The only medical aid on the island was provided by an orderly, who seemed to keep everyone fairly fit, Tikopia being a healthy island, but death, when it came, prompted an ancient and unique ceremony. Men and women daubed themselves with tumeric, a root which when crushed produced a yellow-coloured dye, grown only by the number one chief, and wore head-dresses of banana and taro leaves, grass or matted skirts to perform the ritual death dance for hours on end. They stamped, wailed and wept, waving their square dance 'paddles' carved with various forms to the beat of the slit gong, chanting their ancient dirges for the spirit of the departed. A whole day would be spent at this dancing, sometimes more, depending on the importance of the deceased. A chief was given a whole week of high pressure dancing with the whole island present. In the past, bodies of men had always been buried in their houses, but now this practice was dying out in favour of the communal cemetery, except for chiefs who could be buried inside or just outside their houses.

Thirty days' mourning followed, when no singing or dancing was allowed. Then came the 'end of mourning' ceremony, which we were privileged to see. On the night before, all friends and relatives gathered at the house of the deceased for a night-long session of weeping and wailing to get into the mood for the next day's dancing. Led by the chief, the men dressed in their best skirts, belts and head-dresses performed their ancient repertoire of dances and songs, starting with sad ones for a couple of hours, then leading up to gaiety and laughter, in the certainty that the departed's spirit had 'ascended to heaven' (now that these people were supposed to be Christian). Then the women, in grass skirts and leis of shells and leaves, topless, performed their gay Polynesian dance, very similar to the Tahitian *tamare* but with less hip wiggling, to the music of guitars and slit gong. A feast followed.

In marriage customs the Tikopians seemed to be ahead of the Western world. The procedure was for the girl to move into her betrothed's house for four weeks. Then if both were satisfied, they were married by tribal custom, that is, by the exchange of gifts between the parents with the man giving more as a bride price. Sometimes there was a later ceremony in church—a small wooden hut with a rough hand-made altar—when the missionary paid one of his occasional visits.

No one knew how old they were. The calendar was not known here until 1959, but even since then people had not kept count of their years. 'What is the point?' they asked. And it was hard for us to give a sound reason. No one worried about approaching old age—they just lived for the present.

On Tikopia the people were self-sufficient, with plenty of water, abundant food, warm weather always, numerous coconut and other trees to provide shelter and clothing. No trading boat called as the island was too isolated, so money was unnecessary. There was no radio station as the batteries went flat. The only contact with the outside world was the Government boat that called perhaps twice in a year. The people of Tikopia lived happily in a world of their own. It all made us wonder what life is really about.

At last, one morning, we sailed away in a windward breeze and bouncy seas to Cherry Island 70 miles North, an island smaller and even more remote than Tikopia. By morning we were in sight of it, with binoculars out studying the surf on the reefs. We anchored a good hundred yards off the shore in a heavy swell, ill at ease at the thought of leaving our ship pitching and rolling to such an extent, yet all of us wanting to visit one more island. The pilot book was as ever depressing, telling us holding ground here was poor. There was no sign of life, the beach deserted.

As we were gulping down one of our last beers, the strip of sand suddenly filled with men. Were they going to launch a large canoe to take us ashore? To our amazement they dived into that vicious surf and swam towards us. How could any human being survive such seas? They did, a score of them, huge Polynesian men around 15 to 20 stone, and they clambered on board naked except for a thin strip of cloth passed between their legs and wound round their waists. We had no language contact, signs only. These rugged citizens of Cherry Island invaded our ship, pushing their way past us to explore the saloon, aft and forward cabin. I'd never seen so many burly men's bare bottoms in all my life. For the first time through all our adventures I felt afraid. The three of us looked fragile amongst all this brawn. They could if they chose knock out the three of us and the ship was theirs. Baccy was their craving, so I produced a few packets of cigarettes that were handed round.

I knew at all costs I had to look calm. I guess each of us has a different way of dealing with fear; my answer is to work with my hands. I fought my way through bare flesh into the galley to prepare lunch, pushed and jostled as I stood there. While I shakily threw something into a pan, Norman and Rob struggled in the cockpit with sign language and endless smiles that seemed to work miracles. I gave Norman a desperate look and he reacted immediately. What an act he put on! First he started yawning, then held one hand to his stomach and the other to his mouth, and eventually held his two hands together in a sign of sleep. The message seemed to get through. The men were rested, they'd had their smokes. They proved to be harmless, just curious. One by one our visitors took the hint and dived back into the sea to leave us in peace.

The islanders had indicated they would later come out for us in a canoe; we felt highly uneasy at the prospect. Could we trust them—or might they take over the ship? Nor did we like the idea of leaving *Shebessa* unattended as there was still a heavy swell and she was pitching about with the chain slackening and then tightening even with the nylon spring we had rigged. We decided not to wait to go ashore but to depart. This was one of the very few times we had not visited an island where we had anchored, and later we regretted it.

Our next hop was 240 miles West to the island of Ndeni in the Santa Cruz group. We anchored in Graciosa Bay, where Mendana, the Spanish discoverer of the Solomons, anchored in 1568. It was like an inland lake, serene and beautiful. A Solomon Island policeman came out in his launch to visit us. Just to see the familiar uniform and then hear his very English name, Joe Higgins, made me quite home-sick.

Entry formalities necessitated our going to the settlement on the crest of the hill where we were told there was a police station, hospital, post office and store. We went ashore and climbed onto the local transport, a tractor driven by a man with hair like a golliwog's. Bumping along the track through the jungle, we stopped now and again to pick up travellers heading for the settlement.

While we were at anchor, the islanders came in their canoes to sell us feather money, handing us a six fathom roll of belt roughly four inches wide, wrapped in sacking, smelling of smoke and blackened through storage in the hut where they cooked. On this island feather money used to be the currency and one of these belts had been needed to buy a wife. The base of the belt had been woven from the wings of sea birds, and into this base tiny red, downy feathers from hundreds of small birds indigenous to the island had once been stuck in with a tree glue. The belts we were shown were very old with only a trace of the scarlet feathers, but they must have been magnificent when new. Norman bought three as they were very rare, carefully stowing them in the engine room.

Matema in the Reef Island group was our next stop. Armed with sticks of baccy like twisted liquorice sticks, we went ashore and traded some of these for bananas and coconuts. A young lad called Philip begged us to give him a lift to his island, Nukopu, ten miles north of our course. We agreed. Nukopu turned out to be surrounded by a huge fringing reef with no passage for us to enter. 'How are we going to get you ashore, Philip?' Norman asked. 'Give me shirt. I wave it,' he said. We waited in heavy seas, keeping our distance from the reef. Then a large canoe headed towards us, looking as if foliage was growing out of the centre—a canoe with disposable sails. Two palm fronds were stuck up as sails while running, then surfing over the shallow reef, the paddlers tossed them overboard and tied up alongside *Shebessa*.

Philip was lowered into the canoe with his worldly goods, a small lamp, a beer bottle full of kerosene with an old cloth as the stopper, a copy of *Pilgrim's Progress*—surely a treasured possession rather than a book he enjoyed reading—and a 40 pound tuna we had caught, a present for the village.

Rob, so full of bounce at the outset of the voyage, had for some time become more and more aloof. Sailing and racing were his passion. He was finding it hard to adjust to mingling with islanders whose ways were so remote from his own, and found it tiresome to have to communicate constantly by sign language. We began to wonder how much longer he'd want to stay with us.

Next morning there was a rap on the hull. The local headman had come to visit us. 'Bad foot,' he said, 'you look at it.' The sole of his foot was as hard as any shoe leather and half an inch thick, yet a sharp stick had penetrated right through, making a nasty wound that was festering. Norman treated him each day, continually changing the dressing. It was relief all round when the pain left him and healing commenced. The day we were to leave, he paddled out once more, this time to bring Norman a thank-you gift, his most treasured possession, a golden cowrie.

We sailed on. Sighting the island of Malaita after 90 miles we ran up the west coast till we found the entrance to Are Are lagoon to anchor opposite a small leaf hut village. It wasn't long before we were surrounded by the local men in their canoes, hands grabbing the coaming as they deposited bundles of shells wrapped up in dirty rags on our deck. They were alive with cockroaches; as if we hadn't enough already! Trading commenced. The islanders pointed to Norman's bathers. I went hastily below and brought up two pairs of old but colourful underpants. Broad grins spread over their faces and within the hour a stalk of bananas was laid on our deck in exchange. A faded hand towel was exchanged for a great many beautiful cowries. I wished I'd been to a jumble sale before we started.

The lagoon stretched for 30 miles, calm water with lush vegetation either side, on the shore small villages here and there and occasional missions run by different denominations. At the South Seas Evangelist Mission in Kiu village we tied up alongside the mission boat. Here we met Frank and his wife, an English couple, both of whom had dedicated their lives to helping the local people. We had become somewhat jaundiced by what we'd seen and heard of the missionaries—so many wanting to change the whole pattern of these people's lives and converting them by fear. Here it was different. Frank had twenty-four boys in his care. As well as teaching them a Christian way of living he taught them a trade as well—carpentry, a knowledge of which they could pass on to their village when they returned home.

In the Langa Langa lagoon situated in the more northerly part of the island were many man-made islands, piles of coral rising out of the water with no vegetation whatsoever, some so small there was just enough room to erect one leaf hut, always built on stilts and overhanging the water. It seemed to us a hard way to live, every drop of water and sack of food having to be carted from the mainland. We couldn't discover why the people some seventeen generations ago went to all the trouble of carting rocks in their canoes to make an island—perhaps from fear of other tribes or of evil spirits where they lived before, or did the mosquitos drive them out?

Towards the head of the lagoon was the man-made island of Alite, so tightly packed with huts on stilts that there was little room for trees to grow and no land to cultivate. 'Come on, let's go ashore,' said Norman. The people didn't resent us, just stared. We had little communication. Four different tribal languages were spoken in an area of a few miles. Only a few spoke pidgin English and we were beginners at that. Norman, Rob and I were led along a mud track by an elderly man with fuzzy hair, his ear lobes slit and hanging down like saucers almost to his shoulders. We followed him through narrow passages between huts to a clearing, the centre of the village. Here the man turned, pointing his finger at me and then at the ground. I got the impression I'd better stay where I was. Norman and Rob were then led across a tree trunk spanning a small ravine to a different part of the village, a 'men only' area, to be ushered into a hut lined with skulls in various stages of decomposition—a gruesome sight. The custom was that when a man died he was buried in a shallow grave. Eight days later it was the painful duty of the eldest son to cut off his father's head and place it in this special hut amid ceremonies with much wailing and dancing—again excluding the women—to remain there for ever.

I became restive. The women were gaping at me, feeling my clothes, my hair and my skin, women completely unlike any I'd ever met before, their faces tattooed with scrolls and strange designs. With a fixed grin on my face I moved around only to be grabbed. 'Go there—you die!' someone shouted. 'Oh Lordy, please God may Norman come back soon.' In the back of my mind I had the idea of running for it and swimming to *Shebessa*. I was highly relieved to see Norman and Rob crossing the bridge, a few shades paler despite their sunburn, but all in one piece.

It was my turn to be led off to see the women's set-up—taboo for men—escorted by a woman who spoke a little English. Outside the boundary of the village was a leaf hut ten foot by eight, bare with a mud floor. I had arrived at the maternity home. Here the mother-to-be came and got on alone with the business of childbirth. Food was brought to her by other women but no male could visit her and she couldn't return to the village for four weeks. The hut had a large leafy tree overhanging it, and these particular leaves were picked by the mother, to be rubbed on her back to soothe her in labour. Such was the way of bringing children into the world on these islands—a natural process and people thought little about it; all right if all went well but if complications occurred they had little chance. Clinics were now springing up in the area but to many that meant walking many miles or a long canoe ride, so most women still had their babies in leaf huts like this one.

I admired the tattooing on their faces, legs and arms. This was done soon after birth, we were told. With a sharp point made from a piece of turtle shell or a slither of bamboo, the mother scored her new-born's face and limbs, scratching a design of whorls or lines—no two were alike. It was up to the mother to dream up a design and lucky if she had an artistic bent. The new-born baby's delicate skin rebelled against this harsh treatment, swelling up grotesquely, sometimes taking weeks to return to normal. The scratches were treated with a mixture of mother's milk and coconut juice to soothe the skin and act as a disinfectant. Poisoning was unheard of.

Babies were a joy to these people, never a handful. It was rare to hear a baby cry. They seemed an integral part of the mother, nibbling at her breast whenever hungry, lying in a sling around her body when she was working or in a bag across her back. Now and again loving grandma took over, letting her grandchild nibble at her breasts, no longer firm but sagging to the waist. Her role was to be the soother, the dummy. The girls when young had full figures, but they aged quickly with the life, soon becoming thin and wiry, their skin shrivelled with the sun.

Shell money was the currency here, each family making its own. It was a big home industry; the harder people worked the richer they became, each family its own mint. Shells, fashioned into beads, were used to buy fruit and vegetables, a pig or a wife. Father dived for the special clam shells which were broken up into small pieces by the elder children, who hammered them with a piece of coral till they were whittled down to the size of a halfpenny. With a home-made drill made out of bamboo and fibre, the point a sharp piece of shell, they pierced each piece. These pieces were then thrown into a fire lit on the mud track, the colours changing and growing richer with the heat. The work went on all day, even the tiny tots helping, sitting in huddles on the ground sorting out the different colours. The bits of shell were then threaded onto lengths of fibre and the strings put together to form a band. Father then took over. The band was stretched between two coral stones grooved to hold it. With a piece of coral and plenty of water he scrubbed away at the band, wearing the shell down till every tiny piece was a uniform size and rounded. The bands were then put together to make belts of varying sizes; a small one a few inches long would buy fruit and vegetables at the local market on Malaita, a larger string bought a pig. A very large belt, yards long, made up of at least ten bands beautifully put together with special colour design, bought a wife. No man could obtain a wife without this great length of money, which was given to the father-in-law, so the family had to start the enormous labour when the children were young, and the more sons there were the more money was required.

We motored to the head of Langa Langa lagoon in calm water to anchor off Auki wharf in four fathoms, sand and coral. By this time Norman and I were weary of trying to make ourselves understood with sign language and our smattering of pidgin English, and living in a world so foreign to our own. We needed time to digest and assimilate all our experiences. Auki, the capital of Malaita, was a small town, its centre a mud track lined with shops—many of them Chinese—either side, and at the top a hotel, where Ceylon curry was the permanent menu; there was also a post office and a British administration. We spent a pleasant seven days here and had the electric anchor winch repaired—a great blessing, as we were tired of pulling in chain every day by hand. The Club, the meeting place for the Australians, English and New Zealanders working in Government departments for the development of

Malaita, proved a convivial place each evening, a comforting change after so long among native villages. Rob was especially thankful for the new surroundings, and here he decided to take his leave of us and fly home.

Norman and I headed for Guadalcanal to take a look at Honiara, reading up the pilot as we went along. It sounded a difficult anchorage with poor holding ground, small vessels being advised to tie up to a wreck lying there.

The passage to Honiara was frequently windless and incredibly hot, the teak decks burning the soles of our feet even though they were hard and leathery. As we neared the island a stiff breeze blew up. As always we had a flag up to give us wind direction. We never fussed in the ocean which flag we used, as often as not a signal flag or a tea towel. The Honiara Yacht Club were fascinated to watch the arrival of a British ketch flying a very tattered blue ensign, and from the mizzen stay the red and white signal flag 'You are running into danger'. The harbour was packed, mostly with fishing vessels. Circling round we dropped anchor within 30 yards of the rusty old wreck, just visible as the water lapped over it. Within minutes we had dragged and leant against an old yawl. We pulled the anchor up and dropped it again, but the stiff cross wind and the bad holding ground shifted us once more, this time on top of a fishing vessel. A dinghy pulled up alongside us and a New Zealand voice called out: 'Bill Culver here. You need a hand in this wind. Give me another anchor and I'll lay it for you.' The second CQR was lowered into his dinghy, which then shot off and within minutes it was laid. We were then able to pull away from the fishing vessel and take stern lines to the wreck—and at last we were secure. Our new friend came on board for a beer. He and his wife Betty owned a 72 foot ex hospital ship, *Kia Kia*, anchored near-by.

Norman had a tropical ulcer on his foot that didn't answer to treatment. We were longing to get ashore to collect mail and enjoy civilisation, but at all costs Norman had to keep his foot dry, with so many bacteria breeding in these tropical waters. Putting his leg into two garbage bags tied up and taped, we rowed ashore, and I dragged the dinghy as high as I could up the beach so that he could step out dry. We received a great welcome from the Yacht Club whom we had entertained hugely with our antics. The Commodore took Norman to a doctor to sort out his foot, a German lady kindly offered to type our articles for publication. We dined at the Club on

Chinese chicken legs in oyster sauce. A salvage diver talked to us of some rare shells he had recently found—Cypraea martini. He had collected twelve of these specimens, the first live ones ever found, also Conus gloria maris, one of the most sought after shells in the world, worth from US$300 upwards. It was an exciting place. The salvage diver had spent many years crocodile hunting, and gave us full instructions on how to catch them, the laws, the best to choose and how to skin them. It was a heady conversation as we had never even seen a crocodile, but we knew funds were getting low, so that maybe we would also have to become hunters and hope to get about A$20 per skin—hard work the idea of which we didn't in the least relish.

One morning we looked over to *Kia Kia* and were dazzled by its new canopy and winch covers. Had its owners suddenly come into money? 'Had them all made at the local prison,' they said, 'they cost next to nothing.' Our canopy and a couple of sails were badly in need of repair, so we also visited the local jail. It was no cold dismal place with high forbidding walls. A few yards from the shore, a small white fence enclosed a few dozen huts surrounded by well trimmed lawns; to passers-by it would have been taken as a housing estate or a holiday camp, save for the warder at the gate. We explained what we wanted. The warder opened the door and yelled: 'George—come here George!' A man in his thirties weeding the garden sauntered over and we were introduced. George was a long-term prisoner in for attempted murder, who in his day had been a sail-maker. We spread out the sails and canopy on the lawn, instructing him in the repairs needed. 'Don't worry, Missus, I like this sort of work,' he said. 'I'll make a good job of them'. He did. Two days later we collected our sails and canopy, beautifully repaired, and paid the bill to the warder—A$1.50!

Sabo Island, home of the famous Megapode birds, 23 miles North-West, was our next stop. Ashore we were lucky to be met by George Rorado and his father Alan. Generations of Rorados had lived here, their income coming from the eggs of the Megapode birds. It was quite a sight at six the following morning to see hundreds of the birds, quite small, about the size of a guinea fowl and black with long necks and large feet, flying in from the bush to congregate along a stretch of sand. Here they dug like fury five feet down to lay an egg, three times the size of a hen's egg, then filled in the hole. At nine o'clock they flew off into the interior, whereupon the villagers, who had been watching the performance from a distance (these birds are very timid) attacked the sand. They dug down five feet with their hands, just about disappearing head first, to try to find the eggs. The area was divided by posts, and each villager had his little area about ten by twenty yards, which could yield up to 20 eggs a day. Alan's family usually sent 300 eggs per month to Honiara, for which they received $15—less cost of transport and living: $8. Theirs was a thriving economy.

We cruised for three weeks, enjoying being alone together, through the New Georgia and the Shortland Islands, most northerly of the Solomons, on our way to Kieta, Papua New Guinea. In this area the main occupation of the people was making carvings and artefacts, many of which we bought or exchanged for the fish we caught. The only drawback was that heavy rain and mist made navigation a perpetual hazard.

One day, trailing our very strong one-eighth inch diameter nylon line, we had a tremendous strike during a rainstorm—it sounded like a real monster as the line on the winch ran right out and just about stopped *Shebessa*. Norman couldn't pull it in at all—so gradually winched it in, fighting all the way. What could it be? Perhaps a big tuna, although they didn't normally fight so much. Then it showed—a great shark! Slowly Norman winched him close alongside, until we could see just how big he was—eight foot at least. He looked horrible with his mean-looking beady eyes glaring at us. 'He's too big to gaff and lift aboard,' said Norman thoughtfully. 'We're not having that thing on board at all,' I said emphatically. 'Get rid of it.' Norman muttered about losing the gear, and anyway that the Munda islanders would be glad of him. But how to kill the creature? Digging out his ·22 automatic, he took careful aim and shot the shark in the eye. Then the most frightening thing of all—the monster leaped right out of the water six feet high at least! Hoping he was in his death throes, we gaped at the creature threshing around, his great mouth opening and shutting within feet of us. Then his last convulsive twist tautened the line like a whiplash and the trace snapped. We had lost him. Norman was very upset and blamed himself for not just dragging him alongside all the way to our next anchorage by which time he would probably have drowned, the force of the water passing through the gills in his struggles too great for the extraction of oxygen, and we could have immediately opened up fresh shark shop.

12
Papua New Guinea

We were sad to leave the Solomons, British to the core and proud of it. However alien they had seemed to Rob, we'd felt at home in these waters. We headed North for Kieta, Papua New Guinea.

Our funds were now very low indeed and we were in a hurry to get ashore and sell the kingfish we had just caught to the local store. Customs were very friendly but the questions on the forms we filled in were unusual. 'Have you any of the following goods on board: firearms, dangerous weapons (including air pistols, switch blade knives, daggers, knuckledusters, sword sticks) or playing cards?' We had two ancient packs of playing cards, with the odd card missing that had blown overboard when we played rummy in the cockpit. These we were allowed to keep. Playing cards were officially banned, a step intended to protect New Guineans from gambling, thus probably saving a lot of bloodshed. In such a stifling humid climate as theirs it would be easy for a loser to get overheated. Cleared of customs, we dunked our fish in the sea to freshen them, then rowed with all speed ashore and sold them to a store for 30 cents a pound.

Kieta struck us as a go-go place where money flowed. The Bougainville copper mine, the second biggest in the world, set back in the hills behind the town, brought prosperity to the island. There were many Australians around. The Commodore of the Kieta Club met us in the street, and took us into the beautifully appointed Club—civilisation once more—packed with Aussies who never gave short change on hospitality. The barman here came from the Carteret Islands, and persuaded us to call at these remote islands—some 60 miles from Bougainville—on our way to Rabaul, capital of New Britain, one of the main islands of Papua New Guinea. One reason why ships seldom went there was that this atoll had a submerged reef surrounding the lagoon, and finding the entrance was a tricky operation.

We seemed to be drawn to reefy areas. They were wild and beautiful; the water was clear, the spearfishing excellent. Constantly we were hearing, reading about and actually seeing yachts that had come to grief. But somewhere smug inside us was the certainty that it couldn't happen to us. We had come through unscathed so far and thought we had the whole thing licked. In the New Hebrides we had been told a definition of a liar was a yachtsman who said he'd never been on a reef. Were we getting over-confident?

We had a drill when approaching reefs. Norman climbed up the ratlines wearing polaroid glasses, carefully scanning the sea. The colour of the water told all. Deep blue meant fathoms of water below and safety. As the blue changed to a lighter hue, then pale aquamarine, shallow water was ahead and patches of brown could usually be seen among it, rocks, coral and coral heads. Norman signalled port or starboard; I reduced speed and edged our way through. The time of day was important. It was not always possible but ideally we liked to negotiate passages through reefs when the sun was behind us or directly above, preferably at low water when there was a swell. In bad weather we never attempted them and needless to say kept well away from reefy waters at night.

The Carteret Islanders, like the Tikopians, lived in a world of their own and were rarely visited. We anchored in their lagoon and spent two wonderful days among these gentle people, before leaving for a two day passage to Rabaul. Waving goodbye to our new-found friends, including a German Roman Catholic priest who had spent 54 years there, we weighed anchor. Relaxed and happy, with the sun high and a favourable breeze we set course to take us easily through the narrow pass in the reef surrounding the five mile wide lagoon. The tiny village receded into the distance. But then the sky clouded over, the wind faded, and the sea dropped until it was like glass, so that we couldn't see the colours of the water—the very worst conditions possible. We motored slowly, with Norman searching for the pass from the ratlines, then BANG!

Shebessa shuddered and lurched. Below there was a cracking noise as if our ship was being torn to shreds. Stunned, I grabbed for the controls to stop the forward motion. Engine into reverse, more power, then the sickening knowledge that we weren't moving; a ghastly split second look over the side showed what looked like two foot of water, coral heads, reef and pale, pale aquamarine water. We were hard on! Norman got his snorkel and was over the side. In a matter of seconds he was back. We had copped the edge of the channel right at the entrance to the pass and it was teeming with fish and SHARKS. We had better try and kedge her off. It was high tide now and minutes mattered. As we were about to launch the dinghy Norman suggested giving her one more go, full blast astern. I put her into reverse and drove her hard. All tensed up, we watched the water and listened. The engine was roaring, then there was the odd crunch that spurred us on—louder now—we were moving! Norman was on the stern, signalling directions. *Shebessa* picked up speed, breaking through the coral with crashing and crunching noises below. Like prisoners released we were free, and slowly and carefully we steered through the narrow passage towards the ocean. All was utterly still, no breaking water, no sun to help us spot the dangers that might have been still lurking below.

At last we were in the safety of the ocean. We drew breath and thanked God for a steel hull and our six cylinder Volvo engine. Our very precious home, and we could so easily have lost her, was intact. We sat back and counted our blessings, no longer smug, after our first but probably not our last brush with the marine world below us.

There was a ripple on the water—the afternoon breeze was coming up. Our nerves needed soothing—and what better way than to set the sails, switch off the engine and enjoy the peace of the ocean en route to Rabaul.

We skirted the coast of New Ireland, a dense jungle, green and lush with little sign of habitation. The intense heat and humidity were now making every movement an effort. Tired after a long day's sail up the coast of New Ireland, we anchored at an open roadstead and slept like logs. At dawn next day we motored to the Duke of York Islands, a small group 23 miles from Rabaul, a peaceful spot where we stopped to give *Shebessa* a spring clean for two days, tying up to a large tree so close to shore that we could all but leap there. With the hull cleaned, we rowed out in the dinghy to take photographs, *Shebessa* looked so beautiful in this setting, with branches overhanging her stern. As I stepped back on board I screamed to see thousands of bull ants which had invaded us from these branches. The creatures, each as big as a sizeable finger-nail, had fierce bites, and the thought of them below was unspeakable. Quickly we pulled out, then spent two hours swabbing and washing the decks till every bull ant was destroyed.

Dripping with heat we neared Rabaul, sloshing water over the deck and ourselves to keep us cool and alert. In a light wind *Shebessa* sailed into Simpson harbour, a horseshoe bay skirted by lush greenery and coconut groves. Rabaul nestled in the corner,

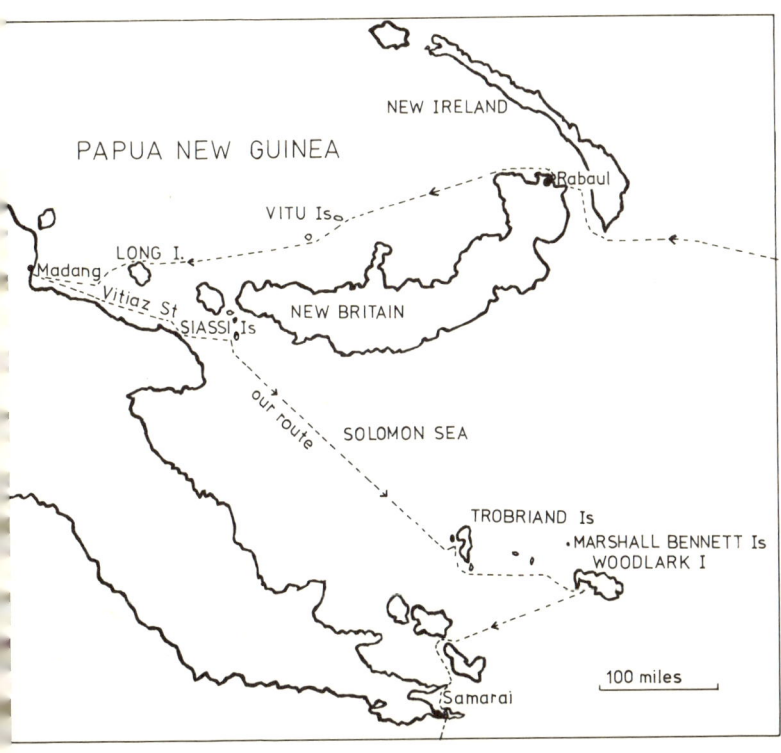

Shebessa's course Rabaul-Samarai

dominated by volcanoes. The three tallest peaks were called Mother, South Daughter and North Daughter. Next to South Daughter Matupit volcano smoked away lazily, the sulphur fumes wafting over the harbour; it had last erupted in 1937. It was a breath-taking sight. The Yacht Club with its lawns running almost to the water's edge came into view as we drew closer.

A speedboat came racing out and a rugged-looking Australian, a committee member of the Club as we found out later, introduced himself: 'Reg Stephenson. Follow me. I'll show you where to anchor.' As soon as we set foot on land we felt at home. The Clubhouse was a meeting place each day with its tables and chairs set out by the lawn and a bar serving long cold drinks and snacks;

members collected there at lunch time and after four for long yarns until dusk.

Rabaul has one of the finest markets in all the Pacific, called The Bung. It has an abundance of every kind of tropical fruit and vegetable one could wish for, all set out in bundles. Everything at The Bung is ten cents a bundle, be it ten lemons, two papaya or eight bananas, making for ease of calculation for the slowest head. Armed with a dollar's worth of ten cent pieces, every week I filled two baskets to overflowing with the local produce. It was our vegetarian period, and we both thrived on it. This was truly shopping at leisure, chatting and joking to the friendly women stall-holders called *meris*. Shells galore, some quite rare, baskets and carvings were also there for sale, many of these wares being carried to the market long distances on foot.

It was good at last to have time to sort ourselves out, and to work on the ship. We still hadn't managed to do anything towards replenishing funds, so I started selling shells by post to conchologists in Australia and America, and gave the local gift shop a basketful on sale or return. Norman went job hunting. Work was difficult to come by, most jobs being reserved for the New Guineans, but Norman found an accountant who needed a hand and luckily this profession didn't come into that category. The pay seemed to us fantastically high. Norman was given an air conditioned office to himself—and better still a fridge in the corner.

The heat was more stifling than anything we had yet experienced. It was an effort to walk one block; our bodies streamed with sweat most of the day, and we felt our brains were melting. Neither of us could think rationally. We rose at dawn, trying to finish most of the daily chores by breakfast time.

Becoming a white collar worker created problems for a man who lived most of the time in an old pair of bathers and bare feet. We scrummaged in bags, long since stowed, to find three reasonable white shirts and a tie. The drill was to go ashore in bathers, then shower at the Club so that one arrived at the office presentable; the problem was remembering to take all the necessary garments. There were days when Norman went without underpants—and once without shoes! His office was a godsend. Making a salad, I'd row it ashore and put it in the fridge and we would have picnic lunches in style in air conditioning. When shopping round town, the only other cool places to relax were the banks, also air conditioned. When I felt dehydrated I would sit there to cool off for a while before facing another hundred years of dripping heat. The bank staff didn't mind in the least.

Despite the intense heat we both kept well, though grew leaner and leaner. Women in Rabaul either put on a lot of weight or lost it; nobody seemed to stay normal. I became a Twiggy of seven stone.

Anchored close by were a young Australian couple from Sydney, Bob and Robyn. Robyn was about to have her first baby. One morning in the early hours I woke to hear banging on the hull. It was Bob. 'Can you give us a hand? Robyn's in labour and we need transport.' Norman in a borrowed car drove them both to the hospital, and a few days later Robyn was back on board with their new daughter Melita, carrying the tiny mite in a strong string bag, made locally to carry vast quantities of produce, known as a billum. Many a morning I'd row by and call out to her. 'Want a hand today? Can I do any shopping?' The answer was always 'No'. Robyn wouldn't accept help from anyone. 'I have to sort things out for myself and manage,' she said. She did, rowing ashore each day to wash the nappies under the tap on the jetty, laying her little one in the shade of a tree, shopping with a billumful of baby over her shoulder, breastfeeding her wherever she happened to be. Rabaul, apart from the joy of living in such a beautiful place, had something very special—a freedom of living, no airs or graces or snobbishness. It was too hot to fuss.

Papua New Guinea was on the way to independence, but the transition period seemed to us rather too rapid. The local people were bewildered and unprepared, as more and more white men who ran the services flocked back home. Few New Guineans had been trained to take over their jobs. Rabaul had in fact nearly ground to a halt. It wasn't even possible to buy a stamp at the post office. With the literacy rate among the lowest in the world, a great many people didn't even know what self-government was. Some inhabitants of a remote Sepik village, when told self-government was coming, ran away, thinking a group of warriors were coming to drive them out of their homes.

Under the surface of gaiety and fun, there was an undercurrent of fear of what would happen on December 1st when the first step towards independence, self-government, came into being. As the time grew closer, many shops closed, mostly the Chinese, and the exodus began, people paying large sums over the odds to get a flight out. Owners of boats checked their engines carefully and filled up with fuel—just in case. Children in the mixed schools came home with disturbing stories. 'Charlie's Dad's going to stab four white men on Self-Government Day' and so on, but thanks to the wise planning of Mr Somare, the Prime Minister, nothing did happen. For four days all bars on the islands were closed, even at the hotels and the Yacht Club, the same for all, irrespective of colour. People stayed quietly at home and there were no incidents.

We decided to lie up for the hurricane season in Madang, a town situated on an inlet amid an island-studded section of the north coast of New Guinea, even more humid than Rabaul, but we'd been told a safe snug anchorage. Without crew since the Solomons, we had been much enjoying having *Shebessa* to ourselves and felt no need now to take on any as our plan was simply to follow the north coast of New Britain, making mostly day passages.

After an overnight passage in squally weather we picked up the coast watcher's lighthouse marking the entrance to Madang harbour, which had been built in memory of the brave people who relayed information of Japanese troop-ship movements during World War Two. Madang was a quiet, beautiful town set along the shores of its harbour, which in itself was a photographer's paradise, the safest harbour in the whole Pacific area, practically landlocked with coves and snug inlets stretching inland for one and a half miles.

After sitting out the hurricane season in Madang, it was a great relief to leave the heat and humidity of this anchorage at the beginning of April to start the homeward half of our circumnavigation. The Siassi Islands, a cluster of tiny islets 120 miles south-east of Madang, were our first objective. Here the world-famous Siassi bowls are carved, 12 to 30 inches long in an elliptical shape, from the native tuan hardwood, embellished with figures of fish and birds and used in the preparation and serving of food. The old ones have now disappeared into the hands of dealers and museums, and the making of new ones is the island's industry for export.

While Norman was working in Rabaul I had looked for crew for our 1974 voyage from Papua New Guinea to South Africa, and had met two boys who were keen to come with us. Jerry, a thirty-year-old Englishman, flew out to join us at Madang, and

Johnny, a twenty-two-year-old Rhodesian, was to join us later at Samarai. Leo, an Australian all of 16 stone with a deep thundering laugh that seemed to bubble up from his boots, also joined *Shebessa* at Madang. We'd got to know him and his charming wife here as we watched the progress of the fine-looking steel yacht he was building, hoping to sail away like us one day with his family. As yet he had little knowledge of sailing and welcomed the chance to gain experience. We agreed to take him for the short sail to Samarai via the Siassi and Trobriand Islands. Afraid of what the sun would do to his skin, he was always to be seen with his vast straw hat covering his wild black hair and shading his thick shaggy beard below. His lap lap, a long length of colourful cotton, was wrapped round his more than ample body all day and cuddled round him at night. This man was the most colourful personality of all the crew we ever had on *Shebessa*, and we were sorry his time with us was to be so short.

This was a period when our loos were a little fragile. Leo, who had hardly been to sea before, found the magnitude of what he was doing had a disastrous effect on his bowels, and time and again he found it necessary to visit the loo. Norman decided that the plumbing really wouldn't stand this wear and tear for any length of time, and so instead a bucket was wedged into an old motor tyre and placed on the stern. Leo took it all very philosophically, in fact he greatly enjoyed his hours of meditation there, his vast frame overlapping the top of the bucket, and he vowed it was the most scenic loo in the whole of the South Pacific. He looked rather like one of those large balls in a circus turn, balanced on a tiny stand, that seals play with.

Visiting the islands Leo was in his element, a natural comedian, a man who was genuinely fond of and interested in the native people of the islands. They were never quite sure about him. Had he supernatural powers? Was he a good or bad spirit? Leo would catch their attention by making strange noises and rolling his big googly eyes. Then he would do his party piece. Slowly he would make his teeth protrude from his mouth, further and further, till he looked quite grotesque. To people who had never seen false teeth or knew they existed, this was magic. They roared with laughter, then grew strangely quiet, trying to sort this man out.

The second man on board Leo christened The Walrus as soon as he set eyes on him. Jerry on arrival looked a cross between Baden-Powell and a gypsy, his scout's hat holding down shoulder-length wispy hair, one large gold loop earring dangling, and khaki safari shirt and shorts. He had a shaggy moustache that flowed over his mouth and was chewed regularly with his food. He had been a crop-spraying pilot in the Sudan and before that had had some experience in the merchant navy. He was a nervous man who never really fitted in, thinking he should be an officer on a liner rather than helping to run a small yacht, but with much teasing and joking from Leo, the voyage with these two was an amusing one.

On Aromat island we saw one of the last of the famous Siassi canoes, 48 foot long, four foot beam, six foot draft, hollowed out of one tree trunk three foot deep, then the sides built up another three foot and fastened to the trunk with pandanus leaf stitching. A platform was laid across this to the outrigger. The two masts were stepped at a 15 degree angle to each other, on which the craziest sails ever seen flapped in the breeze. Diamond-shaped, made of pandanus leaf, rigged with the points vertical, they gave a sort of slot effect enabling the craft to make the 50 mile passage to New Britain laden with copra and up to 25 people in ten hours. These vessels were an extraordinary sight. In Madang we had heard there was a great shortage of goods on the islands, so had brought as much patterned calico, rice, sugar and twist tobacco as we could carry, and here started trading for carvings and shells. But it was tobacco the islanders craved, and the cry of 'Baccy, baccy' was heard every time we anchored.

From the Siassis was a hard sail—three days to windward—for the 250 mile passage to the Trobriands, the 'islands of love'. On these very primitive islands the people lived in leaf huts built on stilts because of the rats and the risk of cyclones or even big storms flooding their homes. It did the eyes of the crew good to see the pretty topless girls dressed only in grass skirts waltzing gracefully along with everything swinging. These islands were just full of children—there was no other entertainment, of course. Here the tradition of universal free love still existed. Our interpreter said this state of affairs could be enjoyed by our two amorous crew for a 'present'. They decided it was time to taste the fruits of the island, so it was arranged for two girls to visit the ship around dusk, prior to a night of love on shore. What should we give the girls to drink? Beer or spirits might knock them out—the boys decided on jungle juice, made from Heinz packaged crystals, a bright green liquid with a sickly sweet taste.

The girls arrived, paddling out in their canoes, two plump young things no more than fourteen. Shyly they sat on the deck with their new beaux and started on the jungle juice while we retired below. Half an hour later they had gone, paddling off towards the shore with no date for the evening, leaving two most dejected men. What had misfired? Was it the jungle juice—or couldn't they face up to Walrus's moustache or Leo's over-ample proportions?

On these 'islands of love' the belief was that copulation and conception had nothing to do with each other. The former was to be enjoyed by all and the latter was brought about by the spirits of her ancestors creeping into a woman's body while she was bathing. A woman conceiving while her husband was away working on the mainland merely proved that she had bathed too much!

Iwa, in the Marshall Bennett group, was a tiny coral atoll. Here we were really invaded by scores of men and boys who snatched the tobacco out of our hands as we doled it out. Calico was also popular, so *Shebessa* looked rather like a draper's shop with me measuring out lengths of calico which the women and men wrapped round themselves. After a long struggle Norman went ashore. Here were really primitive people—they had a school but no teacher, a mission but no missionary, and no boats came. Norman was surrounded by people wanting to trade carved sticks, bowls, metal nut grinders, anything for tobacco. One old fellow with great glaring eyes tore up to him with a handful of carved sticks, thrust them into his hand, leered close with his wild-looking face and literally screamed 'Baccy, baccy!' Norman hastily put a stick in his hand, whereupon the old man took a bite out of it and rushed off to his hut.

So to Samarai, a small island on the south-east tip of Papua New Guinea, once a thriving and important place but now run down. It was a hard passage to this island, presenting a navigational nightmare in plenty of wind, rain, strong currents and poor visibility, so we were thankful to find a quiet anchorage 400 yards offshore to partake of civilisation once more and collect our mail. At this point Leo returned to Madang and home comforts. We were to miss his gargantuan shape and humour to match. Jerry, while passing through Papua New Guinea on the way to Madang to join *Shebessa*, had been offered a job with an airline; finding that the job was still open, he now decided he was better in the air than at sea, accepted the offer and with our blessing departed.

13
Indonesia, Here We Come ... We Hope

At Samarai we were joined by two new crew for Indonesia. The sandy-haired Rhodesian Johnny hadn't had much experience but appeared willing to learn. Peter, a stockily built young man from Adelaide, was a keen sailor and was planning to buy a 19 foot sloop in England to sail back to Australia. We set off for Cairns, a thriving town on the Queensland coast from where we planned to sail inside the Great Barrier Reef to Cape York, the most northerly point of Australia, and Darwin.

It was a miserable four days' passage, heavy seas and squally weather with Johnny sick and dizzy and Norman not feeling his best. Cairns and the land of plenty were more than welcome.

Over a pub lunch we met someone who gave us some useful advice. 'Hope you've stocked up with pumpkins,' he said. We hadn't. 'They're a marvellous vegetable, keep for years and you'll need them to get rid of sharks.' 'Sharks?' queried Norman, astonished. 'Sharks. If you've got a tiresome one following the ship, boil up a pumpkin whole. Feed the shark with some garbage, then toss him the pumpkin straight out of the boiling water. He'll swallow it whole and it'll blow up inside him.' We ourselves swallowed his story and bought pumpkins. We never had occasion to throw them to a shark but they were a great stand-by as a vegetable, keeping in good condition for eighteen months.

We were all looking forward to our cruise through the Great Barrier Reef, having read and heard so much about it, but seemed to have joined too far North; the more inhabited areas of the reef were to the South of Cairns. The sailing was magnificent, always a moderate to strong ESE wind on the beam or on the quarter, and the anchorages had good holding ground; but there was an utter emptiness about this part of the world, no sign of life for hundreds of miles. We had been to many lonely places, yet never felt so alone as we did here, seeing island after island uninhabited. Perhaps we'd grown used to having smiling brown faces clambering around our ship. Even the sight of another yacht on the horizon would have been welcome. We had been warned not to attempt night passages off the Reef but this meant twenty-one days to Thursday Island, more days than we could afford, if we were to reach Durban before the start of the Indian Ocean cyclone season starting in October, so it was early to bed and many a night we set off in the early hours, reaching Thursday Island fourteen days after leaving Cairns.

Thursday Island used to be the home of the pearl diving industry. A few of the beautiful old luggers, with their graceful yet sturdy hulls, were still there, but no longer used for this purpose. Anchored in an eight knot current, it was difficult to get ashore and back. It was a real hick town, buildings in disrepair and the hotel an ancient barn with a rough sawdust bar where the customers were always in various stages of intoxication. The big industry now was crayfish, ships coming in laden, but only the tails were for export—the rest were thrown overboard. The waste of it all!

From here to Darwin took eight days through the Gulf of Carpentaria, eight long days with weird weather, *Shebessa* swinging all over the place and rolling. We were all tired, our muscles continually strained to cope with the motion. Once across the Gulf, as we entered the Arafura Sea, the wind really whipped up, *Shebessa* scorching along at eight to nine knots. The strong tide pushed us around; the pale-coloured water was unnerving. Markers led us to the big sprawling town of Darwin, and we dropped anchor off Stokeshill wharf amid other yachts, an uneasy anchorage with strong winds and rough seas in the mornings but reasonably near town. Later we moved to Fannie Bay which was more sheltered, to enjoy the hospitable Darwin Sailing Club. Darwin wasn't the hick place we had expected. It had been described to us as an old city best known for its eccentrics, dust and tropical heat: 'People go round there with corks hanging from their hats to keep off the flies,' we'd been told. Now tourism and the iron ore industry had put it on the map, it was in fact a thriving town with solid buildings and well stocked shops, though prices were sky-high, a young people's town where money was made fast. A yachtsman's wife could take a job at the Club as barmaid for a few hours each night and collect a hundred dollars a week.

We heard later that only six months after we left, Darwin was flattened by a cyclone.

From Darwin to Dili, Portuguese Timor, across the Arafura Sea was only 380 miles, but our seven day voyage seemed more like seven years. We left Darwin on June 16th for what we hoped would be a fine sail for three days to Dili with the South-East trades behind us for a change. A couple of hours out a strong wind warning of 30–40 knots came over the radio. By dusk the sky behind us had taken on a dirty sort of look and all evening the wind freshened. At 2200 hours the mizzen was dropped, the main reefed and a small jib put up to replace our yankee. The sea got up quickly in this shallow water—and did we roll. Dawn brought a fabulous sight as the sun shone on the foaming crests as they surged up astern with *Shebessa* lifting to them, then surfing down the faces with the wind whipping the tops off ten feet high waves. Steering was hard work.

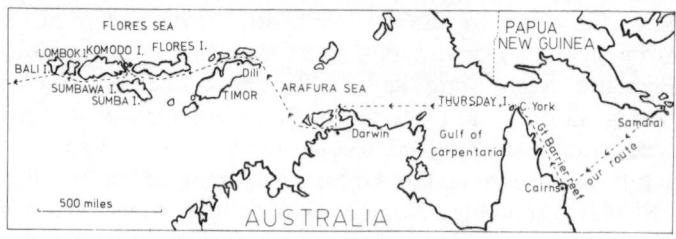

Shebessa's course Samarai-Bali

It was early morning on the 18th. Norman was on watch. Over the years I had become very aware of the slightest change of movement in the ship. I woke with a feeling that something was amiss. We were slaloming, taking more punishment than usual, and I could hear the waves slopping into the cockpit. I put my head out of the hatch and called to Norman. 'What goes on? Is everything OK?' 'Come and give me a hand,' he said. 'She's not responding much to the wheel.' I threw on a jacket, went up and took over the wheel while Norman tried adjusting the sails, but I found it almost impossible to steer a course and within minutes I had no control at all. We had *no* steering!

It wasn't a nice situation in these conditions—but we weren't unduly alarmed. When the steering had broken before we'd managed to fix it. This time we finally found the trouble lay in the differential which drove the rudder. All our steering went through the differential, be it the emergency tiller or the wheel. If we could have removed this, some sort of steering arm could have been fitted onto the rudder flange. Norman and Peter made many attempts to move the mounting blocks without success. They'd been put on for keeps. We had become accustomed to breakdowns and running repairs, Norman often having to improvise with stocks available on board, but gradually it began to sink in that this time we were in a spot of bother that we couldn't fix.

Norman put up the brown boom staysail forward of the mast to steady us. We were all strangely calm, yet the anxiety and strain was there; we knew full well the liferaft might be on the cards. Should we try and make Timor, another 250 miles, or turn back for Darwin? The forecast was for continuing gale force winds and these we would have to bash into without a rudder. No chance! It had to be Timor. During the day, through spray and blinding rain, we'd sighted an oil rig, Big John, the only sign of life in this desolate part of the world, and had taken a bearing on it. Our radio telephone might be in range—but if we got through what then? We couldn't afford to be towed back to Darwin. At least if we were in real trouble the rig could call for help, so best to try and keep in range. Norman called them on the radio. No response. Then Darwin. No response. Finally—any ship—any ship . . . the line was dead. The aerial to our set fed through the deck, invariably packing up in bad weather. Even the radio we had put on to cheer us up seemed to go sour, playing time and again the popular hit tune 'It's hard to die'. We switched off!

It was as if we were in a car out of control, the wheel spinning this way and that, now a useless toy that had no power to steer; we were being carried along at an alarming speed, unable to turn or stop. Were we to share the fate of the Flying Dutchman, endlessly sailing the oceans of the world? This was the weirdest sensation we had ever experienced in our three and a half years of sailing round the world, to be carried along by gale force winds with enormous waves breaking over us, unable to control our direction, like a piece of flotsam at the mercy of the sea.

Some sort of steering in addition to experiments with the sails was vital, so we set to to build a jury rudder. The timber we carried wasn't strong enough. Attached to our mainmast were the two aluminium poles, 12 feet long, for booming out our foresails. These must be the answer. So they were unshackled and laid on deck. Then Norman found a length of brass threaded rod, which he cut up into six bolts, and two pieces of 34 inch by 16 inch plywood sheets. The sheets were bolted together and lashed on each side of the two aluminium poles at one end. This was our new rudder, our sweep. It had to work.

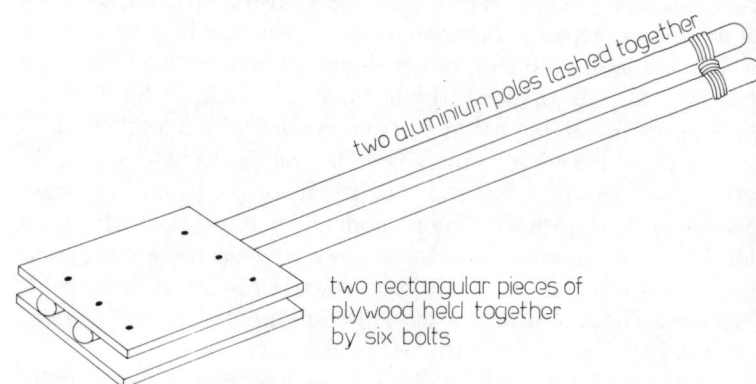

Shebessa's jury rudder: the two aluminium running booms, bolted at one end to two rectangular pieces of plywood, were lashed at the other end to the upright stanchion, one pole either side of the horizontal stanchion. Used manually as an oar

The brown staysail was carrying us along at two knots. Spirits began to rise now that everyone was busy doing something constructive. We made another rudder out of the boathook and dinghy oars as a 'bow rudder'—just in case. We were still being tossed around like a cork and moving about the ship was slow. We all became very aware of the fact that we must take the greatest care. Nobody could afford to put a foot wrong. Man overboard or any kind of accident was not on.

Night watches were taken as usual. It was strange to be standing there without a wheel to hold and nothing to do except peer into the blackness in case a ship loomed up, heaven forbid. By morning the wind had veered a little and the gale was abating. We made experiments with the brown sail, sheeting her hard in, watching the compass till she slowly swung us round to 310°, our exact course for Timor. We were jubilant. What a sail! It was incredible that it could keep our 20 tons exactly on course downwind. So it was straight to the east end of Timor, through the narrow passage between it and the island of Leti—what would happen after that we shuddered to think. We had to head West along the north coast where strong winds zoomed down the mountains, then negotiate Dili harbour with its narrow channel lined with reefs.

We perfected the sweep. A spare stanchion was found; lashed upright to the taffrail it made a vertical support. The booms were threaded each side of the horizontal stanchion and lashed together at the forward end. We were ready. It was hard to get enough elevation to immerse the blade in the big following seas, but using it as an oar, *Shebessa* would at least be able to alter course. Our confidence continued to rise. It was time to experiment with more sails. We had a nice 12–15 knot wind on the port quarter. We held our faithful brown sail on the tack to windward and put up a number one yankee on the starboard stay. By sheeting in the yankee we could make the ship turn to starboard, let it out and she went to port; a slight slalom, but no matter. We just played the winch, and started raising the mizzen by varying amounts—which we discovered had a tremendous effect on steering. What a blessing the mizzen proved to be; the advantage of a second mast was apparent.

By dawn of the 22nd the island of Timor was in view, stark and beautiful but with an inhospitable coast, rugged cliffs and high surf. We raised the mizzen to push our nose to port. Tension rose as we neared the passage. The pilot, as always, was gloomy, telling us of tide rips and confused seas, so we had our emergency stores and gear at the ready—but it wasn't as frightening as we expected. Cocky now, we changed the yankee for a number two genoa and had the same result with more power in the sheeting position and more effect from the mizzen.

Almost through the passage I suddenly saw a jet of water shooting up into the air about 200 yards away on the port side. A whale—we hoped he wouldn't come closer: but he did—50 yards off, his vast form was just below the water. Pray heaven he stayed there, but he didn't. In a gush and flurry of water he dived, and we all held our breath in fear and trembling he would come up under our ship and tip us up. We never saw him again, but our nerves had been jangled once more. Dili was only 90 miles away. Should we go all out to arrive the next evening or take two days to be sure? 'Let's make a run for it' was the unanimous decision.

At dusk we tacked away from the coast away from danger if the wind dropped, to get through the fearful pitch-black hours of night. On Peter's watch a light appeared on the port quarter and he woke Norman. The mizzen was put up to steer us away but still the light came closer. A steamer passed within a hundred yards. Morning sights of Liran and Atuaro islands put us still 30 miles out. There had been an adverse current. Entering Dili was going to be a tricky exercise—best to let all other vessels know we hadn't one hundred per cent control. Looking up the Portuguese words for 'rudder broken', I painted on a large piece of old canvas the words 'leme fracturo', and this we tied to the guard rail on the bow. It was a frustrating morning with variable winds. Tired and strained, we had carefully to rehearse our drill for getting through Dili Pass.

At last the huge crocodile head shape of land came into view, identifying the entrance to Dili, then at 1500 hours on the opposite quarter the lighthouse. But now with sudden strong winds from the North-East, plans had to be changed. It was hard to see the floating drums marking the entrance to the harbour between the two reefs, but at the critical moment we headed downwind, pulled the mizzen across to have the wind on the beam, and headed for the buoys. With Johnny on the sweep, Norman on the mizzen, Peter playing the sheets and myself on the engine, we steered towards the wharf. Tense but triumphant we swept in, dropping our sails in record time as we neared the jetty, then anchor down. Splosh! What a wonderful sound! We'd made it after the longest seven days we had ever known.

In Dili we received the greatest co-operation, kindness and generosity, from Government officials and ordinary people alike, that we had ever experienced. Our steering problem was solved by the most efficient Government engineers. The steering shaft was resplined, the star wheels reversed, bearings repaired—they were masters of improvisation as there were no new bearings available—and the differential was filled with oil. We were able to enjoy Dili before setting off on the 600 mile hop to Bali via the Sumba Strait, then along the south coasts of the islands of Lomblen, Flores, Sumbawa and Lombok.

In Dili there was a delightful mixture of races, customs and ways of life; Timorese, Portuguese and Chinese all getting along fine with each other. The native Timorese were gentle folk, tiny in stature, the women colourfully dressed in a kind of sarong, carrying their goods on their heads, going about their business—mostly agriculture—smiling and laughing, doing their utmost to be friendly to us strangers. Dili reminded us of Rabaul, with its beautiful mountains reaching right down to the sea, the clean and tidy town spread along the shore amid sandy beaches, and fishing villages further out, with clear water and some reefs for added interest. The territory was benignly administered, it seemed to us, by Portugal through its Governor and his officials who employed as many of the native population as possible. We were saddened to read later of the bloody revolution here with street fighting, as we could not imagine these gentle people shooting at each other.

The native market, open every day, teemed with tiny shops in narrow streets, selling materials and goods from Singapore, Indonesia, Mainland China, Hong Kong and local sources. People from the mountains thronged down from their remote villages on tiny Timor ponies to spread their wares—fruit, vegetables, tobacco, betel nuts, basketware, handwoven rugs, buffalo horn carvings, turtle shell rings—on the ground, squatting there all day and calling out their prices. Haggling was the way of business, and you had to be hard even amongst friends to obtain a fair bargain. Close by were muddy paddy fields which huge water buffalo ploughed just by walking through—they were a grotesque sight, all shining with thick slimy mud.

Cockfighting seemed to be a semi-religion among the men—women were not allowed to attend but an exception was made for me as a visitor. The arena next to the market was packed with men lovingly holding their birds, arranging matches and shouting challenges, with onlookers flashing wads of notes and money changing hands with bewildering speed—there seemed to be a system of trust—amid tremendous noise all the time, until a match was arranged. Then the money really went around, everyone betting on one or the other, the owners accepting all wagers. The latter each sat sharpening a steel spur—a three by three-eighths inch steel knife—on an oilstone until it was like a razor, then each lashed his tightly to one leg of his bird before flinging it into the ring to face the other.

Why do cocks hate each other so much? Heaven knows, but immediately their neck feathers fanned out they were into each other with their murderous spurs flying and the crowd yelling in frenzy. Crash! Down one went with a great red gash down his chest. Dead! Just like that. It was incredible how quickly the fight was over. Sometimes they lasted a minute but that was rare. More frenzied shouts and cheers from the winner with his supporters as he proudly held his prize cock aloft, while the loser disconsolately threw the carcass of his bird outside the fence, then started to pay out.

Formalities in Dili were minimal, so after paying ten escudos for a stamp on the clearance and thirty for water we were away on July 6th for the island of Komodo, to try to get a glimpse of the giant reptile called the Komodo dragon, which we had been reading about in the pilot book, before going on to Bali. I didn't exactly whoop for joy at the thought of the hunt. I had it firmly implanted in my brain from childhood days that dragons were definitely scary animals—enormous creatures breathing fire that would devour you in one gulp. Peter and Johnny were eagerly looking forward to this adventure, but I had a feeling of foreboding. The pilot described the animal thus: 'Komodo, a peculiar creature, sometimes called the Komodo dragon, owing to its resemblance to that legendary monster, is found in the forests of Komodo. These beasts possess colossal strength, attain a length of ten feet, and attack the numerous wild horses on the island, and sometimes even man! In hopes of seeing these monsters, treks have to be taken into the mountains, through terrain alive with venomous snakes, scorpions and poisonous spiders.'

For four days there was very little wind. In this part of the world there seemed to be more whales than wind—we saw five spouting and surfacing at once, luckily at a safe distance. An incident now occurred to add variation to our difficulties.

Johnny had been a changed man since the drama of the Arafura Sea crossing. Was it a delayed reaction? He became petulant and morose, spending much time alone on deck and unreliable when steering in a light wind. This behaviour culminated in his allowing *Shebessa* to gybe on his night watch, and the subsequent flogging of the main caused it to split right along a seam. In fact we learned a valuable lesson now: how to fit a jury main. We hanked on the number two genoa to the tightened main halyard. It couldn't be sheeted tight enough when on the wind, but when the wind was abaft the beam it worked like a dream—more improvisation—and more sewing.

We passed the Flores coast, with the fantastic sharp-pointed conical volcano of Inerie, and in the early morning light saw the outline of Komodo, a wild rugged coastline, with surf pounding in and throwing huge spray high into the air. The sea became violently disturbed, water was flying around the cockpit, breakfast dishes crashed around the saloon. It was like an overture putting us all in the right frame of mind for what was to come. Fighting the strong current, we worked our way along the south-west side of the island, silent in awe of the majestic scenery, high peaks, fantastic colours of the stone faces—deep red, rust, white and grey-blue—and the weird forbidding shapes of the rocks and caves. I felt we were looking at a page out of Grimms' Fairy Tales. Beyond were grassy slopes and, dotted over them, tremendously tall palms rising into the sky, with small tufts of green at the very top, absurdly out of proportion to the height of the trees. The water was evil-looking, like thick treacle whirling around, reminding us of the Messina Straits of Sicily. At last we sighted the narrow entrance to Letuhoh Bay with its long sandy beach, where things looked tranquil, the only sound being the loud pounding of the surf as it rolled in. We had an uncanny feeling of being all alone, with no habitation, no sign of life—it was fitting terrain for dragons.

We anchored, piled into the dinghy and rowed ashore to start our first exploration of Komodo. The sand was a pattern of tracks—deer, goats, wild boar, snakes and then, more prominent than the others, a deep slaloming track with large claw marks each side. 'The dragons are here all right,' I thought; 'we're getting close.' Automatically I picked up a big piece of driftwood to protect myself. Carefully we picked our way through the grass and undergrowth, skirting the beach, then came across a river bed with a clearing nearby. Tucking ourselves behind a bush, we sat down quietly and waited. Silence reigned, broken only by a dead leaf falling into the undergrowth and the cries of the white cockatoos, who had seen us and were warning their friends. Pigeons flew back and forth and finches perched above our heads. Into the clearing of grass, well trampled by animals, came a family of wild boar. Then a goat ambled by and in the distance we heard the call of a deer. It suddenly seemed very normal—we could have been sitting in the Australian bush—and I was fascinated to watch these wild creatures leisurely going about their business. Patiently we waited until dusk, but no dragon came into view.

Early the following morning, Peter and Johnny set off for a day's hike in search of the dragons. After breakfast I was sitting in the cockpit writing and watching the many sharks cruising by when I happened to look up, and couldn't believe my eyes. There on the beach, not much further than a hundred yards away, was a huge dragon, all ten feet of him, lolloping along in a very ungainly manner, but powerful with a prehistoric look, and fitting into the scene beautifully. As he swung his way along, dragging his huge tail, he moved his head from side to side and we saw his white forked tongue flicking out, his scaly hide a greyish brown colour, showing up against the sand, but good camouflage in the scrub. So this was the mighty dragon. He looked like an old gentleman taking his morning constitutional! But if we met him face to face, it might be a different story.

Quietly and quickly Norman and I rowed ashore. As we drew nearer the beach, we were able to study the monster more closely—his tough hide, like lizard skin but pebbly, his armour-plated head, his long sharp claws. We dragged our dinghy through the surf and up the beach, but even with the pounding surf to drown any noise the dragon immediately sensed we were there. He became alert, stopped in his tracks, reared up on his hind legs, holding his head high as if sniffing the air, then turned round and glared at us. He was flashing his tongue from side to side, as if thinking, 'Who are these interlopers in my domain?' We wondered what he would do—attack us? But instead he scurried off into the long grass and was gone.

Later that day we were lucky enough to see two more dragons. One crossed our path only 20 yards ahead of us and quietly disappeared into the undergrowth, then ahead of us we saw dust rising on the track and there, almost blending into the surroundings, another was moving in the same direction as we were. He suddenly quickened his pace, which wasn't very fast, retreated to a dried up gully and was lost. At dust Peter and Johnny returned from their long trek, disappointed they hadn't seen a dragon—but they had speared two crayfish for supper, which was some compensation.

The fears of Komodo began to leave me. This was such a peaceful spot and unbelievably beautiful, even in the dry season, with the ground hard and covered with loose red rocks under the grass. It was teeming with wild life and yet with no sign or sound of the struggle for existence these animals must have. The beach was endless entertainment. Pa and Ma Boar appeared again with their young searching for food, a crab perhaps, Pa rubbing his snout in the sand as he walked along, making a deep furrow, and the babies sniffing around. We saw no evidence of water on this island—even the river beds were dusty and rock hard when we were there. The

Komodo dragon has close Australian relatives. In the evolutionary pattern it is the same genus as the Australian Lace Monitor, but whether the two reptiles had a common place of origin is lost in time. Perhaps Noah simply dropped them off in their respective countries as he passed by!

We moved on towards Bali amid tide-rips and whirlpools and a strong South-going current, but we had plenty of south-easterly wind so had a fine sail across Sape Strait at eight knots. Light winds followed along the coast of Sumba which with the now East-going current made it a slow ride with sails flogging in the swells, then violent squalls. It was up and down sails all day. When 145 miles from Bali we decided to go to Belanak Bay on Lombok to anchor, then set off early next day for Bali, 30 miles away, to arrive in the forenoon. But coming upon heavy seas pounding the rocky coast, we decided it would be safer to stay out at sea, making tacks under reduced sail every two hours to keep within four miles of the coast.

Peter, a reliable helmsman, going on watch at 0200 expecting to be well out at sea, woke the skipper with a yell of urgency. Norman rushed up to see land on port, land on starboard, land ahead! *Close.* 'Start the engine!' he screamed as he tore the wheel from the hands of Johnny, still drowsily at the helm, and turned hard to port to steer due South away from those rocks ahead. Where the devil were we? A study of the chart revealed that we could only be in Belanak Bay. Our helmsman had steered us exactly where Norman had refused to go in daylight! Under the sheer pressure of need to express my feelings, I immediately wrote these lines:

Johnny Crew

(Written after 2 a.m. en route to Bali,
during a sleepless night).

I'll never sleep while you're on watch, never,
You silly young idiot, trying to be clever.

You sleep and you read and loll around;
It's a wonder to me we've not gone aground.

You may like to travel and see other lands,
But our lives and the ship are in your hands.

You contradict each word your skipper utters.
We're tired of your adolescent mutters.

We made a mistake. We chose you as crew.
We thought you'd be strong and honest and true.

This is your watch and you're meant to steer.
If you can't do the job, be gone with your gear.

A few stars came out, so we could see when the west end of Belanak Bay was cleared and we could turn towards Bali. But we had to find Sophia Louise Rock, ten feet high and a mile offshore, to establish our exact position. With a lookout in the bows and one each side three pairs of eyes anxiously searched. 'There—forty yards off the starboard bow!' called Peter suddenly. There was a terrific phosphorescence around the rock, making it a spectacular as well as welcome sight. Confident now, we steered for Bali.

14
Bali to Swaziland

Bali, known as the Island of the Gods and the Morning of the World, lies at the southern tip of Java, one of twenty-six provinces that make up the Indonesian Republic. Was this island going to be as fabulous as we had imagined it? As we sailed towards the port of Benoa, gay lateen rigged canoes, each with outriggers either side, skimmed past us, looking like giant spiders on the water, superbly handled by their Balinese crew competing in an annual race. In the harbour we anchored, then, warned of thieving, stripped the decks of sheets, blocks and shackles, anything that was likely to be pinched. We locked up the ship well, and went ashore to clear customs. The customs officers treated us with the greatest courtesy and, to our amazement, were not in the least bothered that our visas were two months out of date. An Australian motor cruiser had arrived two days before us with no documents at all. They found their own way to enter Indonesia, handing over a pile of much sought after *Playboy* magazines. Here lipstick, old jeans and magazines were great currency.

We said goodbye to Johnny here. It was a great relief. Our nerves couldn't have stood a repeat of the last voyage. We had been incredibly lucky so far with just about all the crew we had had aboard, but you can't hit the jackpot every time. Peter, a much more settled person, stayed on with us to enjoy Bali.

Lined up near the jetty were some strange-looking vehicles, small three wheeler vans with open sides and back and two benches inside, propelled by a motor cycle engine, each officially allowed to carry ten passengers. These were called *bemos*, the local transport to Denpasar, the capital, half an hour's ride away. We climbed aboard, squashing up together as more and more people poured in. A man appeared with an enormous sad-looking turtle which took up most of the floor space. We lifted our feet, resting them on his shell. A large lady sat down with a wicker clothes basket piled high with hundreds of eggs. A man with four live chickens was breathing down my neck. The engine burst into life and we shot into town, weaving in and out of the traffic, missing cars by a whisker, the driver jamming his brakes on now and again to let out passengers or take on more. In a narrow street opposite the market our bemo came to a final halt. We disgorged onto the pavement a sticky crumpled mass, relieved to stretch our arms and legs again.

The streets of Denpasar were noisy, colourful and bustling with life, a fascinating mixture of East and West. Raucous noises came from juke boxes blaring from nearly every shop, while in the streets beautiful women walked by erect and poised. They had to, as rarely did we see them without vast stores balanced on their heads, sacks of flour, rice or a stalk of bananas. They stood erect while their menfolk piled on more and more for them to carry. Street hawkers kept stopping us, opening their bags or a piece of rag, revealing wood carvings, bone statues, paintings and jewellery. Little English was spoken. One street was set out as an open market, throbbing with life, stall after stall of every fruit and vegetable imaginable, stalls making pancakes, *Semur Sapi Sate*—beef, pork and chicken or turtle meat served with peanut sauce dip—and other strange-looking foods. On the sides of the street were trestle tables and benches. Behind these were set up huge cauldrons, some filled with cooked rice, others with tasty Indonesian dishes, each trader having his own gas bottle and rings for cooking. Here on the open street we ate many a meal, no having the slightest idea what we'd ordered. We left it to the cook but each dish was different, highly spiced and delicious.

Peter went to collect our 32 lb gas bottle which was being refilled in town. Grabbing it in his arms he struggled along the hot dusty street, when a nine-year-old child tapped him on the shoulder and made signs to drop the bottle. She was just a slip of a girl, but within seconds she'd swung the heavy bottle up on her head, balancing it with superb poise, and strode off to the bus station. Peter, utterly demoralised and deflated, followed. It was too much for him.

There was so much to gaze at in Bali, full of the complex life of cultured people. Most followed the Balinese Hindu religion, as much a part of their life as their livelihood. The many homes we passed all had their own small family shrine set on stilts in the garden overlooking the square walls. The walls were set inside the gate, built square as evil spirits weren't able to turn corners. The women of all ages were beautiful, their shapely bodies moving with grace and poise as if they were trained ballet dancers, their faces unlined and serene. They seemed to have an inner peace that radiated from their faces, believing in reincarnation and in living a good life now in preparation for the one to come. Even the women doing menial tasks such as road making, collecting stones in their small wicker baskets to spread on the road, made every move a pleasure to watch. In Indonesia, as on all the islands of the Pacific women seemed to do more manual work than men and actually seemed to enjoy it.

We took a bus into the countryside to see miles and miles of rice paddy fields in terraces full of toiling peasants. The irrigation systems, hundreds of years old, flooded each field in succession. We drove through villages famous for certain crafts—Mas for carvings; Celub for jewellery; Batubulan a colony of sculptors, peaceful and serene; Ubud for paintings—and many others.

Tim Elliott, a young American, had come down to Benoa after touring Indonesia, looking for a ride to Mombasa, Kenya where he had friends. As Mombasa was to be our first stop in Africa, he joined *Shebessa*. Twenty-six years of age, Tim had spent two years with the anti-malaria section of the Peace Corps in Malaysia

He had a good sense of humour and it was fun listening to his tales of the primitive living in the Malaysian interior. Our plan was to sail via Christmas Island, 600 miles West, to Sri Lanka and the Maldives, then via the Seychelles and Mombasa down the Moçambique Channel to Durban rather than the common southern route to Reunion and Mauritius. We wondered what the vast Indian Ocean had in store for us.

Fantastic sailing for the first week—the fastest we have ever experienced before or since. With the steady South-East trade wind we covered 1,119 miles in seven days with a record day's run of 170 miles, though with far too much rolling for my liking. Fish were scarce—maybe we were going too fast—except for one occasion in pitch dark when the lure struck and we hauled in an extraordinary specimen, a real denizen of the deep (we were in 2,500 fathoms), three feet long, three inches wide, a shiny bluish colour, with three irregular big teeth in the huge upper jaw, more like an eel than a fish, a slimy, horrible-looking creature with huge, oversize eyes. No one fancied him for the pot so he was cast away. Months later, reading Thor Heyerdahl's *Kon Tiki Expedition*, we found they had caught the same fish in the Pacific, a Gempylus, claiming it was the first time it had been seen alive.

One rough evening, with *Shebessa* well heeled, the lee rail awash, Norman, from the foredeck where he was changing a sail, called Peter to help. Crouching low he came up but on the lee side, against our rule always to pass along the deck on the windward side. As he grabbed the guard rail it broke and he half-fell over the coaming, but clung on by one leg. Before Norman reached him he had somehow managed to pull himself back and grab the hand rail on deck. How lucky he had been: it would have been hard to rescue him in those seas. Peter was always happy to work on deck even in bad conditions and had become somewhat overconfident—but he took a good deal more care after this experience.

On the fifth day we decided to give Sri Lanka away as it lay rather too far to the North, and make straight for the Maldives 600 miles south-west of Sri Lanka, so our course could still have some westing in it instead of trying to sail directly across the Doldrums. The cyclone season in the South Indian Ocean extended from October to June. It was now August 25th and we were 3,500 miles from Durban. By cutting out Sri Lanka, at least 14 days would be saved—useful as we wanted to reach Durban by the end of November after seeing as much of the Indian Ocean islands as possible; from there we would eventually sail on to Cape Town to prepare for the long haul back to England.

While we were in South Africa we hoped also to have time to see something of Bri. As a sociology student at York University he had interrupted his course to come to Swaziland to work with a society promoting adult education, returning to take his degree at Leicester University. Then while studying there for his Phd, he had gone back to Swaziland, this time to do work in various different fields. I dearly wanted to find out what the magnetism was that drew him there.

It was hard to win with the Doldrums anywhere. First the wind changed to South-West, so we were hard put to it to complete our record week, then followed frustrating sailing—winds from every which way, calms, squalls, torrential rain, electric storms, sails up and down, with plenty of motoring till we reached the RAF staging post of Gan island, the most southern of the Maldives, which consist of 1,200 islets set in 19 groups of atolls extending 470 miles to the North, each surrounded by a barrier reef—those reefs again! Gan island was loaned to Britain for 30 years by the Maldives Government after these islands gained independence from Britain in 1960.

The 2,235 mile voyage from Bali had taken 16 days at an average of 140 miles per day, tremendous sailing for *Shebessa*, so we were glad to have a rest for a week enjoying a little bit of Old England in the hospitable company of the RAF. Each Sunday the Gan radio station broadcast messages to the men from their loved ones at home. Norman and I were asked to give a talk on our voyage and to read out the postal messages. I was the only female on this island among hundreds of men. The boys, though living in paradise, missed their womenfolk and wanted to hear a female voice again, even it if was a grandma's.

Norman had been suffering for some time from a skin infection. A doctor on Thursday Island had diagnosed it as a fungus but the cream prescribed hadn't cured the itch. The RAF doctor took one look at him and said 'Worms'! They were easily picked up just by leaning against the wall of a native hut. Like a puppy Norman was duly wormed and at last cured.

We received permission by radio from the capital of the Maldive Islands, Mahé, to visit the northerly atolls and they radioed the headmen in all townships to expect us. The pilot made their way of life sound intriguing. 'The inhabitants of the Maldives are

Moslems and are not permitted to barter or accept gifts of any sort without the permission of the Sultan and this order is enforced by the headmen of the villages. If it is required the Sultan will authorise a representative to accept Ceylon currency in exchange for foodstuffs, chiefly chickens, eggs and fish. Coral fish abound. Turtles, sharks and porpoises are plentiful. The swordfish is common and sometimes found 18 feet in length.'

Our arrival at the outlying island of Fua Mulaku 40 miles North-East was the event of the local year. Dozens of small boats, called *dohneys*, laden with people including the chief with his retinue of twelve, put out from shore to see this strange ship as many had never seen a yacht in their lives before. We spent the evening ladling out drinks—soft, as being Moslems they prohibited alcohol—and cigarettes, and listening to accounts in Maldive English of these people's hard way of life.

In the morning the chief, dressed in his best western suit, arrived to take us ashore to his office, the 'centre of local government'. Treated to lovely large milky drinking coconuts we sat on chairs while the chief and his number two sat on a bed which was swinging from the roof, rather like an English garden lounger. This was the normal way a high class person slept and sat. There the two administrators sat, swinging to and fro as all the local dignitaries, but no females, filed in one by one to be introduced to us with much smiling and shaking of hands.

Then followed a tour of the village. Like a king and queen on a state visit we led a procession of the dignitaries along every wide, clean street, with the entire populace standing outside their mud and coral-limestone square houses watching impassively. The women were dressed in a poor type of cotton sari, the children, seemingly thousands of them, in a motley array of clothes, the men in a knee-length black skirt, but no fez. In a couple of the houses into which we were invited, only the men were allowed anywhere near us. The women were kept behind a grille of wooden bars where they crowded, gazing solemnly at our every move, they or the children not being allowed even to bring in the coconuts. This is the pattern throughout the Maldives—it's no fun being a female there.

A special lunch was given to us in the chief's office: mostly chicken curry with rice, and lots of side dishes of vegetables and yams. There were no eating utensils of any kind; one had to crush up the yams in one's hands and eat with the left hand only—a messy business indeed. After another tour of inspection during which we visited our interpreter's house to meet his fourteen-year-old wife, there were more visits with the same routine of coconut drinking. We eventually returned to *Shebessa* almost on our knees.

Thirty-one miles North lay the entrance to the huge Suvadiva atoll, 45 miles long and 35 miles wide, along the perimeter of which lay a number of inhabited small islands, some of which we visited. On Tinadu the town somehow supported 4,000 people. Here we heard that when the Maldives were granted independence the people refused to accept it, wanting to stay British. For this 'crime' they were all banished to various other islands to split up the agitators! Only lately had they been drifting back.

After a few days of prolonged and heavy rain we unanimously decided to take off for better weather. But our passage out of the Maldives was a rough one indeed. Great black clouds formed overhead, and a heavy swell quickly built up, sending up mountains of water that smashed against the reefs—a spectacular send-off. We soon sailed straight into a terrific approaching squall which recurred at intervals for the rest of the day. A 40 knot wind split the mizzen down the middle in the night, and next morning we had to rig a jury mizzen. We used the storm jib. Hanked to the mizzen's wire halyard, raised by the topping lift, sheeted on the end of the boom with the staysail halyard, it worked with about fifty per cent efficiency. Sew, sew, sew!

The last 1,200 miles to the Seychelles took ten days. Reaching the island of Mahé, we crept up the coast towards Port Victoria. The big surprise here when we rowed ashore was to be welcomed by our great friends John and Peggy Finlinson who, knowing our itinerary, had succeeded in making a holiday coincide with our arrival. And later we had a marvellous seven day visit from Bri on his way to England from Swaziland. Mahé began to feel like home, all touristy as it was.

Mahé was another crossroads for yachts and yachties, where last minute changes in plans were made. With the Suez Canal about to reopen one could use it for a fast trip to Europe, or pluck up one's courage for the voyage across to Africa and down the Moçambique channel to Durban—or just stay in Mahé. We met one single-hander who was leaving for Africa the following week. But he had been saying that for *twenty-eight years*! Norman asked him if he would sell us his self-steering gear but he said 'Sorry, but I'll be wanting it when I leave next week.'

Bri asked us to visit him in Swaziland for Christmas, so we decided to cut out Mombasa, and Tim was quite happy to fly there to save time. Peter was impatient to get to England to buy his Hunter 19 sloop, and when he found a yacht planning to leave for the Red Sea, he transferred with our blessing.

Two youngsters asked for a ride to Durban, both called Mike: a tall Rhodesian blond youth aged twenty, and a shortish curly-haired English boy of nineteen. As neither of them wanted to change their names we called them Big Mike and Little Mike. They were both very sick for the first three days, but then settled down better, though still hating the discomforts caused by a lot of bad weather. It was to be a rough passage, testing even us seasoned sailors.

We planned to let the wind decide whether we called at Madagascar or the islands towards the mainland. With the West-going current and southerly wind, Madagascar in fact proved beyond our reach, so on the fifth day out it looked like a landfall on the Cosmoledo group, an atoll with a few small islands on the rim. All atolls way out in the ocean seem at first like paradise, but after a walk across to the windward side, sometimes in mud up to the knees after heavy rains, they don't. This time was no exception—but back at the anchorage after a swim in the warm clear water and a few rock oysters which we found on flat rocks in the sand it was paradise again.

We motored on. We lost the trade wind approaching the Moçambique channel; the wind changed to North-East either light or very strong, with rougher seas. On our fourth night out from Cosmoledo, in the channel itself, occurred our worst experience ever.

We hadn't seen a ship for days, but on my first watch I saw one. It appeared to be going to cross our bows about two miles away, so there seemed no problem. But when I looked again it was closer. I called to Norman, who rushed up on deck. The ship, on our beam now, looked stationary. The spreader lights were switched on and we turned more to starboard. Then she came to life and seemed to be coming straight at us. Panic! Norman dashed below to free the prop, and when he reappeared the great thing was a couple of hundred yards away.

'Start the engine!' What to do? If we motor to starboard she'll get our stern, if to port she must hit us amidships. Reverse! Flat out astern! But it seems she *must* hit us. Now *Shebessa* stops and ever so slowly starts to move astern. Will we do it? Somehow we get our bow back a little to stop ourselves ramming or being rammed, and the great ship slithers past towering above us inside *twenty feet*.

We spat at her: no sign of life on board. Norman and I were a couple of nervous wrecks, but luckily the two boys woke up only at the end of it all to see the ship's lights through our ports.

This was the pattern of the next few days, eternally dodging tankers—there seemed to be hundreds of them by day and night, all seemingly on autopilot, so we just had to keep well away. This wasn't easy in the misty, changeable weather. For the first time on a long voyage Norman and I started to yearn for a long rest.

I'd had that unsettled feeling inside me all day. Nothing was wrong but I was restive and uneasy. A swallow had joined the ship and settled himself in the saloon to stay. Birds have a built-in system of knowing when bad weather is brewing. At 2100 hours I woke Norman and Mike for their watch (we had two on watch at this difficult stage). The sky, previously clear, was massing dark clouds to the South-West and there was a sort of reddish glow. Suddenly the cabin was blindingly bright as fork lightning shot around us. I drew the curtains but still it flashed through the hatches, then a crashing of sails, *Shebessa* lurched and we were all in the cockpit. There was thunder overhead, blinding rain and the wind whipped up to tremendous force, the sea a haze of flying spray and spume. Norman took the wheel and fought for two hours to keep control with the lee rail awash and water half way up to the portholes as we stormed along with number two genoa and mizzen, gust after gust more and more vicious. He hadn't even had time to put a shirt on and his body glistened as the rain streamed off his chest and back. Even the cooker and the curtains swung out and stayed at the same crazy angle. Our swallow was cowering among the cushions.

The mizzen had to come down as time and again it crashed, each gust felt as if it was bringing us closer to being flattened, but Norman couldn't leave the wheel. It was taking all his strength and experience to control the ship and our two young boys were not experienced enough to bring it down. Then like a gunshot there was a tremendous rip. The mizzen had blown out into ribbons, thrashing around in the wind. Would the number two hold? This was no ordinary gale—it felt like a cyclone. All the elements, the most deadly forces, were unleashed against us. We were completely at the mercy of the wind driving us where it wanted—please God no tankers now.

I eventually had a go at the wheel while Norman and the lads crawled forward to claw down the genoa without damage, then the remains of the mizzen. We lay ahull under bare poles drifting South at two knots. Norman managed to get the boom staysail up, then the wind changed to South-East and force nine! So we hove to, but were drifting North away from Durban. The engine was started in case a close quarters situation developed while we were helpless—and sure enough, out of the mist loomed a Japan Lines tanker. About turn quick.

Having had no sights we tacked later, under boom staysail, yankee and jury mizzen, towards the coast, at last meeting St Lucia light 110 miles from Durban—it wouldn't be long now. Big Mike suggested that he and Little Mike should be rowed ashore! But it turned out to be two more days before we reached land.

We made a night arrival in Durban. The area looked like Wall Street, with twenty-three fully lit ships in the roads and the city lights behind. It was forbidden to enter the harbour channel before clearing, so after jilling around we finally anchored on the east side of the breakwater and SLEPT.

In the morning a pilot boat came to lead us to the harbour for clearance. Our 1,200 mile passage had taken fourteen days of sheer hell and we hoped we should never experience its like again. The two Mikes disappeared onto dry land very fast indeed—and we thoroughly sympathised with them. We saw only Big Mike again a couple of times. It was a shame the two had had such a gruelling initiation into ocean cruising—it probably put them off sailing for ever.

Durban harbour was packed with yachts, and we had to tie up to an old hulk a good 200 yards from the shore and outside the breakwater. There was no respite. We might as well have been on the high seas, having to fend off at all hours of the day and night as the wind whipped up, causing heavy swells. On our last legs and in driving rain we were taken by the launch to the Point Yacht Club where many an old yachting face welcomed us. Like us, most of them had had a rugged trip and were thankful to draw breath for a while. For some it was the end of the road. They'd had enough and their yachts were put up for sale, others were nearly broke and hoping to find work. This wasn't as easy as they had anticipated: first of all a permit had to be obtained, often taking as long as three months to come through, and unskilled labour was for blacks only.

Formalities here were a hassle, more so because we were so weary. We thought we'd been cleared in the harbour, but no—there were offices to visit and forms to fill in. We enquired about public transport. 'Take a taxi,' we were told. 'The bus is for the blacks.' 'Oh, they won't mind us,' we said—to be greeted with stony looks. Our funds being as usual low, despite the heat we walked many a mile over the next few days visiting various offices to complete the documentation before we were finally cleared.

We were excitedly planning our trip to Swaziland to stay with Bri. But the immigration officer dampened our spirits the first day. 'No yacht personnel can leave Durban unless each puts up a deposit of R500,' he said. At this stage of our journeying it was like asking for the moon. 'But why?' I asked. 'You're an alien,' he replied, 'and if we have to deport you it has to be at your own expense.' This wasn't the welcome we had expected. The law caused yachting folk a great deal of discontent, spoiling many a dream of touring the country to see the game parks. 'Of course if you can get a South African to stand surety for you, you'll be free to move,' the immigration officer continued. We didn't know a soul in Durban, but later a member of the Royal Natal Yacht Club, Douglas Cawdron, came to our rescue. He was a Yorkshireman married with four children and living in Durban, whose pride and joy was his yacht *Andrew Miller*, and whose ambition was to cruise the world. He very kindly signed the necessary forms to give us our freedom.

The city of Durban, a jungle of concrete blocks and skyscrapers lining the shore, seemed to us a land of plenty, and was in fact the cheapest place we'd visited for food. Outside officialdom, the white population we found among the world's friendliest. All white people looked prosperous, well catered for and their life seemed orderly. But we had absolutely no contact with the black people, and we could never get used to this. Having spent years with many different islanders we'd ceased even to think about colour, looking dark and weathered ourselves. Segregation struck us as extremely odd, with two of everything, a black lift, a white lift, black loos, white loos, black buses, white buses. What on earth, we wondered, did honey-coloured people do?

A few days before Christmas we flew to Swaziland for our stay with Bri. This little landlocked kingdom, about the size of Wales, is wedged between South Africa and Moçambique. Here King Sobhuza II, the longest reigning and probably the last absolute monarch in the world, benevolently rules barely half a million people steeped in age-old tradition, but is now leading them from obscurity to a firm place in the modern age. The country has great mineral wealth, mostly iron ore and asbestos; much sugar for export; a thriving tourist industry; a game park and the only casino in the southern part of Africa, at the Holiday Inn, five miles from Mbabane the capital.

As we stepped off the plane, we gazed at country not unlike the highlands of Scotland, majestic mountains reaching up to 6,000 feet, rolling hills and lush green valleys, all as yet unspoilt by man. Large areas were covered by pine forests, the sweet smell permeating the air. There were no villages. Each man had his piece of land with its own *kraal*, a group of reed beehive-shaped huts anything from two upwards; he could have as many wives as he could afford but had to provide a separate hut for each of them. These *kraals* were dotted over the plains and the hills, melding into the landscape.

We were overjoyed to be with Bri again, and in a country he had been drawn to for many years. He took us to our temporary home, a lovely old farmhouse on the outskirts of Mbabane. Nestling in the hills, the capital has one main street which is rapidly changing in style, new government buildings and modern banks springing up among the old-style small shops. Nowhere in the world had I seen a street filled with so many colourful and fascinating people. Swazi women even on the hottest day wore long cotton skirts, and some had wool caps on their heads; all carried their babies on their backs in a thick blanket tied in front across their busts. Some young girls wore western dress while others were in the traditional costume, a toga-like garment, the *mahiya*, two scarlet patterned pieces of rectangular cotton attached on one shoulder. The men's dress varied as much, from the few conservative collar and ties to the *mahiya* with a loin cloth of goat-skin. I felt a salesman in trunks would have had a lean time here.

The Swazis, who in town mostly spoke English as well as their own language SiSwati, were gentle kindly people and this was reflected in their facial expressions and warm smiles. Here where the clock was of little importance, people had time to be pleasant. I was deeply impressed by their old world charm and good manners. We felt completely at home.

Early in January the most important festival of the year took place, the Incwala—a sacred ceremony, not a tourist attraction. Visitors were allowed to attend if they were properly dressed and didn't take cameras or umbrellas. Bri drove us down the Ezulwini valley to Lomamba, the scene of this event. As we stood in the vast grassy veldt and gazed around, I felt I had stepped back into what seemed like prehistoric times. Here in the Valley of Heaven, the very heart of Swaziland, thousands of loyal subjects of His Majesty King Sobhuza II had collected from all over the kingdom, some walking in from a hundred miles away to take part in this feast of the first year fruits. The ceremony has its climax on the day of the full moon nearest to the New Year, the day when the King is joined by his people in symbolic rites marking the change of the year and the rebirth of hope for fertility and security. Only among the Swazis does this ancient African tradition still exist. Its meaning is the taking in of new strength by the King for the ensuing year, and through him by the people, for the Swazis believe that the power of the nation and its wealth in crops lies in the health and virility of their King. So to this end he must take one or more new wives each year. By the time we saw him he had ruled 54 years and had untold children!

The King's loyal and devoted subjects were brown-skinned men, bare save for the shaggy bovine tails around their necks draped to their waists, leopard and goat skins around their loins, and armlets and anklets of feathers; each carried skin-covered shields and wooden spears with posies of feathers tied to them and feathers stuck in their hair—different colours for different ranks. The chiefs, huge powerfully built men, wore fantastic head-dresses made from the feathers of the black Sakabula, the widow bird. The whole scene made a thrilling, awesome and somewhat unnerving sight. The thought ran through my mind—what if they were to go berserk?

Here in an enormous reed-enclosed arena we were experiencing the climax of weeks of preparation for this special day. The Bemanti, messengers of the water, had been down to the ocean to collect froth from the top of the curling waves, as the foam is the strength of the sea. Others had scoured the forests for special medicines, especially the Lusekwane shrub, a type of Acacia, whose leaves are a symbol of resilience and fertility. These things and many others had been obtained for the King. Numerous ceremonies had already been carried out, culminating the previous day in the driving of a great herd of steers into the arena. The King had struck one on the head, then the young men had had to chase it, fell it and knock it unconscious with their bare fists—quite a feat—after which it had been dragged away to be secretly killed and some of its blood used for anointing the King.

Now today brought a fantastic sight as the warriors and chiefs filed into the arena, gradually, as the afternoon progressed, spreading out into a huge semicircle, swaying and chanting. Suddenly from the far corner of the arena there was a dazzling burst of red. It was the King's wives—over a hundred of them! Each was dressed in a scarlet *mahiya*, and together they appeared a shapeless mass, dancing but hardly moving, each holding a reed with a small feather flying near the top. Then the number one wife moved out alone to face the mass of wild-looking warriors.

It was an oppressive afternoon with thunderclouds collecting and small bursts of rain followed by sunshine. Tension built up as the moment for His Majesty to arrive drew near. Church dignitaries appeared and there was a stand for Consular Officials. Then from the Royal enclosure there was another burst of colour as in stately procession the King's daughters came into view, again over a hundred of them. They were bare-breasted, in fact totally bare save for their belts of highly coloured beads, woven into an exquisite pattern, hanging from their waists—the shortest mini skirt ever, reaching only half way down their bottoms, with their brown rounded cheeks peeping out below.

When would the remarkable King himself come, the seventy-five-year-old who symbolised unity in Swaziland, revered for his wisdom and power—and a strange supernatural power too, the power to bring rain on the day of the Incwala, to start the crops growing in the New Year?

Another flurry of brilliant colour and he was in the arena. With his bodyguard he advanced—a fine well-built man in no way stooped by his years, recently supposed to have been sick but today appearing full of vitality, draped in skins and wearing three white feathers in his magnificent head-dress of black Sakabula feathers.

With his chiefs gathered round him he toured the arena, inspecting his warriors. Then as part of the traditional ceremony, he turned and started to walk out of the arena, the pretence being that he had been rejected by his people—as had actually happened in previous reigns long ago. But he was followed by the chiefs who, amid much chanting, stamping and waving of spears, brought him back to face the multitude and to reign for another year. The Incwala ceremony was over.

Then all at once the whole valley was rent by a deafening clap of thunder. Fork lightning flashed over the arena, the heavens opened and torrential rain cascaded down. The lightning and thunder seemed directly overhead; we all winced as it struck and pealed, the Royal daughters breaking ranks in fear. The hail lashed down and everyone fled for cover. Dripping wet we made for our car, the arena now, as the Incwala finished in the traditional way, a sea of red mud.

What was this power the King had to bring on rain on this particular day? But hadn't he overdone it a bit this year! We wondered about it all as we drove away in the rain, past the camps of the warriors, out of the Valley of Heaven into clear sunshine.

And so the days flew by, exploring the countryside and learning about the Swazi way of life. As I was obviously in my seventh heaven being with Bri again and in this friendly land, Norman suggested I stayed on for six weeks while he returned to Durban to do repairs, find crew and take *Shebessa* to Cape Town, whence we would set off on our last passage back to England.

Bri and I now rented a small cottage in the grounds of a lovely house close to town. I woke each morning to gaze on blue-grey hills and a wild green valley below me, a scene of great beauty and tranquillity. There were even small monkeys swinging on the trees nearby, and a profusion of flowers to study. During these weeks I had a chance to recharge my batteries, and indulged in my favourite hobby, painting, with all the time in the world to do it.

At last, rested and revitalised, I flew to Cape Town to join *Shebessa* again.

15
Cape Town to Rio

Back in Durban there had been plenty for Norman to do on board—the sails to be repaired by a sailmaker; the bearings in the steering repaired at Dili to be replaced with new ones; and lots of other jobs as there always are on a yacht, as well as finding crew for the run to Cape Town. The Point and Royal Natal Yacht Clubs had been very friendly and hospitable, with all their facilities provided at no cost to us. Arthur Jones the Secretary and Bob Lambert of the Royal Natal were particularly helpful. At both clubs many blood-curdling tales were recounted of how horrible the voyage around the Cape of Good Hope could be, with gales and rogue waves off the coast that had overwhelmed yachts, but in spite of this four youngsters volunteered to join Norman for the passage to Cape Town, and Dougie Cawdron also asked to come to get experience.

In fact it had turned out a pleasant voyage, with Dougie a tower of strength—and good company, for he was a man of dry Yorkshire wit and high spirits, always bursting into song. With the wind always fair the 750 miles were covered in six days, the strong Agulhas current giving a hundred miles free. It was a happy ship that tied up at the Royal Cape Yacht Club. The boys all returned to Durban, while Norman set about preparing *Shebessa* for the last long voyage to England. Many firms were generous to us here, filling *Shebessa* with goodies.

At the Royal Cape Yacht Club Norman heard many stories of the delights of Rio. He had always had a secret yearning to go to South America some day, and over the past few weeks had begun to wonder whether here might be the chance. 'It'll be a long haul to England and not much to see on the way,' he said to me as soon as I arrived in Cape Town. In fact I myself hadn't been relishing the prospect of this long uninterrupted passage either. Slipping over to Brazil, then heading North for the West Indies to return home via Bermuda suddenly looked a much more attractive idea. What was another year? I eagerly agreed to the new plan. We started collecting charts and pilot books to cover our new itinerary.

Picking crew was always a difficult task, and especially so in Cape Town, with so many wanting to join us for Rio and the West

Indies. 'Don't take an Afrikaner for a start,' Norman was told. 'They're moody and difficult to live with.' This advice proved quite wrong. Norman took on Steven de Koch, an Afrikaner engineer, as his first choice and he proved to be a great crew. Steve was a gentle, quiet man, utterly happy as long as he could suck his pipe with Jock of the Bushveld tobacco after meals; he was fascinated by a new way of living and within a month or two of hard studying with Norman became an efficient navigator. Another South African, Russ Shipton, an English teacher, was the second choice. A tall, lean man with hair to his shoulders and a beard as long, he too had little experience, but a strong desire to see the world, and a willingness to help with any task during the day or night. His most treasured possession was a complete Shakespeare, in which he buried himself in his free time, often quoting us long passages; it was like a bible to him.

Dougie Cawdron wanted to come on with us as far as Rio for the experience. Then a young Englishman came to see us just before we left Cape Town. Brought up in South Africa, a champion diver, Dave Buckley was like a rubber ball, all bounce and energy, rarely without a grin on his face. He would make six, more than we had ever had on board before, but we had to say 'Come too if you don't mind the crush.' Luckily they all had money and were happy to pay their way.

We found Cape Town a superb and friendly city; it was the best we'd struck for stocking up. Here double baked bread could be bought, each loaf sealed in a polythene bag, loaves that kept fresh for at least 28 days, as if newly baked. I ordered two dozen and when Steve went to collect them and pay, they were presented to him free. I have a feeling they would have lasted much longer, only we weakened and ate the last loaf fairly soon. All canned goods were cheap, as were fresh fruit and vegetables.

On March 12th, 1975 we were ready at last, and headed out into heavy seas. There wasn't much chatter. We all felt strange, I getting my sea legs again, the boys orienting themselves to a new ship in the worst possible conditions. It takes time for anyone's body to adjust to continual violent motion and more so for our crew, tensed up at the start of their first long voyage.

Over our years of voyaging we had had eighteen men on board, some for short hops, others for many months at a time. Practically every one of those men suffered at the start with sea-sickness, some vomiting their hearts out, others just queazy. Apart from Ken whom we had taken from Tahiti to Rarotonga, they all adjusted in a matter of days. Pills we didn't encourage. They reduced the nausea but also made the men incompetent, and drowsy day and night. On a small yacht there's an unwritten law that a man has to stand his watch and only in real sickness is relieved. By trial and error we found the best cure was hard work on deck, and at the start of a voyage Norman always had an absorbing project for the men to do. Feeling like death they were ruthlessly dragged up and given a job in the fresh air with mumbles of 'Just our luck to pick a rugged old skipper like this one', but as they became absorbed in the job on hand, they gradually forgot how rotten they felt, and their bodies relaxed and acclimatised to the motion of the ship. Norman and I were incredibly lucky, neither of us ever suffering from seasickness.

The weather, bad enough already, deteriorated still more and the wind blew cold. We were all frozen. At our request the boys had brought the minimum of clothing, so all our sweaters and socks were pooled. In Durban Norman had called on a dear English lady, well into her seventies, called Hannah. It had been raining cats and dogs when he was about to leave her house. 'You need a mackintosh,' she said. Delving in her cupboard she came out with a superb black Scottish fisherman's coat that would defy any hurricane, and this she sold to Norman for a few Rands. How we blessed Hannah and that coat. It was christened the BBC, the big black coat, and was worn by each of us in turn as we went on watch.

It continued to blow like mad, with huge disturbed seas. One morning in the early hours, while Russ was on watch, a loud crash and shudder woke us all up. The wind now on the stern had backed the mainsail, throwing it from port to starboard with incredible force, despite our preventers, tearing the sail in two below the first batten. We had spent a lot of money in Durban having our sails resewn and now we were to be back at the same old game, hand sewing yard upon yard of sail, carefully placing our needle in the holes that were already there.

It was Doug's day for washing up duties. After supper he sat with the bucket between his legs, washing away and singing as he always did when he was working. Being Sunday it was hymns, 'Abide with Me' and 'Onward Christian Soldiers'. At last his work was finished. Thankfully he threw down the washing up cloth and carried the bucket of dirty water into the cockpit, then with a good swing tipped the contents into the sea. Apart from the splash, there was a loud clanging noise, alerting each one of us. Our entire cutlery drawer and set of cooking utensils had gone clanging to the mighty deep, and there we were, six of us with one teaspoon between us!

How was I going to stir a stew or a sauce? With a chisel? We took it quietly. We had to readjust, having sandwiches next day for lunch, cheese and egg on fried bread with chips for supper, but bread was getting low. Each of us had his own knife and these became more and more evident at table. It was quite an art balancing porridge on a sharp jackknife to the tossing and rolling without slashing our mouths. With pencils as chopsticks we struggled on, all doing our best not to make it too much of an animal affair. The chart was studied and finally it was decided to change course and head North-East 350 miles into the wind for the nearest island, St Helena, the tiny speck of land in the South Atlantic 1,200 miles from anywhere on which Napoleon lived in luxurious exile with a staff of fifty and 3,000 English soldiers and sailors to guard him for six years until his death in 1821. There we would buy new cutlery.

Early on Good Friday morning the forbidding-looking island loomed up before us, a great mass of volcanic rock reaching up to 2,000 feet, with perpendicular faces. We anchored in Jamestown harbour and then wondered how on earth we'd get ashore. There were no beaches. In the left hand corner of the bay was a concrete landing stage, and stretching from it was an overhead rafter from which a number of tousled ropes hung over the water. The swell was strong, dinghies in close proximity to the concrete being lifted high, then crashing against the concrete or being swept out on a receding wave. My heart was in my mouth. Eventually, we made it.

The people here were dark-skinned, being a lovely mixture of Malays, Indians, Chinese and Portuguese, plus a smattering of all the nationalities of the myriad sailors who had called there. Everyone from yachts and ships who called was made welcome. There was a shortage of men because of the lack of jobs on the island, many going to Ascension Island to find work. It was a great place for young men yachties—we lost ours immediately.

Norman's dental plate had split among the storms from Cape Town. He'd stuck it together with Araldite as a temporary measure. We called on the local dentist. He looked aghast.

'*Araldite*? It's a wonder you haven't been poisoned!' His mechanic fixed him in a matter of hours for 75 p—some service and on Good Friday too.

A ribbon of small blue, white and yellow painted stone houses lined the winding street to town. Here the next day we met an islander called Dot, dark-haired with sallow skin, a gay spark of a woman, mother of eight children. In former days she had run a café, and she promised to help us out with our cutlery problem. At noon I met Norman on the balcony of the pub in the high street, both laden with shopping. Our crew appeared, some of whom we hadn't seen since our arrival. Dot, joining us with a bag of assorted cutlery, turned her attention to one of our crew and in a voice so loud it seemd to rebound off every building in St Helena, shouted: 'You slept with my daughter last night. Why didn't you ask my permission?' In a quiet voice our man retorted: 'May I sleep with your daughter tonight?' 'By all means,' said Dot.

On Easter Monday we sailed away with all our crew, some more weary than others ... We turned our thoughts to Rio.

The voyage proved that the Atlantic pilot charts can be wildly wrong because we never really found the South-East trades at all as we sailed along the twentieth parallel. What wind there was came from the North-West bringing heavy rain, so we were pounding to windward in the heavy swell. Often *Shebessa* was completely becalmed; we made the most of it whilst waiting for wind by swimming and cleaning the bottom.

The island of Trindade, a Brazilian possession lying 1,400 miles from St. Helena and 800 miles from Rio, is a turning mark for the Cape Town to Rio yacht race, so it seemed right for us to call there, especially as the Admiralty pilot said the island abounded in wild goats and pigs. After two weeks without meat the prospect of shooting a pig or a goat followed by a beach barbecue was mouth-watering. Also the prospect of finding shells on this isolated island was enticing. The island, as we approached it in the afternoon, presented a fantastic sight with the great cliffs of Morro Acucar and Ponta da Tunel at the south end rising stark and majestic straight out of the ocean, with other sharp peaks beyond. The anchorage at Enseada Portuguese opened up; there looked to be a lot of buildings off the beach—and a large ship—the Brazilian Navy! No chance of a wild pig now. We found later this was a permanent meteorological station with a commanding officer, a doctor and 38 men.

There followed two days of hospitality ashore with us sleeping in the hospital and having drinks and meals in the mess, as we were lucky enough to be there at the change-over of commanding officers which happened each eight months, with some ceremonies. We were introduced to the Brazilian national dish, Fejuado, a stew of pieces of pork and black beans from which comes a black gravy, poured onto rice with a grilled steak and chips on top. This, after a few Cachatas—the very potent national spirit—made a very happy meal.

Trindade was an unusual island, two and a half by one and a half miles. It was really an extinct volcano with the highest peak 2,000 feet. Most of the ground was steep, and the interior was like pictures of the moon—lava and huge rocks everywhere, very stark and bare. A wrecked destroyer lay off the beach around which we enjoyed very good spearfishing. At the end of the island were two huge sandy beaches where each night turtles came out of the sea to lay their eggs. We saw a huge one which must have weighed 400 lb.

On leaving we were presented with all manner of stores, including a barrowload of bananas—three stalks—which lasted all the way to Rio. We found later this was typical of the Brazilian Navy, as wherever we went in Brazilian waters, if we needed assistance the Navy were always happy to help.

We covered the last 800 miles to Rio in six days with the help of a steady SE wind and the friendly Brazil current of one knot. We eagerly scanned the horizon just before dawn for our first sighting of Rio de Janeiro, generally lauded as the most beautiful harbour in the world—except for Sydney of course. Yes, there was the Isle de Ras light 20 miles out blinking a welcome. At dawn the great illuminated statue of Christ with arms outstretched, 125 feet high on the summit of 2,308 foot Pico de Corcavado was visible, then lovely Sugarloaf mountain, a conical-shaped peak, 1,294 feet high with a cable car on its summit, showed up in the early sunrise. We passed Copacabana beach, with high rise apartment blocks all the same height completely dominating the huge half moon shaped stretch of sand and land behind, just a couple of miles outside the entrance to the harbour in the bay of Guanabara. We rounded Sugarloaf—then the whole vista of the Bay opened up. What a magnificent sight! The Iate do Rio de Janeiro Yacht Club stretched a mile along the front, with hundreds of boats anchored off, and behind reared the huge white buildings of the city with a background of high peaks away in the distance, the morning sun throwing out all the colours imaginable, the sun bright and warm—the place seemed a fairyland, and immediately we got a feeling of tranquillity and peace even though jet planes passed overhead.

We anchored off and waited for officials, but none came. There was a lovely informality about bureaucracy in Brazil. The Club ferry came out and took us ashore, where the officials of this very exclusive luxury club—entrance fee US$10,000—invited us to use all the facilities which included two restaurants, repair shops, showers, free ferry service, free coffee, free phones, and to regard the Club as our own. And 'Bring the passports over some time!' The Club typed a letter giving our full particulars, we took this to the police in town, they produced an entry permit and that was it. No customs, no immigration formalities; what a change after the three days of hassle in Durban.

The Iate do Rio de Janeiro Yacht Club was a millionaire's paradise, an exquisite long ranch-type building with tiers of tables and chairs set out below, the décor the last word in colour and design. The place was packed with Brazilians sporting the very latest fashions, like models who had stepped out of *Vogue* magazine—no sign of old jeans here—relaxing in the sun and sipping their drinks.

We looked like a group of hobos, five bearded men and myself, all in clapped-out clothes. Going ashore we passed a huge gin palace motor boat, the staff dressed in Persil white suits and bow ties, but what stopped me in my tracks was the real live grass growing in the cockpit, a beautiful green lawn. Rio was certainly exciting, but after so long at sea, bewildering too. It took me more courage to walk through that club than it did to fight a storm at sea. The toilets and showers were the last word in cleanliness and plumbing, with an attendant always there. Each time I called the smiling girl presented me with a fresh bar of soap.

Rio is a vast, bustling city of seven million and, judging by the traffic, about the same number of cars. More Volkswagens are built in Brazil than in Germany! Everyone, including our taxi-driver, drove as if on a race track, full blast with hooting all the way, the brakes slapped on at the very last moment, the whole car shuddering as if about to turn over. We weren't acclimatised to this sort of living. Public transport was more in our line. A great network of bus services covered the area and was very cheap—the equivalent of 8 p took us anywhere, there were no stages. Shops were loaded with everything and not expensive except for imported goods which carried 175 per cent tax.

But the greatest charm in Rio was its people. Whenever we made an enquiry in the street and said 'No speak Portuguese, only Ingles', all was smiles, handshaking and eager sign language. The people were a delightful mixture of colour from the pure blacks here since the slave days through all the variations down to the white Portuguese stock, and there were no colour restrictions of any kind.

We were tied up stern to to the outside wall surrounding the small motor boat harbour in front of the Club, with our anchor well dug in to hold us off. It was a calm sunny morning. Dave let the pawl off the anchor to pull *Shebessa* in so that Norman and Steve could jump ashore. I went below to wash my hair. Just as I had my head in the basin—CRASH!! *Shebessa* shuddered, I grabbed to keep my balance, hearing the horrible sound of splintering wood. I rushed into the cockpit only to feel *Shebessa* being lifted up by another enormous wave and crashed once more against the wall. Dave rushed to the anchor to take up the chain, Russ and I to the stern, but we had no hope of fending off against such force. The pawl had not been put back on the winch so the chain had run out—it takes only one mistake on a ship for disaster to strike. We had been warned about these terrific surges for which Rio is notorious, but had been assured that they never came in April or May. I stood and wept at the sight of our ship, her stern caved in and buckled, the coaming in a thousand splinters, the stern locker lid a mess, the guard rail drooping, the stanchions pushed forward at crazy angles. I dreaded Norman coming back to see his wrecked home...

Shocked as he was, he took it calmly and set about finding how to carry out repairs. The Club gave us all assistance and after a few days' bashing with great heavy metal hammers, and with the help of joiners and painters, our lovely old girl, no longer perfect, looked at least presentable. But at what a cost! Cashwise, only US$100 plus three bottles of Scotch, but *Shebessa* would never be quite the same again, and our nerves had been badly jolted.

Dougie left us to return to his family. He'd been happy in all conditions at sea, but was ill at ease on shore among foreigners, unable to make himself understood and highly suspicious of their different food. 'These Pork and Cheese,' he said of our host nation (he seemed to think of it as still part of the mother nation), 'knock up some odd meals.' We left Rio at last with Steve, Russ and Dave in fine fettle and sailed up the coast to the Abrolhos archipelago, which we had heard was a delightful spot.

Before us were five small stark islands, lumps of volcanic rock rising out of the sea, the only inhabited one, Santa Barbara, with a light, the strongest in the Atlantic—800,000 cp. Civilisation was nine box-like houses and the large lighthouse. We nearly sailed on, but anchored just for a look. The four army families living here to service the light welcomed us warmly, advising us to go around the corner to anchor between two other islands, Redonda with a straggly line of ten coconut palms waving on the skyline, and Siriba with three, surrounded by clear water and reefs.

The stillness and utter peace, the freshness of the air and sea around us began to work on us all. On Redonda we climbed the hill to sit on the cliff among hundreds of boobies nesting there, squawking and clucking in continual motion, turning their heads from side to side, for ever on the alert, hiding their tiny angular brown chicks under their downy feathers. Most laid two eggs but when one hatched out, ate the other and both shells! Above the Frigate birds hovered, ready to snatch the babies or grab the fish dad was bringing to feed his wife and children. Siriba 400 yards away was the nesting ground of the Bosun birds, strikingly beautiful with their vivid red beaks and extraordinarily long narrow tails, which had entertained us on many a long voyage. They seemed more sensible than the boobies, nesting in less exposed areas, on tiny ledges, in caves or in holes in the rock. Each morning an enormous old turtle came to see us, resting with his head above the surface, now and again diving under *Shebessa*, a friend who must have been all of a hundred years old.

Salvador, the next place we visited, the oldest city in Brazil, was on two levels with a lift from the harbour to the town 110 feet up. In the sheltered harbour, a colourful area with endless entertainment, we met a South African couple whom we had last seen in St Helena, Bernhard and Sue Sacks, on their 35 foot yacht *Meander* setting out on their cruise to discover the world just as we had done more than four years previously—but they were now without

Meander. A few miles out of town was an open fruit and vegetable market, and they'd decided to sail there rather than take the bus. Entering the narrow passage to the tiny harbour they had hit rocks but managed to get in, beach the boat and repair the hull. Engine repairs had to be done in Salvador. The Navy offered to tow them back. In rough weather they sailed to the harbour entrance where the naval vessel was waiting. In the hiatus of passing a line to the ship, *Meander* was caught by the wind and tide, smashed against the sea wall and capsized. Bernhard and Sue and their poodle were saved but the yacht and its contents were lost. The Brazilian people rallied round finding them accommodation and eventually a job for Bernhard. Our hearts went out to them, but they kept their morale high and as we left were planning to build another boat. Here was just one more instance of a hoped for circumnavigation ending abruptly.

Tucked into the harbour corner were the local trading boats, *saveiros*, selling their wares—beans of various colours, sacks with many types of the flour used for sprinkling on food, even live hens and pigs. We saw a pig being bought. A line was thrown to the boat and tied round the pig's neck; it was then thrown overboard and dragged ashore amid shrill protesting squeals. On the quay, stalls sold exotic fruit, vegetables and fish. Towering above this scene was the beautiful old market building, Mercado Modello, which sold everything imaginable from leather goods to dried prawns. Under its porticos numerous cafés, each with its own gas stove, tables and chairs, were set out on the pavement, the women continually touting for business. Coffee was served out of thermos flasks by small children for a couple of pence.

There was laughter and gaiety of living here against a backcloth of sad, crumbling beauty, old buildings of exquisite architecture despite their peeling façades, some belonging to the sixteenth century. In the street close to the Mercado Modello we saw an exhibition of the famous Capoeira, a game of great skill and dexterity between two men, like a dance and fight to music. Crowds gathered on the pavement to watch while a group of musicians, shaking their tambourines, stirred the contestants. The youths punched and kicked to the rhythm, not touching each other but going through the most incredible display of acrobatics to miss a blow or a kick in the stomach. The Capoeira was introduced by the slaves as a means of attack or personal defence, as they were not allowed to carry weapons.

Salvador was a town of sharp contrasts. We sat in the great golden Saint Francisco church, a mass of gold leaf, so ornate that it seemed incongruous with the dirty smelly streets crowded with crippled beggars and destitute families lying on the pavements. Rio was the go-go place for tourists, but Salvador, covering the whole spectrum of life, was, we felt, the heart of Brazil.

16
Home—via Revolution

We had intended to sail along the north-east coast of Brazil, Surinam, Guyana and then Trinidad, spending the rest of 1975 in the West Indies. In Recife we had second thoughts. Chris had written to say our second grandchild would be arriving early in the New Year, and I wanted to be with her this time and give her a hand. We and *Shebessa* were ready for a spell of rest after more than 40,000 miles of tramping the seas. To our amazement Steve, Russ and Dave were keen to head for England. We knew that the 4,600 mile passage would be a difficult one, being so far West with the North-East trades to buck and the Doldrums and Horse latitudes to get through—and then there was the talk in the pilot of hurricanes around the Azores every three to four years, a thought that niggled us. In the end after much discussion the fors exceeded the againsts and we decided to head for home.

England now became the main topic of conversation. We knew so little of what was going on there, unable to decipher much news from the Brazilian newspapers. Occasionally we turned on the BBC World News, mainly to get the time signal. Listening to that programme, you'd think nothing good ever happened anywhere in the world—just a series of disasters, wars, famine and hijacking. Our South African boys' main thoughts were the girls in England. Were they on a par with the Brazilian girls or would they be all goose pimples, white faces and red noses?

We set sail for home on July 13th. Carefully we threaded our way through the narrow shallow passage leading from the Recife Yacht Club to the open sea, silent, each saying our own farewells to Brazil and getting our minds adjusted to the long passage ahead. We had become used to land and coastal waters, and had to gear ourselves up again to the sea's constant violent motion, with muscles grown soft. The words Norman often quoted ran again through my mind: 'Ports rot ships and men.' There was a feeling of apprehension all round. This might prove to be our hardest voyage. Were we morally and mentally ready to cope?

With Steve, Russ and Dave on board plus a shipload of shells, artefacts and other objects gathered after four and a half years' wandering, there was little room for stowage. At sea Norman always slept in the saloon and I had the double bed to myself, but not on this voyage. Half our double bed was now laden with twenty dozen eggs, twenty loaves and dried meat, held in by a leeboard. What strange bedfellows. I mustn't kick or stretch too hard or I'd drown in scrambled eggs. I woke to find ants crawling all over me. I'd had no time to check over the eggs we'd bought in the market. I peered into the cartons to find they were alive with ants. Twenty dozen eggs to clean was quite a project for a morning with the sea tossing me around the cabin like a ball, but one by one they were carefully washed, the cartons cleaned and all repacked with Dave's help and by some miracle we didn't break one egg.

We'd all been together now for six months and despite the inevitable dramas and ups and downs we were a very happy ship. On 42 foot of boat we had got to know each other better than friends we'd known half a lifetime at home. The boys were wonderfully patient with us and our idiosyncrasies and we tried to be with theirs. Dead on the dot of eight, Norman would switch on the radio at full belt, nearly blasting them out of their beds. I had a bit of a fetish about tidiness, hating to see piles of dumped clothes. 'Who do these belong to?' I'd call out, holding up some grey tattered T-shirts. 'Now let's see,' Dave would say as he strode over and sniffed each one to identify his own. It was a new method of sorting out clothes, by smell rather than looks.

Fourteen days out the wind lightened considerably and we had to motor on and off for three days approaching the Verdes. Where were the trade winds? If we didn't find them for a couple of hundred miles more, then found they ran out around 30/35° North and we had run short of fuel too, we might be in some difficulty reaching the Azores. The hurricane phobia nagged us again. We decided to refuel at San Tiago, capital of the Verdes: even if it meant giving away 70 miles of eastings it would be worth it to be full of fuel and perhaps collect fresh stores.

We motored West to arrive late at night; the town on the hill was visible but there was no main light and no leading lights, so we had to feel our way into the harbour to anchor finally at 0400 hours among some fishing boats. We ran up our Q and Portuguese flags and slept. I woke to look at a barren island of yellow and brown scrub, the air full of dust. Cabo Verde—hadn't somebody made a mistake naming this place?

An hour later we were invaded by six men in peaked caps—presumably the customs officers—and one young army chap, the leader, looking like a commando in green uniform, black beret, jungle boots, huge dark glasses and a *gun*! All had surly looks on their faces. I sensed trouble was brewing. Best to be terribly terribly English on these occasions. Norman and I stood in the cockpit and shook hands with each of them. This seemed to floor and embarrass them, then Jungle Boots with hand on gun started in. 'Where are the photos you took of our warship this morning?' In the dark we had anchored close to an old MTB, a beaten up hulk of rust, manned by a few soldiers and a very old man in a peaked cloth cap. Steve came forward and said he'd taken a few shots of the local fishing boats. 'We want the photos,' insisted Jungle Boots. 'But they're still on the reel and not processed yet,' we told him. 'We will do it and bring them back to you,' he said, impatient now and glaring at us.

Jungle Boots called up two of his men and ordered them to search the ship, then turning to Norman said 'And take that flag down.' 'Are you independent?' asked Norman brightly. 'Of course!' the answer was snapped—'for one month, since July 5th. You didn't know?' Our ignorance didn't please him. 'We have our own flag,' he said. 'We're world news.' Well, we had listened occasionally but hadn't heard of this great event. Apparently Cabo Verde had joined with Portuguese Guinea, 500 miles away on the coast of Africa, into one state and many African guerrillas had come over. 'You know of our leader of course?' 'No.' 'Impossible you can be so ignorant. He is Pierre Carval! Aristides Pereira is our local leader. I am the Commandante. I was a guerrilla fighter in Guinea. Why did you come here?' He glared at us all the time. Why did all these so-called leaders wear dark glasses, we thought. 'Just for fuel and bread,' said Norman.

What the customs men were looking for we never found out—they were not interested in booze or cigarettes. But every camera when found was brought for the inspection of the Captain. He insisted on taking the 35 mm roll from Dave's Nikomat and the film and camera from Steve. We never plucked up the courage to ask him whom they were afraid of. Who would be interested in this barren, desolate, dusty, poor-looking place?

'You can now go ashore, get what you want and go.'

We walked along the shore road, past broken-down houses and poor-looking African people, up the hill to the town. The place was busy, with soldiers everywhere and young people lounging around. The bank people were courteous, there was no problem changing money, but there was nothing much to buy. The alleged supermercado had no sugar—there was none on the island—no meat, no eggs. Diesel at 25 US cents a litre was easy to obtain. The local people were very pleasant to us, though obviously worried about the future. How could these people survive alone? The town was plastered with slogans, 'United Africa', 'Independence or death', and photos of Lumumba, Castro, Carval, Nkrumah, Pereira—all with dark glasses. The soldiers, most of them Africans, were enjoying it all, strutting around with guns and seeming all-powerful, while the locals just went about their daily grind of trying to get a living.

As we loaded the diesel that afternoon, Jungle Boots didn't leave us alone. 'I come and see you later tonight,' he called out from a near-by ferry. While on board, he had demanded our passports. Norman had put them on the table but when Jungle Boots started looking at our cameras, had quietly whipped them away and they'd been forgotten. Would he come back for them? If he hung on to them or dropped them over the side like the camera, we'd be in dead trouble. We were all strung up.

The fuel operation over, at last we were all on board, tired and filthy dirty. 'We don't want Jungle Boots on board again, we'll get the hell out of this place as soon as it's dark,' said Norman, and this we did, hoping the rusty old gunboat wouldn't pursue. In a light east-south-easterly we motor-sailed between Cabo Verde and Africa. After one hour the engine overheated. Luckily the wind had got up, and so it was all sails up and motor off. A terrific swell soon set up which tore into the shore of the island, breaking in tremendous surf. We were in a potentially dangerous situation if the wind changed, maybe from the East, presenting us with a lee shore against these huge swells, bigger than any we had seen since Rio. We reached away to clear the island. Just as well as sure enough, the wind did veer suddenly to East-South-East. Visibility was down to a mile. A fog of red dust blew over us, settling in a fine film over everything on board, yet we were 300 miles from Africa. The pilot book mentioned the 'Harmattan', an East to North-East wind blowing desert dust from the Sahara. This condition persisted for no less than 36 hours. Please God we would get out of this area soon. The thought of being stuck on Cabo Verde or the African coast appalled us. The sand seemed to have penetrated into every nook and cranny of the ship; we even ate it, it was like having a dusting of Parmesan cheese on every dish, without the delicious taste. Norman and Steve had changed the fan belt and then replaced the impeller, but it still hadn't solved the problem of the engine overheating. All the hassle and effort of filling our tank with fuel and now we couldn't use the engine!

It was always the same at sea. Just when I began to despair the wind changed and life became wonderful again. Suddenly we had a North-North-West wind clearing the foul air, the wind then veered to North-East and we were creaming along with the misery of the past days forgotten, free in an ocean world we had all grown to love.

After a few days of relaxation the wind started blowing like stink—so much for the light trade winds forecast for this area at this time of the year. It was reduce sail again, down to number two yankee and the main reefed right down. Our green table cloth blew off the line, a sad loss. We also lost our last two buckets overboard. An empty milk can with a rope tied through it became our water-catcher. I took stock of our food. The dried bacon had gone mouldy, and the onions and potatoes weren't keeping, though continually put out in the air to dry. We had eight tomatoes left and one cabbage. Sugar was going down at an alarming rate.

Suddenly the wind died. Had we hit the Horse latitudes at last? I anxiously watched our food supplies, trying to make them stretch out. The sea became our swimming pool again while we waited for wind, with 400 miles still to go to the Azores. On August 7th, we crossed our outward bound line from the Canaries to the West Indies on 22°S 27°W. *Shebessa*, Norman and I had circumnavigated the world. We even recognised the waves! It was a day of celebration. We opened our last tin of ham for supper.

On August 9th, a ripple came across the glassy water, then a zephyr of breeze, and soon we had a fair westerly wind to take us for a fine sail direct to Horta in the Azores. We suddenly began catching fish, and with dorado (the largest 34 lb), bonito, tunny and a 45 lb thresher shark aboard, I ceased to worry about food.

At dawn on August 18th, a vague outline of land under a cloud as black as ink came into view. We found we were between Pico and Fayal. We sailed into the busy Horta harbour with twenty-one other yachts, there at the end of the England to Azores race.

Our welcome was the reverse of that at Cabo Verde, from kindly people ready to help all travellers on their way. Here we could relax before the final voyage to England. Fayal was a warm homely town, nestling behind volcanic hills, the slopes above the town from a distance looking scored with blue streaks. The border of each road and lane winding through the island was lined with a profusion of blue hydrangeas. Never had I seen such an abundance of flowers. Café Sport was the meeting place for yachties, with Peter, the owner, happy to change money for us at the same rate as the bank—a café full of atmosphere, with showcases of whales' teeth engraved with ships and other designs.

On August 24th we set sail for home 1,500 miles away amid calms and gales. At dawn on September 7th there was a rainbow; we had seen thousands but this one came right through the horizon and sea to touch *Shebessa*—we could see it on both her port and starboard sides. We searched for the pot of gold.

We were at the end of our odyssey, four and three quarter years of wandering the oceans of the world, 45,000 miles. England, dear England at last! The wind died on us ten miles out of Falmouth. Life can be so frustrating. Unable to use the motor we patiently waited for the odd puff to ghost us into the harbour.

The customs launch came out to guide us in. The customs officer made formalities a pleasure, cleared us, we rowed ashore ... and stepped on English soil. Though my legs didn't really seem to belong to me and inside I was churned up with a mixture of excitement and relief, we staggered along the street to the yacht club, gazing at shop windows on the way. Kippers—we hadn't had kippers since we'd left home—Cornish pasties! These were our first buys in England, as well as a mountain of fruit and vegetables. The packet of bacon I picked up, I dropped as quickly. The price appalled me.

Our first need was a phone box to ring the children and let them know their wandering parents were finally home. At the bar of the Yacht Club we ordered dinner. The barman's wife was the cook. As I made my way to the powder room, I heard him telling his wife there would be more for dinner. 'Oh, Lorky no,' she said. 'I can't—not tonight loov.' 'But you moost,' he said. 'You see they've been round the world and they're hoongry.' The first meal after a voyage always tastes the best. This one was superb.

A howling gale blew us in 22 hours to Cowes, and thence to the Hamble, the river Norman had left on a cold December day in 1970. At Swanwick marina our crew packed up and set off for London. It was a sad farewell. We'd grown to know each other's every move and mood, like a closely knit happy family. Just so we wouldn't forget them, they hung up a line of their tattered T shirts from the shrouds; wonderful boys—I just hoped London would receive them well despite their erratic appearance. Russ hadn't even a pair of shoes.

Leaving *Shebessa* shipshape, in great excitement we set off to stay with our daughter Carrie in London. Prices made us wince. struggled by underground instead of taking a taxi, with hand luggage overflowing. We arrived to find Norman had only one shoe, one of his only pair of land shoes—we were wearing our canvas ones for comfort. Our feet didn't take kindly to shoes after being barefoot for so long. (Has anyone found a brown shoe size 10 on the Waterloo to Earl's Court line?)

Thereafter things began to deteriorate. Norman, feeling cool, searched for his only sweater. He couldn't have lost that too. It was eventually found, washed, and hung up to dry. Clothes kept disappearing for days and we were left stranded with only gear for the top or bottom half, but never complete. Our clothes, that we had cared for and treasured for wear in port, seemed to wilt and fade as we wore them, pants shrinking and tiny specks of rust here and there spreading to four times their size. We revelled in the luxury of baths, and yet we were continually being sprayed with toilet water by our loving family. The mustiness was all too much for them and we hadn't noticed. To cap it all, there was the dinner party at a smart restaurant when not one but all the buttons fell off Norman's reefer jacket. The world cruise had been too much for the thread, so on all fours, in dim light, we grovelled under the table in search of them, a demoralising experience.

Why didn't things work for us on land? We'd managed very well at sea. We became progressively clumsier. We felt hemmed in. We weren't used to ornaments, knick-knacks, chairs and so on, and maddened everyone by automatically turning off taps to conserve water, when they were required to be running. Crossing roads and dodging traffic was an exhausting experience. We didn't say much to each other, but ill at ease, kept a stiff upper lip. Each day there were the pin pricks, the phone calls from friends: 'I'd get a wig if I were you, it's the only answer.' 'I've booked an appointment for you at the Face Place. It might help.' Were we such freaks? We'd cut each other's hair for five years. It looked healthy but I suppose wasn't quite up to town standards, and our faces did have that weatherbeaten look, not unlike prunes when we smiled. Even our fingers seemed suddenly knobbly and scarred, to be hidden as much as possible.

Since we came back to land we've been trying our utmost to conform and please. But I doubt if we'll ever make it in this alien element. The sound of the sea always rings in our ears, and our eyes scan far horizons.

Postscript

Nearly five glorious years have passed. Now we can answer the question asked by so many people—'Why do you live this way?'

We're free and happy. Voyaging is a whole new way of living, and one we intend to continue. We can go where and when we please. We make our own pattern of living. We're not bound by regulations and restrictions, only the law of the sea and the laws of the countries we visit. We're not slaves to fashion and so life has become simple and uncomplicated. Our taste in pleasure has changed. The things we enjoy doing most are free and by far the most satisfying.

We're not alone. We belong to a large yacht club, the cruising yacht club of the world, where membership is free. There are scores of people like us roaming the world, with everyone ready to help each other. It all makes us wonder—why didn't we start ten years ago?

Can you see why we live this way?

Why don't you?

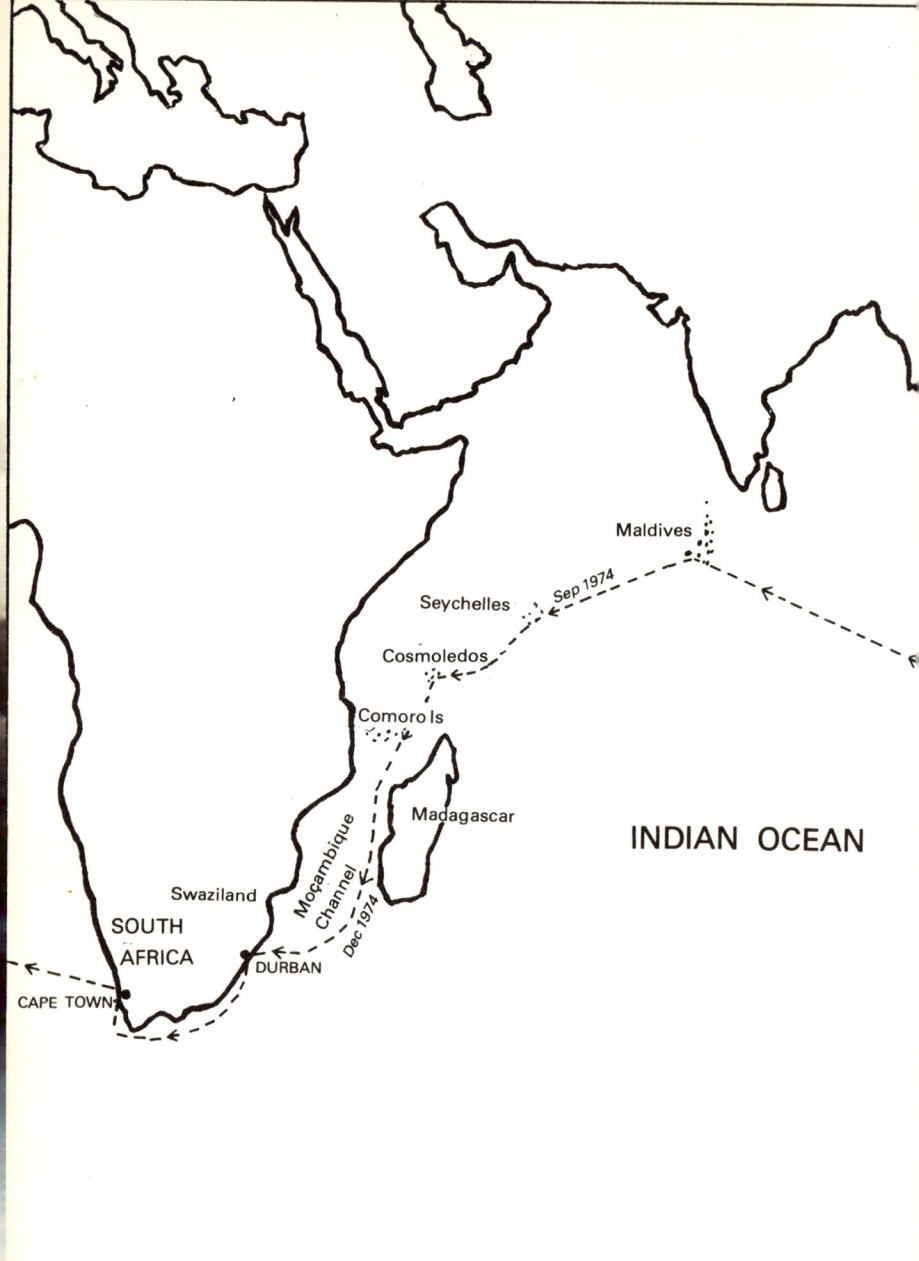

The voyage of *Shebessa*, 1970–75: 2